Conservative Innovators

Conservative Innovators

How States Are Challenging Federal Power

BEN MERRIMAN

THE UNIVERSITY OF CHICAGO PRESS   CHICAGO AND LONDON

The University of Chicago Press, Chicago 60637
The University of Chicago Press, Ltd., London
© 2019 by The University of Chicago
Published 2019
Printed in the United States of America

28 27 26 25 24 23 22 21 20 19   1 2 3 4 5

ISBN-13: 978-0-226-62028-2 (cloth)
ISBN-13: 978-0-226-62031-2 (paper)
ISBN-13: 978-0-226-62045-9 (e-book)
DOI: https://doi.org/10.7208/chicago/9780226620459.001.0001

Library of Congress Cataloging-in-Publication Data

Names: Merriman, Ben, author.
Title: Conservative innovators : how states are challenging federal power / Ben Merriman.
Description: Chicago : The University of Chicago Press, 2019. | Includes bibliographical
    references and index.
Identifiers: LCCN 2018051862 | ISBN 9780226620282 (cloth : alk. paper) | ISBN
    9780226620312 (pbk. : alk. paper) | ISBN 9780226620459 (e-book)
Subjects: LCSH: Central-local government relations—United States—History—21st
    century. | United States—Politics and government—2009–2017. | United States—Politics
    and government—2017– | Federal government—United States—History—21st century. |
    Government litigation—United States—History—21st century. | Deregulation—United
    States—History—21st century. | Political participation—United States—History—
    21st century. | Conservatism—United States—History—21st century. | Kansas—Politics
    and government—21st century.
Classification: LCC JK325 .M47 2019 | DDC 320.973—dc23
LC record available at https://lccn.loc.gov/2018051862

♾ This paper meets the requirements of ANSI/NISO z39.48-1992 (Permanence of Paper).

Contents

Preface

This book is mainly about political activity in the United States between 2009 and 2016. As it takes several years to study a topic and write a book about it, this work therefore began as a study of ongoing events. (I here acknowledge that I was appropriately warned about the difficulty of undertaking that sort of study.) By the time I was finishing the book, it had become a study of the past—a past scarcely removed from the present in chronological time but rather more distant in mood. It therefore seems important to say at the start that, although this is a book about conservatism in the early twenty-first century, it is not a book about the Trump administration, except to the degree that the Trump administration represents a continuation of processes already in motion. It is certainly not a book about the Trump Era, whose beginning was proclaimed by many after the 2016 election. I confess that I am not sure what era this is.

To write about things so close to the present leaves the researcher singularly vulnerable to being made to look foolish by the later course of events. This risk has been somewhat lessened in my case because I have not sought to explain partisan fortunes or forecast the extremely unpredictable course of elections. My goal has been to hear and transcribe the disharmonies produced when the clamor of partisanship is laid over the slower and somewhat steadier rhythms of the bureaucracy and the courts. This book ventures few predictions for the future, but I feel relatively safe in the one it does make rather firmly: that disharmony is not likely to fade soon. If it does fade, I will be glad to have been wrong.

Lawrence, Kansas
May 2018

Acknowledgments

Work on this book spanned graduate years at the University of Chicago and faculty years at the University of Kansas. In that time, I benefited from the intelligence and kindness of people too numerous to count; to single out more than a few for mention would do injustice to the generosity of the rest. I thank Chris Graziul, Jessa Lingel, and Sarah Wilson Merriman for their constancy. I also thank Andrew Abbott, Chuck Epp, Mark Hansen, John Levi Martin, Chuck Myers, and the reviewers at the University of Chicago Press; each of them, at one time or another, did the most essential thing: they did me the great favor of reading this entire work and freely shared what has seemed to me unfailingly sound advice about how to make it better.

In the conduct of this research, I received financial support from many sources, some of it generously offered to me before I could give a very clear account of what it was I was attempting to study. At the University of Chicago, I received support from the Department of Sociology's Charles R. Henderson Fund, the Social Sciences Division, the Office of Graduate Student Affairs, and the Urban Network. Other institutions supported travel to conduct research and present work in progress: the Minda de Gunzburg Center for European Studies at Harvard University, the Graduate School of History and Sociology at the University of Bielefeld, and the Robert J. Dole Institute of Politics at the University of Kansas. I am grateful to all these organizations for their support, which often arrived in what would otherwise have been very lean times.

This work is relatively short for a scholarly book, but its works-cited list is a long one. Behind this simple fact is an important truth: this argument stands on a great body of existing knowledge. That knowledge was always readily available to me, for free, in a number of fine academic libraries: the Joseph Regenstein, John Crerar, and Social Service Administration Libraries at the University of Chicago; the Watson and Anschutz Libraries at the University of Kansas; and the Leonard H. Axe Library at Pittsburg State University. I am grateful to the faculty and staff of these libraries and to these universities for their continued support of the mission of academic libraries—a bookish person like me cannot ask for a better home.

CHAPTER ONE

Choosing Conflict

The Emerging State Challenge to Federal Power

The US federal government grew dramatically over the course of the twentieth century. Congress raises and disposes of sums measured in trillions of dollars. The modern presidency is the symbolic center around which the rest of American political life revolves. Holding the symbolic role entirely aside, the president sits at the head of a bureaucracy of millions. The Supreme Court, which a century ago was occupied mainly with business disputes, is now routinely called on to settle some of the country's most urgent, divisive political questions. This view of the growth of federal power is a familiar story, and a true one.

However, generations after the New Deal, the civil rights era, and the Great Society, it is worth remembering how much of the ordinary, important business of American government is still conducted by the states. The very fact of a person's birth in the United States will be recorded in a state-issued document, a birth certificate. The basic means of establishing one's identity in a host of routine interactions—a driver's license or the equivalent—is also state issued. Most young people study in public schools operated with heavy subsidies from the state government, which may also have a substantial role in deciding what classes students take, what textbooks they read, and how their academic progress is measured. Most people seeking a higher education will enroll at institutions operated by states.

People who marry will do so under a state's law; entrepreneurs form their businesses under state law, too. Those who register to vote are most likely to do so at a state office. However they register, their names are duly recorded on a state-maintained roll. Aside from a few elected offices that appear on ballots everywhere, the range of choices voters have about their government will depend on what powers state constitutions have afforded the electorate. It is wholly in the power of states to decide how free local governments are to make their own decisions. For ordinary Americans, federal tax day comes once a year, but, in much of the country, people pay taxes to their state every time they walk into a store.

Although the federal government provides much of the money, the main programs of aid available to people who are poor or in need are administered by states, according to rules over which states have a great deal of control. Many environmental standards are defined federally, but it falls to state government to make sure that the water coming out of the tap is safe to drink. Even in matters like immigration, the federal government is heavily reliant on state and local governments to carry out its policy. Such examples—all of which are relevant to the particular matters of law and policy discussed in this book—suggest that state governments are important and powerful even in an era when politics seems to have become more national. The activity of state officials has, in fact, had a decisive effect on political life in the twenty-first century, and, though the current happenings in the White House and on Capitol Hill seem especially momentous, this book will argue that state government is likely to become more rather than less important in the coming years.

The Obama administration began in 2009 with what appeared to be a strong mandate to change American government. In short order, it was pushing through legislation to jump-start the faltering American economy, reform the finance industry, and dramatically expand access to health care. When the administration ended in 2017, things looked rather different. Important parts of the health care reforms, the Patient Protection and Affordable Care Act (ACA), had never gone into effect; those that had looked vulnerable to repeal. The administration's environmental protection and immigration agenda remained mostly unimplemented, having spent year after year mired in complex lawsuits. Although the administration had a strong interest in protecting civil rights, many rights protections—especially the right to vote—became much weaker during Obama's tenure. The two major political parties drifted further and further away from each other ideologically, and bipartisan cooperation, which was not particularly extensive before, seemed little more than a distant memory—American political life had become as polarized as it had been at any time in recent history. This book is an effort to explain what changed in those eight years. That explanation has everything to do with state governments.

The beginning of the Obama administration prompted a rapid intensification of a partisan polarization that had existed before. This quick process occurred after a long period of time in which executive powers had grown. These two patterns, in conjunction, created remarkably favorable conditions for state-level executive officeholders, such as governors and attorneys general, to challenge the Obama administration's policies. Those state offices grew in parallel with the expansion of the federal government and now provide their occupants with ample resources and discretion over how those resources are used. Especially after the 2010 general election, many occupants of those offices were staunchly conservative opponents of the Obama administration—and of the federal government more generally. Those officials were remarkably successful in pursuing a handful of familiar conservative goals through a blend of new legal and administrative behaviors. Early in the Trump administration, there were signs that those approaches were shifting familiar patterns of partisan disagreement: conflict between different levels of government is becoming more important.

The Conservative Innovators: New Means for Familiar Ends

This book is about a group of state-level conservative political figures who have, in the past decade, used the strong powers of modern state-level executive offices to seek changes in policy at all levels of government. This has included a strong challenge to federal power that has produced important, tangible effects on policy: state litigation prevented the implementation of major immigration reforms as well as major environmental policies such as the Clean Power Plan. A combination of litigation and state administrative behavior slowed and weakened the implementation of the ACA and has eroded federal voting rights protections. Conservative state opposition to the Obama administration also set in motion trends in judicial thinking and political patterns of intergovernmental relations whose eventual outcomes are not yet known.

The political actors at the core of this argument have important similarities. They are nearly all white men somewhere in middle age. They are all Republicans, and, except for a few who might regard themselves primarily as libertarians, they regard themselves as conservatives. A great many of them were educated as lawyers in the period since the emergence of the conservative legal movement within the academy. It is likely that many of them know each other: governors, attorneys general, and secretaries of state have the opportunity to interact within both partisan and nonpartisan organizations meant to facilitate exchange between such officeholders. For all that, there is not much evidence that this group is entirely self-conscious of itself as a movement pursuing a particular program. It appears closer to the mark to say that it is a group of individuals who have an affinity rooted in educational formation, political ideology, and party allegiance and who have acted similarly in response to a similar structure of opportunities. Because these actors do not have a specific name or subscribe to some statement of principles, it is worthwhile to summarize at the start the goals and commitments suggested by their administrative, legal, and policy actions:

1. Continuously reduce taxation and government expenditure, preferably by automatic or compulsory mechanisms.
2. Where possible, use private or market means to provide services currently delivered by government; limit the political influence of public sector labor unions.
3. Reduce the scope of federal agency discretion, particularly in environmental and regulatory matters.
4. Resist the implementation of the ACA; expand state discretion in the implementation of federal health and social welfare programs.
5. Limit federal regulation and increase the state regulation of elections.
6. Limit government oversight of commercial activity and the labor market at all levels.
7. Finally (for some state officials), strictly enforce immigration law by resisting federal efforts at liberalization, expanding state power to undertake enforcement independently, and curtailing local discretion.

This list provides something definite to refer to, and these actors will, subsequently, be described simply as *conservative*. These ends, plainly stated, reflect familiar conservative aims: relatively unfettered economic activity, limitations on taxation and spending for social welfare or public goods, and devolution of powers from the federal to the state level. The novelty to be found in recent years arises from an expanded repertoire of means used to advance these ends, including changes in administrative behaviors, changes in legal strategy, and a continuous interplay of administrative and legal actions.

Administratively, some state officeholders have shown a new readiness to exercise powers they have always possessed. Many states refused federal funds, most notably federal funding for Medicaid expansion. States have also been more likely to take an uncooperative stance on federal policies that rely on state implementation; the devices of noncooperation are numerous and substantial. In several areas, states have also shown an interest in using interstate compacts as a means of formally coordinating state opposition to federal policy.

Legally, a major feature of the shift is greater state involvement in litigation against the federal government. This possesses several dimensions. First, many states have taken a direct role in cases that might previously have been handled by conservative public interest law firms. Direct state incorporation of these priorities has provided conservatives with the large, stable supply of legal resources available to state attorneys general. It has also made it possible to press certain kinds of legal claims not available to private actors. Second, state-initiated litigation against the Obama administration produced quantitative increases in the number of cases reaching the Supreme Court and in the number of states participating in such cases, either as parties or amici.

The legal arguments and strategies used have also shifted. State litigants have been less reliant on traditional states' rights arguments or claims grounded directly in constitutional provisions about federalism. Rather, many of their most notable successes have been in cases dealing with administrative law and procedure—the body of statute and precedent that serves, in practice, as the legal framework of the modern federal administrative state. Conservative state litigation has also been more likely to have some grounding in novel positive rights conferred by state laws or constitutions. This is an emulation—very probably conscious—of a state-based positive rights strategy that progressive groups used with great success over the course of the twentieth century.

Further, there has been a continuous interaction between administrative and legal behavior. States have often enacted policies or laws that make it possible to test or revisit a settled question of law, further explore the possibilities of a new ruling, or employ administrative techniques that are newly permissible. In some areas, litigation and state policy activity provide redundant means of seeking the same goal. In others, state policy actions, federal actions, and litigation proceed iteratively. This iteration has been especially powerful because many states have shown a lively interest in searching out lateral applications of new precedents and have no shortage of time, money, or legal will.

Although the past decade of behavior of conservative state executive officeholders tends toward a readily intelligible set of ends, this activity did not necessarily follow a consciously defined strategy; indeed, because so much of the action is responsive to new opportunities opened by litigation outcomes, the current strategy could not have been defined a priori. The state challenge to federal power has arisen from a creative, somewhat improvisational manner of combining means. Thus, even though the legal dimension of this activity has many of the qualities of earlier judicially focused movements, this action does not strongly resemble a campaign or mobilization that is playing for a particular outcome or legal rule. It suggests, rather, the emergence of litigation as a way of political life, an inefficient, slow, costly, but powerful means of exploring the law for different avenues toward a general end.

Federal Power: A Negotiated Institutional and Partisan Arrangement

The state activity studied here is clearly responsive to the policies of the Obama administration and was in important respects enabled by the mobilization of the Tea Party. However, the possibility of this particular approach arises from the interrelated set of arrangements that gave rise to a large national government in the United States over the course of the twentieth century. That institutional and intergovernmental settlement rested on a mix of material self-interest and party consensus; its basis in the Constitution and statutory law is relatively weak and to some degree dependent on the judiciary's willingness not to consider certain questions about the behavior of the federal executive. Over time, this particular approach to building a large national administrative and welfare state has significantly strengthened the executive at both the federal and the state levels. The manner in which national government has expanded has gradually made it materially and legally easier for states to challenge its activity.

While the US Constitution outlined a schematic structure for government, it included remarkably few details about the practical business of administration. A handful of vague, brief clauses have been the most important constitutional founts of federal power (see Rohr 1986). Nor has the Constitution been subject to later amendment that does much to specify how a national administration should work or how powers are to be allocated between levels of government. The development of a large, functional national government possessing a meaningful measure of legitimacy has therefore been a result of continuous negotiation and adaptation. Two patterns have been especially significant in this development. First, many powers of government are shared rather than exclusively national. The expansion of national government has relied to a great degree on voluntary state compliance, secured by fiscal inducements or states' sympathy with federal policy goals. Second, political parties have played a large role in producing a reasonably stable intergovernmental consensus; where federal activity has arisen and persisted, it is often because both major parties find it materially or ideologically agreeable, though not necessarily for the same reasons.

Although a country the size of the United States could never have been run without some form of large, continuously administered government (see Mashaw 2012), the present form of American government should not be treated as inevitable. At important historical moments, matters could conceivably have developed differently even if certain paths, once started on, have markedly constrained subsequent developments (Orren and Skowronek 2004). And, although many of the institutions of American government now appear well entrenched, they ought not to be regarded as permanent. They could be disarranged by the simple withdrawal of cooperation by certain political actors—a bold step but in many areas of policy one firmly within the legal power of the states. Serious pressure for the judiciary to scrutinize the legal bases of national government could also yield significant changes. As this book will show, certain of these foundations are surprisingly fragile.

"Fiscal" federalism is widely recognized as a defining feature of the intergovernmental system emerging from the New Deal and the Great Society. But patterns of federalism defined through fiscal transfers and federal investments are much deeper; the intergovernmental politics of spending have always had a defining role in American government structure. The pattern was already visible in the development of a railroad network before the Civil War (Callen 2016), and the exigencies of the Civil War likewise spurred a marked expansion of the federal government (Bensel 1990), shored up to a great degree by expanded power to raise revenue. A negotiated, cooperative federalism sustained by fiscal transfers was already emerging by the opening of the Progressive Era (Johnson 2007), and the creation of a permanent federal income tax in the early twentieth century created a situation in which "the federal government had limited powers but vast funds" (Tani 2016, 4). The period from 1900 to the early 1930s was therefore one that saw a remarkable range of state experiments in social welfare provision (Clemens 1997; Amenta 1998), whose varying success partially dictated the structure of the federal social welfare programs emerging from the New Deal (Howard 2002).

The New Deal rested on a novel and expansive view of the powers of the federal government. The boldest assertions of this power were rejected by the Supreme Court or, in the case of the integrated regional authority model exemplified by the Tennessee Valley Authority, checked by determined political resistance (O'Neill 2002). The arrangement arising from the New Deal, then, was one of state implementation and government restructuring secured—often begrudgingly—by fiscal transfers (Tani 2016). Legally, the period saw a dramatic expansion of state as well as federal powers (Gardbaum 1997). The result has been a complex, non-zero-sum political ecology that includes both bureaucratic and partisan actors (see Zackin 2011, 402–3) and a wide range of lobbies and interest groups that emerged as major political powers immediately before the New Deal (Hansen 1991; Clemens 1997).

Subsequent institutional development has largely continued along these lines. By the latter part of the twentieth century, intergovernmental relations were characterized by a vigorous pattern of jostling and negotiation (Oates 1972; Wright 1982). A defining question in this negotiation is the relationship of funds and mandates; states, predictably, generally prefer maximal discretion in how they can use federal funds and are most often resistant to positive mandates with little or no associated funding (Gormley 2006); at times, the structure of federal mandates has inspired considerable national debate (Mashaw and Calsyn 1996).

This abstract, summary view of intergovernmental fiscal linkages obscures an important reality: governments do not negotiate. Government is a collection of individuals who hold particular offices in which they carry out certain activities; the most important of those figures are elected partisans or appointees of elected partisans. A working administration and a reasonably stable, cooperative model of intergovernmental relations has therefore relied, in part, on the ability of political parties to coordinate officials' actions, especially where law or formal institutional structure cannot directly mandate or execute this coordination. It has been noted above that the Constitution makes little formal provision for administration. It can be added that the Constitution not only did not contemplate a role for parties in American political life; it was drafted by people who were actively hostile to them and sought to fashion a set of government institutions that would frustrate their emergence and influence (Hofstadter 1969).

Yet parties—and a party system—immediately arose to provide a means to staff an administration, facilitate the interactions between branches of government, and simplify the task of lawmaking (Aldrich 2011). Indeed, before the administrative transformations of the twentieth century, even harsh critics of political parties acknowledged that a working government could not have arisen in the United States without relatively strong party organizations (Goodnow 2002, 164, 197). Although the separation of powers was meant, in part, to weaken parties, in practice parties have served a crucial role in safeguarding the separation of powers (Levinson and Pildes 2006).

Given their enduring role in making government administration function at all, it is unsurprising that parties have played a major role in defining a working intergovernmental arrangement. This is true, first, in the sense that the checks against accumulation of national power have been on the whole political rather than legal (Wechsler 1954; Kramer 2000). State political control over elections is an especially important mechanism (Nussbaumer 2013). At important historical moments, parties or party factions have significantly limited the expansion of the federal government, often for ill. For instance, the New Deal had a limited effect on labor rights or civil rights, in no small part because the southern Democrats in the New Deal coalition strongly opposed this (Hofstadter 1949; Katznelson, Geiger, and Kryder 1993). Indeed, southern Democrats delayed civil rights reforms by a generation (Finley 2008), and the eventual reforms were to a great extent judge made and backed by few direct, federal enforcement powers. Rights expansions in the period after the civil rights era have, likewise, been limited by party competition. New federal positive rights generally come with few associated administrative powers; this pattern of fragmentation and reliance on private enforcement is very much the result of the recurrence of divided national government.

The expansion of federal power, then, has proceeded as far as an implicit bipartisan consensus allowed. The preference of the Democratic Party for a large national government is plain: from the New Deal and the Great Society onward, the party's core policy objectives in rights and social welfare provision have plainly supposed a large federal role. The preference is less obvious, but still observable, for the Republican Party: the Southern Strategy and the Reagan Revolution, for instance, both relied on the rhetoric of states' rights but were top-down strategies for national party advancement (Aistrup 1996; Black and Black 2002). In practice, devolution during periods of Republican control of national government has been quite selective (Conlan 1998); the typical pattern has been a realignment of federal government priorities, not deeper re-structuring of government (see Callen 2017). (Among other things, this selective handling leaves devolutionary arguments permanently available to Republicans when they may confer electoral advantage.) In the long, relatively settled period after the New Deal and the civil rights era, the sharpest partisan divisions over the appropriate scope of government activity have tended to assume an interbranch rather than an intergovernmental character—this was the characteristic pattern during Newt Gingrich's tenure as speaker of the House, for instance (Skocpol 1997; Thierault 2013). Until the recent period examined in this book, Republican-controlled state governments were not apt to refuse federal funds even when they complained about federal overreach. And beneath different rhetorical arguments about government activity is the crude fact that federal spending and the scope of presidential power expanded steadily, irrespective of the particular configuration of partisan control of the national government.

The Growth of National Government and the Expansion of Executive Power

By any measure one cares to invoke, the national government grew dramatically over the course of the twentieth century: it is true of revenue and expenditure, the growth in social welfare provisions, number of federal employees and agencies, and total quantity of regulations, and thus, very generally, the reach of government into everyday American life. The expansion of national government in absolute terms has also produced growth in the power of the executive relative to the other branches of government. This is true of the president and the federal executive branch. Significantly for this book's argument, this is perhaps even truer of state executive branches. The remarkable expansion in the activ-

ity and symbolic importance of the American presidency over the past
century has been much studied. The beginnings of this long growth are
often tied to the presidency of Theodore Roosevelt, whose vision of a
strong presidency was, in many ways, fashioned in the image of the increasingly powerful Progressive governors of the period. Since then, the
presidency has become stronger, and the federal administrative state has
grown larger. (This discussion sets entirely to the side the growth in the
symbolic importance of the presidency and in the expansion of military
and national security powers—long-term trends not strictly related to
the matters of policy examined here but certainly an additional factor in
executive preeminence.)

The frequent recurrence of divided government has made Congress
less likely to enact laws that confer clearly defined, strong powers on particular agencies (Farhang and Yaver 2015). Although this may be readily understood as an attempt to limit the power of the executive branch,
fragmentation is also self-limiting: it weakens the ability of Congress to
create policy that strongly reflects its own preferences. The increased
complexity of national government also means that, in practice, major
legislation is defined substantially by the agency rulemaking process:
most political groups report that participating in rulemaking is as important as or more important than lobbying Congress (Kerwin and Furlong
2011). The implementation of major legislation can involve the making of
hundreds of rules, providing ample opportunity for interested parties to
shape—or temper—the effect of major legislation (see, e.g., Pagliari and
Young 2015). Further, the budgeting process has come to define much of
the activity of Congress—the vital work of Congress increasingly proceeds through unconventional lawmaking, especially legislative mechanisms associated with the budgeting and the reconciliation processes
(Sinclair 2011). The centrality of budgeting in the modern activity of
Congress is a further indication of the relatively expanded importance
of the executive: the financing of the executive has become the defining
concern of the legislative branch.

Similarly, over the course of the twentieth century, the federal judiciary has acceded to a large expansion in executive powers. This is not
to say that the judiciary is weak. Although its role as a positive cause of
social change is still much debated, the Supreme Court has certainly figured in enormous changes in American public life since the 1950s, and it
is increasingly called on to settle intensely political questions. By careful
stewardship of its symbolic power, the Court has also been remarkably

successful in establishing itself as a credible arbiter of such questions and in securing compliance with rulings despite very limited powers of enforcement (see Hall 2011). These matters are discussed in much greater depth later in this book.

Here, it is sufficient to observe that the judiciary has been, for quite some time, an ally of executive power. The Court largely endorsed expansive interpretations of constitutional provisions that made the New Deal possible (see Sunstein 1987). Through the latter part of the twentieth century, the courts elaborated a set of doctrines of deference to federal agencies in their areas of expertise; this deference was vital to the development of a large, regulatorily active administrative state. The US solicitor general—the judicial avatar of the federal executive—has enjoyed a uniquely influential position during this period. In the late twentieth century, the presidency fared extraordinarily well before the Supreme Court (Epstein and Posner 2017).

Although the expansion of social welfare provisions and individual rights protections has flowed, to a great extent, from federal activity, this arguably had a more pronounced effect on the balance of power at the state level. Materially, many modern state executives tower over their legislatures. Administering federally supported social welfare programs, enforcing federal regulations and standards, and spending federal money all imply a large state administration. In simple quantitative terms, state governments have grown dramatically—in aggregate, they employ nearly five times as many people as they did in the 1950s (Moncrieff and Squire 2017, 85). By contrast, state legislator pay has declined in real terms since the 1970s, and, over that same period of time, state legislators' staffing has been virtually unchanged (Moncrieff and Squire 2017, 90): many states have retained an ideal of an amateur or semi-professional citizen legislature with low legislator pay, little permanent staffing, and relatively short legislative sessions. Yet the business of modern state government requires continuous administration. In many states, the legislature is simply not a regular presence in the operation of government, and, when in session, such legislatures are highly dependent on the policy expertise of the state executive (Boushey and McGrath 2016). Further, legal and constitutional changes in many states over the past generation are somewhat favorable to the executive. Some states have sought to limit legislative power through term limits and campaign finance restrictions; forty-nine states require the legislature to pass balanced budgets, a marked contrast to Congress's routine deficit spending.

At the same time, many states enhanced gubernatorial powers, such as the ability to reorganize state government structure by executive order or line-item veto power in budgeting. Put simply, long-term expansion of American government has made the executive the locus of political action at the state level.

This argument about state legislatures' relative weakness may appear to run against media accounts (and some social scientific research) suggesting that the American Legislative Exchange Council (ALEC) has played a significant role in the rightward drift of policy in many states.[1] There are good reasons to doubt any strong form of this claim. Most notably, ALEC functions as a broker for policy ideas and does not possess resources to lobby for or actively advocate the passage of bills (Medvetz 2012a). Consequently, passage rates of its model bills are low nationally, and its most obvious function is to speed diffusion (Garrett and Jansa 2015). It may be added that a more detailed examination of the success of ALEC provides suggestive evidence for the marginalization of state legislatures. Setting aside the obvious role of partisanship and legislature ideology in predicting the adoption of ALEC bills, two factors are especially notable. First, such bills are most likely to be adopted in unprofessionalized legislatures where members have limited staffing and policy resources (Hertel-Fernandez 2014; see also Jansa, Hansen, and Gray 2018). Further, the states with the highest passage rates of ALEC bills (as reported in Hertel-Fernandez and Kashin 2015) are also among the states with the strictest campaign finance laws (Barber 2016, 300) and thus legislatures where traditional lobbies may be unusually weak. Frequent adoption of ALEC model policies, then, is likely not directly related to the activity at the core of this book. But the blurring together of the two phenomena is understandable as they may arise from the same set of underlying conditions: high rates of adoption of ALEC policies are an indication that the political climate of a state is conservative and that the executive officeholders in that state may be, relative to the state legislature, unusually powerful.

As the large volume of federal money flowing through state administrations would suggest, formal and informal patterns of intergovernmental relations are mediated to a considerable degree through the state executive. Even as it became embroiled in conflict with many Republican state executives, the Obama administration devised an extensive and relatively successful model of executive federalism in which state and federal administrations coordinated directly, bypassing the legislative branch (Bulman-Pozen 2016; Bulman-Pozen and Metzger 2016). Governors have become a powerful intergovernmental lobby (Jensen 2016), and, at the opening of the more conflictual period examined in this book, Nugent (2009) noted that states had become steadily more successful in securing favorable national outcomes.

Another group of executive officeholders—state attorneys general—has also become more important. The federal government's limited direct role in rights protection has resulted in increased reliance on litigation as a tool of rights enforcement (Farhang 2010). This has resulted in an expanded role for state attorneys general: states have been especially active litigators, a trend seen particularly in consumer protection lawsuits of the 1990s (Nolette 2015). The state attorney general is, increasingly, a powerful official with high public visibility, and the position often serves as a stepping-stone to higher office (Provost 2010). Similarly, serious aspirants to the presidency are more and more drawn from the gubernatorial ranks rather than congressional office.

The expansion of executive powers, then, also has important implications for the structure of American federalism. The growth of state government and the concentration of state power in the executive confer on executive officeholders ample legal and policy resources and considerable discretion in their use. Figures like governors and attorneys general are visible and, setting their underlying values commitments wholly to the side, may judge that they stand to derive political benefit from a well-publicized disagreement with the national government.

At the same time, concentration of power in the state executive also dramatically simplifies the task of interstate coordination. The success of states in intergovernmental lobbying is one demonstration of this, but these conditions also simplify coordination against the national government. Cooperation between state executives can involve a dozen or so full-time, well-staffed officeholders rather than hundreds or thousands of semiprofessional legislators who must secure the cooperation of a majority of their colleagues to undertake actions of tangible consequence. This is significant. In general, central governments in federated polities will be more powerful when it is difficult for mid-level units to coordinate (Bolleyer 2009), and the difficulty of effective coordination increases rapidly as the number of political actors involved grows (Hooghe and Marks 2003). The expansion of American government has thus proceeded along paths that have made it easier for states to coordinate while potentially increasing the symbolic and material rewards for coordinating against the national government. This is precisely what happened during the Obama administration.

The Tea Party Mobilization as Catalyst

The preceding section showed that modern American federalism is, to a great degree, a negotiated arrangement arising from material inducements to cooperation, some measure of bipartisan support for a large national government, and judicial deference to the executive. It also showed that a large national government developed along pathways that increased the potential ability of states to reject features of this arrangement and perhaps increased the political incentives to do so. But these arrangements evolved on a multigenerational time scale. Viewed in those terms, the increase in the frequency and intensity of intergovernmental contention under the Obama administration was sudden and requires some explanation. Some of the factors are associated with legal changes operating at a certain remove from partisan politics and are discussed in detail later in the book.

This section will argue that the Tea Party mobilization served as the catalyst of this conflictual turn. First, the Tea Party mobilization intensified and accelerated processes of partisan polarization that had already been observable in the American electorate, yielding both patterns of tenure in office and a general orientation or mood that promoted conflict. Within the Republican Party, it is particularly associated with a shift toward an antigovernment, libertarian view. Second, the Tea Party had a large effect on the 2010 elections, with significant consequences for the activity of elected officials. Nationally, the 2010 election opened a period of bitterly divided and unproductive national government. At the state level, the election yielded enormous gains for Republicans and saw unusually conservative candidates winning office. Many of these officials—some of whom certainly could not have won office in an ordinary election year—play a central role in the activity examined in the body of this book.

Party polarization did not, of course, suddenly arise in 2010. Ideologically, the sentiments of both the American voting public and elected officials have been moving away from the median for some time. Some of this polarization has been driven by a sorting process by which issues and stances have become more firmly associated with particular parties

(Levendusky 2009). For instance, until the 1990s, there was not a significant partisan division on environmental issues or in perceptions of the trustworthiness of science (McCright, Xiao, and Dunlap 2014). Indeed, the development of climate science in the mid-twentieth century was strongly associated with the Cold War and national security concerns (Baker 2017), and it was President Nixon who played a key role in the creation of the Environmental Protection Agency (EPA). From the 1990s onward, environmental policy—and, with it, science itself—has become a deeply polarizing political issue (McCright, Dunlap, and Xiao 2014).

In a setting where voter participation and information are relatively low, ordinary aspects of the electoral and policy process exaggerate ideological polarization along partisan lines. Both the presidential and the legislative nomination processes yield candidates whose views are distant from the ideological center but close to the values of a smaller set of highly involved partisans (Cohen et al. 2009; Masket 2009). Even when public sentiment has clustered around a central point, the views of partisan elected officials need not, and generally do not, reflect that underlying set of constituent preferences (see Hill and Tausanovitch 2015). As government activity becomes more polarized both in fact and in media representations, people may come to perceive that public sentiment is more polarized than it actually is and thereby develop more extreme positions (Ahler 2014). Although it would be an oversimplification to view perceptions of polarization as self-fulfilling, it requires no great imaginative leap from everyday experience to suggest that the present moment is one in which political polarization has become in some respects a self-reinforcing process.

Partisan polarization also has a substantial geographic component. At the national level, the American electorate has been relatively evenly divided for the past generation. Divided control of the national government has been the most common state of affairs since 1980. Each of the last four presidents won at least one election in which he did not receive a majority of the vote; two won the Electoral College while securing fewer votes than a rival candidate. The persistence of a relatively evenly balanced (but sharply split) national electorate has translated, at lower levels of geographic aggregation, into high levels of partisan dominance. The long-term realignment of the white southern electorate to the Republican Party—a process that was, itself, not completed at the state level until 2010, when Republicans had a landmark electoral success in

North Carolina—has now resulted in strong partisan alignments in each of the country's major regions (see Lang and Pearson-Merkowitz 2015). This is also true at the state level: following the 2017 general election, thirty-four states were under "trifecta" control, in which a given party controlled the governorship and both legislative chambers. At the level of the metropolitan region, there has also been steady partisan sorting driven by patterns of migration, with the result that Democratic supporters are very heavily concentrated in cities (Cho, Gimpel, and Hui 2013; Nall 2015). At the state level, the geographic distribution of political sentiment constitutes a large component of overall partisan polarization (Shor and McCarthy 2011).

Although the Tea Party movement arose in this general environment of partisan polarization, it was specifically responsive to the opening of the Obama administration. The mobilization was to a great degree driven by hostility to Barack Obama's person and policies (Parker and Barreto 2013), particularly the development and passage of the ACA (Ashbee 2011; Banks 2014). The 2010 election, influenced heavily by the Tea Party, resulted in a resounding win for Republican candidates at all levels of government.

The control of offices, in itself, had some important consequences. Republican control of the House opened a period of remarkably divided, unproductive national government (Bonica 2014; Binder 2015). Intransigence proved to be a simple but sometimes effective means to secure desired cuts in government spending—seen, for instance, in the debt-ceiling crisis and government shutdown. The singularly uncooperative Congress also spurred the Obama administration's turn toward unilateral executive approaches to policy-making. This book will show that these approaches were especially vulnerable to state-initiated legal challenges. Unilateral action also very likely reinforced patterns of specific hostility to the Obama administration that had spurred the Tea Party movement in the first place. At the same time, the 2010 election yielded significant successes for Republican candidates at the state level, especially in executive offices. It is these figures who would, in the following years, develop legal and administrative challenges to federal power—a much more flexible and sophisticated set of actions than those available to congressional Republicans, whose main tool for realizing goals was simple inaction.

The Tea Party mobilization and the 2010 election did not produce simply a shift in the number of offices controlled by the parties; they are also associated with an ideological shift within the Republican Party. Republican elected officials moved sharply away from the ideological median from 2010 onward and did so much more rapidly than Democrats (Hacker and Pierson 2015; see also Perrin, Roos, and Gauchat 2014). As the behavior of Congress suggested, part of this shift has been a consolidation or completion of a longer movement away from a pragmatic approach to government and toward ideological consistency even at a high cost (Grossman and Hopkins 2015). Although the visible performance of ideological purity may be to some degree oriented toward constituents (Vasi, Strang, and van de Rijt 2014; Patty 2016), an important result of the Tea Party movement was the creation a vocabulary of self-identification partially distinct from the sentiments or behavior of constituents. Although the Tea Party was, at the time, commonly represented as a sort of insurgency, the candidates who took up its label and rhetoric most enthusiastically were mainly incumbents (Martin 2013). Further, there was a marked difference between the geography of grassroots support for the Tea Party (see Cho, Gimpel, and Shaw 2012; DiGrazia 2017) and the congressional districts whose members belonged to the fluctuating set of congressional caucuses representing the Tea Party tendency (see McNitt 2014). Just as many notable Tea Party–aligned members of Congress do not represent the most conservative constituencies, many state executive officeholders elected in 2010 went on to govern very well to the right of public opinion.

The Tea Party's mobilization was, by all available evidence, a grassroots phenomenon with important local as well as national dimensions (Skocpol and Williamson 2012). But its development provided a focus or attractor for a pattern of staunchly libertarian, promarket, and antigovernment sentiments that were already, to some degree, present within the Republican Party. This was true for donors, interests, and policy advocates as well as elected officials. The Tea Party movement also coincided with a decline in large business influence on the Republican Party. Historically, large businesses have been an important part of the interest group coalition of the Republican Party, a ground for critical appraisals from figures like Mills (1956). The influence of business had been, on the whole, a moderating one—business involvement in politics tended to be relatively nonideological and strongly favored stasis or slow, predictable change (Laumann and Knoke 1987; Walker and Rea 2014). Given that large businesses are geographically extensive, they also, to some degree, recognized national government as having an appropriate role in creating uniformity and in preserving a stable macroeconomic environment (see Schifeling 2013). The capacity for political coordination of this traditional business elite has been waning rapidly in the twenty-first century (Schifeling and Mizruchi 2014), owing partly to demobilization as this coalition has secured core goals (Young and Pagliari 2015) but also to genuine disorganization and fracturing (Mizruchi 2013; Mizruchi and Hyman 2014; Chu and Davis 2016). At lower levels of government, too, businesses have been receding from party political life (see Pacewicz 2015, 2016). As this traditional business elite has waned, a more libertarian and antigovernment pattern of activism and donation has grown in strength. This is associated particularly with the Koch brothers and a network of organizations affiliated with the Kochs. This network expends an enormous amount of money on politics and does so in ways aligned more with a strong antigovernment principle than with the pragmatic pursuit of stasis or access (Skocpol and Hertel-Fernandez 2016). Its activity has often been successful in shifting states' policies to the right even where the underlying structure of public opinion is wholly unchanged (Hertel-Fernandez, Skocpol, and Lynch 2016). That this represents a genuine transition may be, to some degree, obscured by the fact that the Kochs themselves own a large firm. This does not mean that they represent an older, familiar set of business interests, and, in some important areas of policy such as Medicaid expansion, established business lobbies and Koch-affiliated organizations have been bitter opponents. This book—focused as it is on administrative behavior and litigation— will have little to say about the Koch network, whose most notable activity is in elections and legislatures.[2]

The Tea Party movement is associated with a rapid intensification of patterns of political division that had already been apparent in American life. Public opinion has shifted away from a middle ground, and partisan officials—especially Republicans—have moved away from the ideological median—and compromise approaches to governing—even more rapidly than the public. The geographic dimensions of polarization have yielded circumstances in which most state governments are firmly under the control of a single party. This combination of factors doubtless figures in the degree of cooperative state action against the Obama administration. Republican officials were drawn closer together ideologically, and in the Obama administration they also found a unifying opponent whose reliance on unilateral approaches to governing galvanized sentiment (Reeves and Rogowski 2018) and created—or exposed—

opportunities for new and more aggressive patterns of resistance to federal activity. These political circumstances coincided with important institutional factors, including significant concentration of resources and discretion in the state executive, and incipient changes in judicial doctrine that would prove to be very favorable for state litigants.

What Happened Next: The Structure of the Argument

The preceding sections have provided a sketch of American government structure and party dynamics around 2010 and showed why the conditions at that moment were primed for a group of state executive officeholders to pursue a more direct confrontation with the federal executive. The long period of growth in the activity of the national government has been, in the main, an institutional and partisan negotiation. That development also created structural conditions that could favor a state challenge. State governments have grown larger, and the state executive has become stronger; a small group of officeholders with substantial resources, discretion, and public visibility may find it much easier to coordinate their actions or circulate their ideas. Federal power has become relatively more concentrated in the executive, providing both a visible potential opponent—the president—and a variety of possible ways to resist activity. Partisan dynamics, operating to some degree separately from this slow process of institutional evolution, also created conditions that favored a stiffer state challenge to federal activity. Polarization has moved members of the two major parties further apart and drawn co-partisans closer together; on the Republican side, actors have converged on a position that prizes commitment to principles and takes a more strongly skeptical or antigovernment line. The body of this book describes the conflicts that arose from these conditions.

Chapter 2 describes how state offices have been used as public support structures for conservative legal activity. State legal action figures in nearly all the strategic behavior discussed in this book, and state litigation against the federal government increased rapidly in recent years. This chapter examines several patterns of state legal behavior: direct litigation against the federal executive, the use of administrative framings to make new state policy in areas historically understood as federal prerogatives, and the states' use of positive rights guarantees to create conflicts between state and federal law. These legal strategies have deeper antecedents.

First, the legal capacity of state attorneys general has grown steadily over a period of decades. This growth owes, in part, to the federal turn away from administrative enforcement of rights protections. As lawsuits have become the primary means of exercising a variety of rights, states have frequently taken on a primary enforcement role in matters such as environmental and consumer protection. Through the 1990s, states became involved in more complex, multistate suits and have become better equipped and more sophisticated federal litigators than they were in the past. Though involvement in these suits was often bipartisan, this activity also spurred the formation of partisan state attorney general organizations.

Second, the federal judiciary has become somewhat more critical of exercises of federal agency power. The large, active federal administrative state that grew over the twentieth century sits uneasily within the American constitutional framework, and the kinds of evidence and reasoning used in agency decision-making are markedly different from those used by appellate courts. Courts regularly defer to agencies on a variety of matters, but that deference has been circumscribed in the twenty-first century; further, the Supreme Court recognized states as having a special claim on the judiciary's attention where federal administrative behavior is concerned. These shifts have made it easier for states to sue federal agencies on a wide range of grounds.

Third, state legal mobilization against the Obama administration began thirty years after the development of the conservative legal movement. That movement, which began within the legal academy, pursued a long-term strategy of developing new conservative ideas about law, establishing its intellectual legitimacy, then seeking to move both ideas and movement supporters from the academy into the judiciary. A significant proportion of the judiciary and many state attorneys general are part of that movement; the movement has also reoriented conservatism toward legal strategies. That movement's earlier success provided a legal foundation for this more recent activity.

It is in this context that states have pressed a variety of new legal claims. First, they frequently engaged in multistate suits against federal agencies; rather than invoking a traditional language of states' rights, these arguments focused heavily on matters of administrative procedure. Such claims succeeded in halting the implementation of the Obama administration's most important environmental protection policies. States also succeeded in extending the line of reasoning used in cases against the EPA to other matters, such as attempts at executive-centered reforms of immigration policy and labor law. This approach has succeeded by sheer case volume and persistence; these cases have not produced any major judicial restatement of basic doctrines. Second, many states have adopted their own immigration enforcement policies. The "self-deportation" approach to subnational immigration enforcement has relied on state assertions of administrative interests rather than more direct federalism claims. Third, a number of conservative states have conferred new positive rights on their citizens, such as a right to a secret ballot in all elections—including union elections—or a right for terminally ill people to try any experimental treatment recommended by a physician. These positive rights guarantees create conflicts with existing federal law.

In many respects, this pattern of legal activity makes claims similar to those commonly found in judicial mobilizations or public interest litigation. However, when state governments press these claims directly, they are able to make use of a wide range of resources and formal claims not ordinarily available to private actors. By making the support structure for conservative litigation public, states have been able to advance core conservative legal movement goals. To a great degree, this approach has grown from conservatives' careful study and emulation of the techniques used successfully by liberal movements during the twentieth century. The legal headway made by conservative state officeholders, in turn, also broadens the range of claims that can be advanced by liberal state officeholders currently involved in disputes with the federal government.

Chapter 3 examines aggressive state resistance to federal policy within cooperative and fiscal federalism, the framework in which the federal government uses budgeting practices to shape state policy and relies on state administration to implement major social welfare programs. Many features of this "uncooperative" federalism are already well understood. A sizable body of research has examined many states' recent refusal of federal funds as well as a variety of administrative techniques by which states sought to resist the implementation of the ACA. Although it had always been within states' power to take this approach, the willingness to refuse money and actively frustrate policy implementation is new—the preceding generation had been one that was characterized by negotiation and conciliatory intergovernmental relations and in which conflict more often focused on unfunded federal mandates.

This chapter builds on that existing account by examining another new feature of state resistance to federal policy: the development of interstate compacts as a means of facilitating state opposition. Compacts have long been used for relatively nonpolitical administrative ends. However, state resistance to the implementation of the ACA prompted the development of proposed compacts with more overtly partisan goals. Some, such as the Health Care Compact, were fashioned to allow states a means of selectively opting out of federal regulations and programs; these proposed compacts would have provided a fallback strategy for states that were also involved in active litigation about some federal policy. A second group of proposed compacts would have provided an occasion to test new legal arguments in areas of policy where state litigation seemed to present new opportunities. For instance, the Interstate Birth Certificate Compact would have provided for the maintenance of a dual system of birth certificates, effectively seeking to extend a state-based restrictionist immigration strategy centered on record keeping. A third group of proposed compacts would have sought to surmount the coordination problem described above: state legislatures are underresourced and contain a large number of officials. It is therefore difficult to use legislative devices to coordinate a state challenge to federal policy. Compacts, which can concentrate activity and information in the hands of an administrative agency, can make such challenges simpler.

The chapter concludes with a detailed examination of one such compact, the Compact for a Balanced Budget, which seeks a radical transformation of the nature of fiscal federalism: a state-initiated constitutional convention to pass a federal balanced-budget amendment. A similar campaign secured over thirty state petitions in the late 1970s and early 1980s. The passage of the ACA, followed by the debt-ceiling crisis, prompted a revival of this policy idea. By 2015, almost all state legislatures had considered a petition for a constitutional convention, and fourteen had formally adopted one. However, a constitutional convention is a complex, unproved, and risky device for seeking change. The Compact for a Balanced Budget has sought to simplify this effort by creating a standing, multilateral administrative agency to maintain records and advocate for a convention. Although the wave of state interest in a convention has passed, the compact is still in regular operation—the interstate compact device allowed advocates to parley transient interest into the creation of a permanent, public administrative agency.

Chapter 4 studies the recent development of a new model of voter restriction based in strong, uniform state election administration. The development of this regime was enabled by the weak, incomplete quality of federal voting rights protections. The Constitution left much of the business of administering elections to the states, and, for most of American history, the federal judiciary declined to involve itself in disputes about states' conduct of elections. In the 1960s, two distinct legal developments created a meaningful degree of new federal protection. A range of court decisions, constitutional amendments, and acts of Congress effectively prohibited an array of practices that had functionally disenfranchised African Americans in the South. A separate group of court decisions established the principle of "one person, one vote," which brought an end to severe legislative malapportionment throughout the United States. Those changes, however, created very few federal administrative powers, and, to a degree, the courts have understood these reforms as addressing special problems rather than fundamental questions for a democratic form of government. Although overt racial discrimination is now impermissible, judicial doctrines continue to recognize simple partisanship as a valid basis for states to make election-related decisions. Because the southern model of disenfranchisement relied so heavily on intimidation and administrative irregularity, the courts have also tended to proceed on the view that regular, uniform administrative practices are likely to be fair.

This chapter argues that it is this view that made federal courts willing to license the development of a model of voter restriction based on state practices that impose documentary or procedural burdens on individual voters. Voter identification laws are the most familiar measure of this kind, but the chapter shows it to be only one device among many. Curiously, it is federal activity that made this model possible. The passage of the Help America Vote Act (HAVA) in 2002 mandated that states make significant efforts to modernize and centralize their elections administrations; this mandate to increase state capacity also created the material conditions for implementing a number of restrictive policies. Relying in part on the provisions of HAVA, the Supreme Court has recognized a state interest in protecting the perceived integrity of elections even without demonstrable evidence of fraud. The Court's reasoning in its first case involving a voter identification law thus provided states with a com-

plete set of acceptable, facially neutral rationales for making it more difficult to vote. Owing in part to a deep aversion to statistical evidence, the
judiciary has also been unreceptive to the most compelling evidence that
new measures do indeed restrict voting—the new model is, by nature,
probabilistic.

The chapter provides a more detailed view of the probabilistic quality of modern voter restriction as well as the growth of state coordination
in this area through a detailed examination of the Interstate Voter Registration Crosscheck Program (Crosscheck). This program, operated by
the Kansas secretary of state, compares the voter rolls of most American states in search of potential duplicate registrations. Using data provided by the Kansas secretary of state as well as other public data, this
chapter shows that Crosscheck likely flags large numbers of valid voter
registrations as potentially suspect. For underlying demographic reasons, rather than any aspect of the program's design, these spurious
matches are likely to be concentrated among minority populations, especially African Americans. State election administrators may use these
matches in a way that will tend to purge state voter rolls of valid registrations; North Carolina presents a prime example of such behavior. Yet
Crosscheck is facially neutral and would almost certainly survive judicial review under existing law. Indeed, such record sharing is encouraged
by federal law, and the forms of evidence marshaled in this chapter are
very different from the much more limited kinds of evidence courts are
commonly willing to examine. In short, the chapter shows that modern
voter restriction has been made possible because of extreme limitations
on federal administrative power in the area of elections, coupled with
judicial reasoning that has attempted to maintain an untenable distinction between administrative behavior and political behavior. States have
thus been presented with a means of administering their way around key
parts of federal voting rights protections.

Chapters 2, 3, and 4 examine dimensions of state conflict with the national government. Although this behavior is oppositional, it is reliant
on a relatively sophisticated use of the legal and administrative forms
of state power. And, while the states involved in this activity are controlled by Republican officeholders, only a subset of Republican-
controlled state governments have taken an active role in these conflicts.
The pattern of involvement is not a simple reflection of ideology on a
unidimensional left-to-right continuum; for instance, social scientists
have regularly pointed to Wisconsin governor Scott Walker as an impor-

tant conservative state executive officeholder, but he has played very little part in the legal and administrative maneuvering examined in this
book. There is thus an implication of a particular vision or understanding of state government that is important for this story—a vision that is
not simply conservative but innovative.

Chapter 5 attempts to describe that understanding of government by
examining Kansas governor Sam Brownback's experiment in limited
government, begun in 2011. Kansas is a useful case for rounding out the
argument. It is one of the states with a central role in the varieties of
intergovernmental contention summarized above. Its executive officeholders have presented it as a model for emulation at the state and national levels, and major policy ideas originating in Kansas—concerning
such matters as immigration, voting rights, and taxation—have in fact
spread to many other conservative states and have also served as a basis for the policy of the Trump administration. Through an executive-
centered pattern of reforms, the state government has gone unusually far
in reductions in state spending and taxation, privatization of key government functions, and experimentation in administrative structure. Governor Brownback wielded unusually strong executive powers and, until the
2016 election, also enjoyed a sizable majority of partisan and factional
allies in the state legislature. His reforms represent something near a
pure ethos of innovation in pursuit of limited government: as the experiment was rolled out, the state was under no fiscal exigency, and neither
the majority of the public nor key organized interests were calling for
the reforms. Brownback staunchly defended his policies even as they became extraordinarily unpopular.

The chapter gives particular attention to a novel administrative agency,
the Office of the Repealer, charged with soliciting public input on laws
and regulations worthy of being rescinded. While of far less practical
consequence than policy measures such as Brownback's tax cuts, the office provides an unusually clear demonstration of the logic of government contraction pursued in Kansas and elsewhere. It functions as a
ratchet on the scope of government and seeks public participation only
from those who accept the governor's own premises about the nature of
government. This discussion makes use of state records furnished by the
Kansas Department of Administration and the Office of Legal Services
of the Tennessee General Assembly.[3]

The activity in Kansas as well as the larger pattern of state opposition to federal policy flow from an executive-focused, ends-oriented ap-

proach to politics. This behavior is conservative in the sense that the actors understand themselves as conservative and hold illiberal views on many issues. However, it also has features that seem to belie a standard idea of conservatism—it is avowedly reformist and experimental and approaches the law not as a settled system of restrictions on government but as a flexible range of tools allowing particular government actors to pursue their goals. The chapter concludes by arguing that this approach has an important historical analogue: Progressivism, which was remarkably similar in its reliance on state executive power, experimentation with administrative form, instrumental approach to law, admiration for the structure of private enterprise, and illiberal views of immigrants and minority groups.

The comparison may be a useful one for stimulating thinking about American political behavior outside a simple left/right dichotomy. Moving past this distinction may be particularly important for a moment, like this one, in which new government strategies are diffusing freely across the political spectrum and settled associations between political worldviews and institutions appear less stable. The comparison also calls attention to the inherently unsettled boundaries between politics and administration. A recurring theme in this work is that objective administrative techniques admit of political uses, and, in many respects, the success of conservative state officeholders reflects a new partisan mastery of bureaucratic practices created in the Progressive Era precisely to curb the power of parties.

This process is just beginning. The concluding chapter considers the ongoing development of the contentious intergovernmental relations of the Obama administration. If one focuses strictly on policy activity rather than public statements, the first year of the Trump administration was remarkably like the latter years of the Obama administration in the form and the substance of disagreements. Important figures such as Vice President Mike Pence, former EPA administrator Scott Pruitt, former attorney general Jeff Sessions, and Supreme Court justice Neil Gorsuch all have existing reputations as state-oriented conservatives. The domestic policy activity of the Trump administration has been oriented toward limited government and regulation along the lines suggested by the state-level actors examined here. Major priorities such as ACA repeal, general rollback of federal agency regulation, and reversal of major environmental protection rules follow directly from the preceding years of conservative state activity. Trump administration actions in immigration policy have endorsed a restrictive approach closely modeled on Secretary Kobach's ideas; Kobach was also appointed to lead an examination of the integrity of the federal electoral system. The key legislative achievement of the first year of the Trump administration—a reform of the federal tax code—adapts features of Governor Brownback's tax plan. More generally, the Trump administration has relied heavily on unilateral executive action to achieve its objectives.

Democratic opponents of those actions have, for their part, made extensive use of state-initiated litigation, which partakes freely of the same sorts of arguments used by Republican state attorneys general in recent years. Indeed, Democratic officeholders have been quick to emulate nearly all the strategies discussed in this book: congressional intransigence, administrative procedure claims, assertions of state administrative interests, guarantees of positive rights, uncooperative stances toward federal agencies, and compact-like coordination devices. The Trump administration's efforts to narrow the size and regulatory activity of the federal administrative state, combined with ongoing liberal challenges to its exercise of executive power, therefore appears likely to continue trends that are giving states a larger role in American government. Further, this activity shows every sign of deepening the partisan divisions that prompted state officeholders to take an active, confrontational approach to relations with the federal government.

The ultimate result of this pattern of contention will depend on questions that are not yet settled. It remains to be seen whether the federal courts will continue to be receptive to state challenges to the federal executive. The Supreme Court currently finds itself in a doctrinal contradiction, but it is not obvious that a major restatement would reduce the flow of state litigation: legal considerations aside, there are compelling political reasons for states to continue suing the federal government. It is also uncertain how far state policies will diverge in areas where federal involvement is dwindling. Legally, relatively extreme divergence appears possible in many areas. The most significant check may be the difficulty of building the fiscal and administrative capacity for bold new experiments in state government; simple inertia is a major curb on policy fragmentation as well.

Finally, the trajectory of American government in the coming years will depend, in part, on what liberals are prepared to learn from conservative successes. This book documents many instances where conservatives have consciously emulated liberal successes in the use of law, leveling what had been a pronounced imbalance in both legal ideas and organizational capacity during the years after the midcentury rights revolution. There can be little doubt that conservatives currently have an organizational advantage in shaping the conduct of state government as well as a fuller vision of what state government ought to do. Modern American liberalism has had a strongly federal orientation from the New Deal onward; it does not have a comparably elaborated vision of state government, although the Democratic political activity of this moment seems likely to shift both formal power and policy initiative to the states.

This book thus concludes that those interested in the future of policy about matters such as social welfare provision, voting rights, immigration, and environmental protection should look to the states. Academic researchers themselves may have a substantial role in defining that future. This conclusion is, partly, a simple reflection on the past. The development of recognizably modern academic social sciences was a crucial precursor to the political transformations of the Progressive Era. The ongoing conservative reorientation in the American judiciary is, in meaningful respects, a process that started with the founding of a student organization. This claim is also a reflection on who is, geographically, in a position to take on the job. Nonacademic intellectual production in America has always been concentrated in a handful of cities (see Haveman 2015) and is increasingly the province of alumni of a handful of elite institutions. Newspapers have few resources to train on the operation of state government—many states have at best a handful of reporters to cover activity in the capital. Social scientists, by contrast, are numerous and widely dispersed throughout the country. But facing up to the task of chronicling the changes in American federalism—to say nothing of reimagining it—will require traversing disciplinary boundaries. This book draws on large, useful bodies of existing research from traditional disciplines like political science, law, sociology, and public administration as well as interdisciplinary endeavors such as law and society. Each provided a piece to the solution of this book's particular puzzle. No discipline can hope to solve the bigger puzzle on its own.

CHAPTER TWO

State Office as a Support Structure for Conservative Legal Activism

In February 2015, Congress held a hearing on an administrative rule that sought to clarify how federal water quality laws should be applied to certain wetlands and bodies of water that flow only occasionally. The EPA's Waters of the United States Rule (2015) had, like other proposed agency rules, been available for public comment on the website https://www.regulations.gov/. Most proposed rules—even important ones—attract somewhere between dozens and hundreds of comments. The proposed Waters of the United States Rule had attracted millions. The hearing began with testimony from EPA administrator Gina McCarthy, who laid out the agency's rationale for the rule. The first witness to respond was Oklahoma attorney general Scott Pruitt, who said that the rule "reeks of federal expansion, overreach, and interference" and rounded out his testimony with a blunt promise: "The rule will be challenged in court" (Pruitt 2015, 2, 3). That promise was carried out: more than thirty states participated in five federal suits challenging the final version of the rule. Two years later, Pruitt, who succeeded McCarthy as head of the EPA, had begun efforts to rescind it.

This story could be repeated many times over. Whenever there has been intergovernmental friction or disagreement in recent years, multistate litigation has rarely been far behind. Republican-controlled states sued the Obama administration with remarkable frequency, and the administration fared a good deal worse before the Supreme Court than its modern predecessors. Success in the courts, in turn, enabled conservative state officeholders to take a bolder position in opposition to the federal government and try out a range of new state administrative behaviors. The legal activity of state officers like Attorney General Pruitt is foundational to all the other activity discussed in this book. This chapter explains what this behavior involved and how it has succeeded.

Part of that success arose from a readiness to try new arguments and follow up on even modest wins—or, in some cases, losses. This activity largely cast aside a traditional language of states' rights. Instead, it relied on adaptations of legal strategies and arguments first developed by liberals or ventured into the labyrinthine world of administrative law. This chapter examines three important kinds of legal claims made by conservative states. The first, exemplified in the conflict over the Waters of the United States Rule, concerns state challenges to federal activity grounded in claims about administrative law and procedure. Over the past decade, the basis on which states can make such claims has widened, and states have succeeded in laterally applying judicial reasoning developed in cases about the EPA to a range of other federal activity. Relying on established state administrative powers, states have also succeeded in staking a claim to make their own policy in areas, such as immigration, that have historically been understood as federal prerogatives. Finally, states have extended new positive rights to their citizens; those rights are, in some cases, also calculated to challenge existing federal policy.

These new sorts of rights claims have developed in a larger context. Even before the opening of the Obama administration, judicial reasoning about the exercise of federal administrative power had been shifting in ways that made it easier for states to file suits. State attorneys general had enjoyed steady growth in their profile and the material resources at their disposal. And the long rise of the conservative legal movement was not only changing legal reasoning and the composition of the judiciary but also reorienting conservatism toward legal strategies. Using the court system to seek major change is a slow, costly, and arduous process. For such an approach to work, actors seeking change must have in place a robust support structure for litigation (Epp 1998). Solidifying legal change frequently depends on the existence of administrators who are sympathetic to the goals pursued by judicial mobilization and prepared to act independently to make the legal changes a practical reality (Epp 2010). The key argument of this chapter is that the confluence of slower processes of legal change and intense partisan polarization has made state offices like attorney general a ready-made support structure for conservative litigation. This, in turn, has provided opportunity for

new conservative experiments in administrative behavior—and the use
of these new behaviors as a starting point for further litigation.

The Rise of the Conservative Litigation States

This chapter will discuss conservative state legal behavior under the
Obama administration across a wide range of legal matters and policy areas. The recent increase in conservative state litigation, however,
was enabled in part by conditions that developed over a longer period
of time. The capacity of state attorneys general to litigate increased substantially in the decades before the opening of the Obama administration. By the end of the Bush administration, the Supreme Court appeared to be somewhat more skeptical about the exercise of discretion
by agencies and had also handed down an important decision that made
it easier for states to initiate suits against the federal executive. And the
conservative legal movement had laid the groundwork for a state strategy centered around litigation: it had, gradually, succeeded in shifting
sympathies in the federal judiciary and trained a large number of tal-
ented conservative lawyers who were to occupy state attorney general offices in record numbers by 2010. Just as this movement had changed the
law, it also changed conservatism—lawyers and legal strategies had become steadily more central to American conservatism by this time.

The Increase in Conservative Multistate Litigation before the
Supreme Court

The volume and partisanship of state litigation before the Supreme
Court increased dramatically under the Obama administration (Nolette 2014). Historically, multistate involvement in Supreme Court cases
has been bipartisan (Lemos and Quinn 2015). Nolette's (2015) data show
two important patterns of change. First, the rate of Republican attorney general involvement in Supreme Court cases has grown markedly
since the opening of the Reagan administration; in the early years of
Obama's second term in office, Republican attorneys general were involving themselves in Supreme Court cases more frequently than Democrats. Second, the number of cases involving conflicts between opposing
partisan blocs of state attorneys general or blocs of state attorneys general opposing the federal government spiked dramatically; in the pre-

ceding generation, the Court typically heard around six such cases per annual term. Over the October 2013 and 2014 terms, the Court heard nearly thirty such cases—over double the historical norm. The most common division in such cases saw a group of Republican state attorneys general litigate or brief against the federal executive. Simple counting of the number of cases of this kind understates the proportion of cases involving partisan intergovernmental disagreement: the Burger Court, whose last decision was handed down in 1986, issued written opinions in roughly twice as many cases per term as the Roberts Court (Epstein et al. 2015, 89–90).

It takes some time for a suit to make its way up the judicial hierarchy to the Supreme Court. State-initiated cases that challenged Obama administration policy began to come before the Court by the October 2009 term; the Court continued to hear a meaningful number of such cases through the October 2015 term. Justice Antonin Scalia's death during that term resulted in a long vacancy that likely would have left the Court evenly divided in many cases dealing with intergovernmental or administrative procedural matters—evident, for example, in the evenly divided per curiam ruling in *United States v. Texas*, a case on the legality of major immigration reforms. It appears that the Court avoided such cases in the following term. From the start of the October 2009 term to the end of the October 2015 term, it heard sixty-seven merits cases in which a strongly Republican bloc of state attorneys general argued the case, intervened, or filed a collective amicus brief in opposition to the federal government or a predominantly Democratic bloc of state attorneys general.[1] Twelve states participated in a majority of those cases in some capacity, most frequently as producers or signatories of amicus briefs. They are, in descending order: Alabama (fifty-three cases), Michigan (fifty), Arizona (forty-six), Kansas (forty-four), Texas (forty-three), Idaho (forty-two), South Carolina (forty-two), Utah (forty-two), Georgia (forty), Nebraska (thirty-nine), Colorado (thirty-seven), and Oklahoma (thirty-seven). The number of Republican attorneys general participating in such cases has grown in approximate proportion to the number of such offices held by Republicans. The average number of Republican attorneys general joining the litigation coalition in cases heard in the October 2009 term was 14.5; by the October 2015 term the average was above 19. The number of cases of this kind and the number of states involving themselves in such cases grew rapidly. However, this recent pattern is the result of the conjunction of intense partisan divisions during the Obama administration and several legal and political patterns that have developed over a longer period of time.

Factor 1: The Expansion in State Litigation Capacity

Litigating against the federal executive is a resource-intensive undertaking, all the more so for the sorts of cases considered here, which have focused particularly on matters of administrative law and procedure—a remarkably complex legal area in which cases are slow to develop. Making such litigation the core of a political strategy became feasible, in part, because of nearly uniform expansion in the legal resources available to state attorneys general in the preceding years. This expanded legal capacity arose, in large part, as a response to the development of new federal rights regimes. Major congressional acts—especially those that have recognized new individual rights—have become over time less likely to grant agencies large investigative or enforcement powers. Thus, adversarial legal proceedings in the federal courts have become a primary mechanism for enforcement, prompting the emergence of what has been called the *litigation state* (Farhang 2010; see also Burbank, Farhang, and Kritzer 2013, 686).[2] For instance, agencies handle only a fraction of employment discrimination complaints (see Edelman 2016); setting aside suits from prisoners, such complaints are by far the largest source of caseload in the federal district courts. States have taken a particularly active role in litigating under such rights regimes (see Lemos 2012). Major consumer protection suits, in particular, prompted significant and nearly universal growth in state litigation capacity during the 1990s (Nolette 2015, 22, 29); such cases often involved the majority of all state attorneys general, and, across a wide range of cases, there are not meaningful partisan differences in states' participation or readiness to assume a lead role in litigation. Thus, the key contention in Nolette is that the structure of post–civil rights era federal rights and regulatory activity has made the attorney general a more powerful office in almost all states.

In addition to simple quantitative growth in the resources available to state attorneys general, these patterns of litigation prompted a notable shift in the way states approach the federal courts. Although the practice was once rare, by the beginning of the Obama administration it had become typical for states to appoint solicitors general to handle federal appellate cases (Miller 2010). The timing of the adoption of a solicitor general model in states corresponds closely with the expansion in multistate litigation discussed in Nolette (2015). Typically, solicitors general have better legal pedigrees and more extensive appellate experience than elected attorneys general (Owens and Wohlfarth 2014). States are more likely to win cases handled by a solicitor general. The advantage likely arises from better handling of cases as well as more discerning initial selection of cases and legal arguments. The level of talent and experience brought to bear may, in itself, be a significant cause of recent decline in the presidency's historical advantage in cases argued before the Supreme Court (see Epstein and Posner 2017). The overall increase in multistate litigation since the 1990s has also made state attorneys general more apt to join together specifically in litigation against the federal government; multistate involvement in federal cases has proved more likely to yield favorable outcomes for state petitioners (Goelzhauser and Vouvalis 2012).

Factor 2: The Court's New Receptivity to State-Initiated Suits

The degree of judicial skepticism about the operation of federal administration has ebbed and flowed over time. That skepticism was increasing immediately before the opening of the Obama administration. Since the emergence of a large federal administrative state during the New Deal, federal agencies have played a direct or mediating role in the formulation of nearly all government policy.[3] Although an act of Congress can serve to define an intention, desired outcome, and basic regulatory approach, the welter of practical detail can be worked out only by the activity of large, specialized executive agencies. Depending on their organizational structure and mandate, agencies take official actions by several means; the most important is the notice-and-comment rulemaking process defined by the 1946 Administrative Procedure Act (APA) (for a general overview, see Kerwin and Furlong [2011]). In this process, agencies publish a notice of proposed rulemaking—in effect, a public draft of the proposed policy. Interested parties have a fixed period in which to submit comments about that proposal. The agency may then promulgate a final version of the rule after weighing these comments. The implementation of a major piece of legislation may require the development of hundreds of rules. A major rule developed by an agency may, in turn, be longer and more complex than many substantial acts of Congress; the sorts of agency rules discussed in this chapter often run to several hundred pages in length.

The development of the modern federal administrative state produced two difficult judicial problems: how to recognize the administrative state as a legitimate feature of the American constitutional order
and how to review administrative behavior appropriately. The Constitution offers little guidance about the actual operation of government.
As chapter 1 noted, an important early function of political parties was
to make an operable government possible. The same is true of administrative entities. Mashaw's (2012, 285) historical account presents administration as having emerged quite early in American government to fill
in a "hole in the text" of the Constitution. But the twentieth-century administrative state is, without question, distinct from what came before
and posed basic constitutional questions that were up to that point un-
answered. Perhaps the most common view is that the growth of the administrative state—and the judicial reasoning that authorized it—was a
significant break with existing understandings of the Constitution and a
break that was practically necessary (Sunstein 1987; Frohnen and Carey
2016). Some critics continue to view the administrative state as ultra vi-
res and intrinsically illegitimate. A major recent work has argued that
administrative law as such is illegal (Hamburger 2014), while another
critic has said: "The post–New Deal administrative state is unconstitutional, and its validation by the legal system amounts to nothing less
than a bloodless constitutional revolution" (Lawson 1994, 1231).

Yet the basic legitimacy of the administrative state is a firmly established judicial fact. The more persistent problem, from the judicial
point of view, is how and when to scrutinize administrative activity, particularly in view of the considerable procedural and substantive differences in the forms of reasoning employed by modern agencies and
courts. Mashaw (2012) notes that judicial review of federal agency decisions began during a time period when agency activity commonly took
the courtlike form of administrative hearings, thus producing a delimited record and a clear official position on the facts at issue. The shift to
rulemaking, central to the more active model of federal regulation that
arose in the twentieth century, fits awkwardly within the traditional form
of judicial review. Rulemaking produces a sprawling record and closely
resembles legislative activity in its process and objectives—commenting
is, in theory, a consultative rather than an adversarial process even if it is
in practice often a means of laying the groundwork for a lawsuit as well
as a kind of lobbying. Judicial review is not afforded until a party has exhausted the available administrative remedies. But, even at that point,

the record is likely to be technically complex, and core factual matters may remain unsettled.

Agency activity must meet certain legal standards that do not constrain, for instance, the legislative powers of Congress (Metzger 2008). But, in part because of the high degree of technical expertise informing agency activity and underlying differences in the substance and process of judicial and administrative decision-making, the federal courts, in practice, took a highly deferential view of agency activity through the latter part of the twentieth century. The Supreme Court's 1984 decision in *Chevron U.S.A., Inc. v. Natural Resources Defense Council, Inc.* produced a much-used formal test for determining when courts will accord deference to agencies. Judicial deference, too, has attracted conservative criticism. Some of this criticism is, of course, primarily about the underlying policies. But other concerns are procedural and include the relative difficulty of establishing standing to challenge agency activity, permissive standards for agency activity to withstand review, and the relative weakness of common judicial remedies (see DeMuth 2016). Taken in sum, these criticisms suggest that it is too difficult for an agency to truly lose a court case. The perception that judicial review was not a sufficient check against agency power figured in the inclusion of limited legislative veto power over agency rules as part of Newt Gingrich's Contract with America. The Congressional Review Act gives Congress a sixty-day period in which it may vote against a new agency rule, though this vote is itself subject to presidential veto.

A series of Supreme Court decisions in the early twenty-first century appeared to nod at a circumscription of the instances under which *Chevron* deference would be offered (Sunstein 2006). In 2007, the Supreme Court's decision in *Massachusetts v. EPA* initiated a more significant break with the pattern of deference that had been the norm through the late twentieth century (see Freeman and Vermeule 2007). The reasoning in that case proved to be an important enabling condition for state litigation against the Obama administration. There, the state of Massachusetts was among a group of government and nongovernment actors who had petitioned the EPA for rulemaking to regulate carbon dioxide emissions. The EPA denied the petition. In the resulting litigation, Massachusetts asserted that this decision had harmed its interests through the prospective loss of coastal lands to sea level rise. The Court's opinion thus dealt with two matters: whether Massachusetts could use such a claim as a valid basis for initiating a suit and, supposing that this claim cre-

ated a genuine controversy to be settled, whether the EPA had appropriate grounds for denying the petition. As the majority opinion acknowledged, the denial of a rulemaking petition is an action that ordinarily sits
squarely within the range of agency activity accorded deference by the
judiciary.

However, in *Massachusetts*, the Court held that the EPA had erred
in this denial. The opinion offered a reinterpretation of the EPA's view
of both the underlying climatic science and the provisions of the relevant congressional statutes. Further, the opinion set forth the view that
states were to be accorded a "special solicitude" in assessing questions of
standing to bring suits of this kind—in effect, suggesting that they might
be allowed to bring a suit where other actors would not, on the basis of
very broadly construed government interests. Intergovernmentally, this
reasoning created a means for states to prod agencies to act where they
had been inactive (see Sharkey 2009) and also provided an implicit basis for states to make wide claims that their interests had been harmed
by federal action. The political valence in the application of this reasoning would depend, of course, on the leanings of the relevant state and of
the federal executive as well as on the nature of the agency action at issue. The opinion in *Massachusetts* was signed by the liberal wing of the
Court, and it was understood, in practical terms, as a rebuke to the Bush
administration's environmental policy. Yet the promise of special solicitude to states also indirectly functioned as a response to conservative
criticisms of the insufficient checks on the activity of the administrative
state. Though that criticism has often been stated as a concern about the
separation of powers, the reasoning here opened a means to challenge
administrative activity as a consideration about federalism.

Factor 3: The Upward Arc of the Conservative Legal Movement

Finally, the high rate of state litigation against the Obama administration was enabled by the larger successes of the conservative legal movement and the growing representation of those ideas in state attorney general offices as well as the legal academy and the federal judiciary. Until
very recently, Democrats had dominated state elections for attorney general.[4] This electoral success reflected a more general pattern: the legislative action, judicial decisions, and expanded administrative activity of
the 1960s and 1970s were, in many ways, a defeat of traditional Amer-

ican conservatism—a form of conservatism that, among other things, did not envision an especially large or important role for the judiciary (see Kersch 2011). As Teles's (2008) landmark history of the conservative legal movement argues, the reforms of this period produced a legal landscape that strongly favored liberal claims as well as institutional conditions particularly favorable for the production and legitimation of liberal experts and expertise. Teles shows that founding figures in the conservative legal movement, then, undertook a slow process of intellectual development and legitimation, legal training, and development of institutional capacity. By the opening of the Obama administration, this movement had grown and matured in a way that has certainly contributed to the success of state litigation.

The conservative legal movement has developed an extensive intellectual and material support structure, yielding a meaningfully large body of well-credentialed, well-placed conservative lawyers (Hollis-Brusky 2011), a process driven particularly by the placement of young conservative lawyers in federal clerkships (Baum 2014). Patterns of hiring suggest that the successes of the conservative legal movement had become self-sustaining within the legal academy by the mid-1990s (Phillips 2016, 31 n. 118), assuring continued intellectual diffusion and training of young lawyers. Although conservative and libertarian professors represent a relatively small proportion of faculty in law schools, on average they have much more direct experience with the federal judiciary than professors from other points on the political spectrum (Phillips 2016, 32). An important coordinating organization for the conservative legal movement has been the Federalist Society, founded at elite private law schools in the early 1980s. It serves as a mediating organization that unites several distinct conservative legal worldviews (Southworth 2008) and has been successful in promoting the federal judicial recognition of legal arguments relatively favorable to states (Hollis-Brusky 2013). Members of the Federalist Society—who now include four members of the US Supreme Court (Alito, Gorsuch, Roberts, and Thomas) and at least 12 percent of federal appellate judges—have shown themselves to be extraordinarily receptive to states' claims on the bench (Scherer and Miller 2009).

Just as the movement has figured in changes in the composition and reasoning of the judiciary, it has changed conservatism. As Southworth (2008) argues, efforts to limit the influence of liberal public interest litigation ultimately yielded an analogous structure of conservative pub-

lic interest firms with substantial support from philanthropic foundations. This process has also gradually moved lawyers and legal strategies
from a peripheral to a central role within American conservatism more
generally.

The conservative legal movement thus advanced its cause through two
complementary strategies: gaining visibility and legitimacy for conservative ideas within the legal academy and training individuals not only for
legal academic careers but also for judicial roles in which they can give
these same ideas a favorable hearing. The pursuit of elected legal offices
has not generally figured in this strategy. However, it may have been the
decisive difference in recent years. The state attorneys general most active in litigation against the federal government since 2009 typically have
ties to the Federalist Society.[5] As will be argued below, the use of state
attorney general offices functions as a public support structure for pursuing the objectives of the conservative legal movement.

This section has established that Republican multistate coalitions have
managed to bring a large number of cases before the Supreme Court under the Obama administration; the number of cases brought before the
court and the number of states involved have increased even as the total number of merits cases handled by the Supreme Court declined to
historic lows. This represents a significant deviation from patterns that
had persisted since at least the beginning of the Reagan administration.
Several factors in the larger environment created this opportunity. First,
state attorneys general have access to a larger stock of resources and have
had more success in the federal courts. Second, judicial thinking about
the behavior of the administrative state had begun to shift in a way that
produced both increased skepticism about the exercise of administrative
discretion and a greater sympathy for state-initiated suits—a pattern that
was not distinctly partisan. Third, the conservative legal movement had
succeeded in leveling ideological disparities in legal talent and capacity
for mobilization; its focus on the academy, begun some thirty years before, had by the Obama administration persisted long enough for large
numbers of lawyers shaped by the movement to occupy eminent positions on the federal bench. These processes functioned as a highly favorable legal opportunity structure after the Obama administration turned
toward executive unilateralism and Republicans won control of extraordinary numbers of state attorney general offices. The following will consider a range of legal strategies employed to make use of this structure.

Administrative Procedure and the Negation
of Federal Authority

Three Supreme Court rulings during the Obama administration attracted especially wide public notice. In *National Federation of Independent Businesses v. Sebelius*, the Court upheld the legality of the ACA's
"individual mandate." In *Shelby County v. Holder*, it ended continued
federal oversight of elections in states with a history of voter discrimination. In *United States v. Windsor*, it effectively recognized that same-
sex marriages performed in states that licensed such unions must also
be recognized federally. These were cases of genuinely great importance
and ones in which conservative states took an active interest. Yet these
most visible cases are not representative of the legal issues that occurred
most frequently during this period; these three cases, as they were popu-
larly understood, dealt directly with basic questions about the power of
Congress or fundamental matters of individual rights.

The prevailing mode of argument, however, has built on the reasoning in *Massachusetts v. EPA* and has dealt with federal administrative
procedure and the scope of states' interests in such administrative matters. This section will examine states' remarkably successful litigation
against the EPA to describe the larger legal pattern employed in administrative procedure cases. It will then show that states have used successful suits against the EPA to consolidate legal doctrines that have been
used to prevent the implementation of other major policies—that is, a
view of states' sovereign interests initially connected to coastal land
came to be laterally applied to many other matters of policy, effectively
consolidating a very broad basis on which states can sue federal actors.

The EPA was a party to five Supreme Court cases between 2007 and
2015: *Massachusetts v. EPA, Sackett v. EPA, EPA v. EME Homer City,
Utility Air Regulatory Group v. EPA*, and *Michigan v. EPA*. Two other
important cases involving the EPA—*West Virginia v. EPA* and various
suits challenging the Waters of the United States Rule—were wending
their way toward the Supreme Court by the conclusion of the Obama administration. In light of this profusion of litigation, one might think that
the EPA is an agency that poses unique constitutional problems or draws
its authority from particularly troublesome or vague congressional legislation. Yet, once the basic legality of the EPA's mandate was established
in the 1970s and early 1980s, the agency was almost totally absent from

the Supreme Court for a period of thirty years. In the more recent round of litigation, it has faced challenges that are about its use of administrative powers.

In *Sackett*, the first of these cases heard under the Obama administration, the Court unanimously held that compliance rulings—the key mechanism by which the EPA actually regulates activity—are subject to judicial review. Eleven states participated in *Sackett*. The three subsequent cases dealt with particular rules on air quality. On average, twenty-one states participated in each of these cases. At issue has been the extent to which the EPA must consider factors such as cost and the structure of individual state economies when making rules; in these cases, the Court continued to hold that the EPA had failed to fully consider the relevant issues during the rulemaking process, with the result that major air quality protection efforts were repeatedly forced back to the notice-and-comment process.

Delaying the implementation of air quality measures was undoubtedly a goal in itself. Delay has also been foundational for a wider strategy. First, the ability to delay implementation of rules through litigation (or the prospect of litigation) and to force repeated rounds of rulemaking provides states with both a stronger position in rulemaking and time to devise complex legal strategies for use against the final rule. An illustrative case is the Waters of the United States Rule, which clarifies and slightly expands the geographic scope of the Clean Water Act—the Supreme Court's ruling in *Rapanos v. United States* had created uncertainty about the legal status of some bodies of water, especially those that flow only seasonally or irregularly. The promulgation of the final rule was delayed by at least three years while the EPA undertook extensive consultation and solicited a new round of commenting (EPA 2015), a delay that owed to intense political interest in the commenting process as well as the certainty of state litigation. The rule met with immediate legal challenges when it was officially promulgated (see Stenehjem 2015). Table 2.1 shows the petitioners in cases challenging the rule as well as the districts in which these cases were filed and the appeals circuits in which those districts reside.

The involvement of thirty-one states in litigation is striking, as is the extremely high involvement of states where a Republican is attorney general. However, this pattern of filings reflects something more than a simple massed approach to litigation—this is not, after all, one multistate suit but several state suits. This is an approach that greatly in-

TABLE 2.1. **State filings against the EPA's Waters of the United States Rule**

Petitioners	District	Circuit
ND, AK, AZ, AR, CO, ID, MO, MT, NE, NV, SD, WY, NM	ND	8th
OH, MI, TN	S. OH	6th
TX, LA, MS	S. TX	5th
GA, AL, FL, IN, KS, KY, NC, SC, UT, WV, WI	S. GA	11th
OK	N. OK	10th

creases the chances that a judge will bar the implementation of the rule
and that the Supreme Court will ultimately hear the case. The filings enabled states to seek an injunction in five federal districts with conservative leanings; pursuing multiple cases also provides scope for states to
test a wider variety of initial objections to the rule. Because these districts reside in five different appeals circuits, there is also a much greater
chance that circuits will disagree about the rule. Circuit conflict is a particularly persuasive consideration in the Supreme Court's grant of cer-
tiorari in a case. And bringing a case before the Supreme Court is, in
turn, important for securing larger doctrinal shifts.[6] A very similar pattern could be observed in the rule at issue in *Michigan v. EPA*. This rule
was first proposed in May 2011 (EPA 2012) and was the subject of an
injunction. Four years later, the Supreme Court ordered that it be re-
opened for comments and drafted anew. The range of initial objections
to it was very wide; it was eventually found to be deficient because of the
EPA's failure to consider implementation costs during the rulemaking
process.[7]

These cases against the EPA were in some respects recognizably preliminary to litigation over the Clean Power Plan, arguably the largest and
most significant piece of federal environmental policy undertaken since
the creation of the EPA. Under the plan, the EPA would have required
a 30 percent overall reduction in carbon dioxide emissions from stationary sources (EPA 2014); the plan is therefore a significant undertaking
to address the basic causes of climatic change. Work on the rule began in
2010, and, as states have succeeded in litigation against the EPA in other
cases, the agency engaged in longer dialogue with states in the drafting
of the rule (see Konisky and Woods 2016). For all its complexity, the final rule does not include very many particular requirements about compliance: states were given an emissions target and a time line for reaching it but enjoy a great deal of flexibility in how they meet this target.

The state response to the proposed rule was unusually aggressive. In

West Virginia v. EPA, a coalition of sixteen states sought to have the proposed Clean Power Plan declared unconstitutional. (This case was dismissed by the DC Circuit Court on the grounds that the federal judiciary has not rendered a decision on the legality of a rule that has not actually been finalized—ruling at this stage would, in effect, have constituted an advisory opinion.) The delayed development of the Clean Power Plan also provided states time to prepare a variety of challenges to the final rule. Oklahoma governor Mary Fallin, for instance, issued a sweeping executive order that would serve to test the legality of any emissions target. Kansas created a special commission that must approve any state plan, laying the groundwork for a legal dispute about preemption of a kind that has been very successful for states before the Roberts Court (see Young 2011). Other states fashioned policies that would provide for other grounds to challenge the rule.

The promulgation of the final rule prompted a continuation of the *West Virginia v. EPA* case. In January 2016, West Virginia, joined by twenty-nine other states, sought to have the Supreme Court issue a stay on the rule's implementation until the DC Circuit ruled in the case. This stay was granted in February in the final round of orders issued before Antonin Scalia's death. The federal government's response to the request for a stay noted that this, too, was extraordinary: the stay has gone into effect before any court had actually issued any ruling on the plan and also stopped the clock on implementation, which would have delayed every aspect of the plan even if it had eventually been permitted to go into effect.

These cases against the EPA consolidated and extended the line of reasoning set out in *Massachusetts* and contributed to evolving judicial views of state standing and the requirements of rulemaking. These same administrative procedural arguments have been successfully deployed to prevent the implementation of other major federal policies. Two merit mention for their substantive importance and clear suggestion of a larger shift in state claims making derived from the EPA cases.

Through a series of executive orders, President Obama sought to achieve a number of reforms to federal immigration law. The most important of these orders would have, in effect, provided several million undocumented immigrants with a legal status that would protect them from deportation. In *Texas v. United States*, a large, overwhelmingly Republican attorney general coalition secured an injunction against the implementation of key aspects of the reform, justified primarily on the basis that the order violated standards for administrative procedure established in the EPA cases. In *Texas v. United States*, the states made a two-part argument about administrative procedure. First, they contended that the executive order amounted to a kind of policy change that is, under the APA, required to go through rulemaking. Second, they argued that, if the order had gone through the rulemaking process, it would have been necessary for the Department of Homeland Security to consider the financial costs the new immigration status would create for states. (Texas specifically discussed the cost of issuing drivers' licenses.) This claim about compliance costs as both a basis for standing and a substantive objection to a policy is strikingly similar to the argument advanced by the states in *Michigan v. EPA*. In the summer of 2016, the Supreme Court handed down a 4–4 vote in *United States v. Texas*; the split decision had the effect of upholding the lower court's ruling that the immigration order could not go into effect.

In November 2016, a federal court issued an injunction against the Overtime Rule, which would have made 4.2 million low-paid, salaried employees eligible for overtime pay. The ruling—in *Nevada v. Department of Labor*—turned on a reading of the APA that relied heavily on recent Supreme Court cases, particularly *Utility Air Regulatory Group v. EPA*. It also pointed to two other cases in 2016 in which district courts issued injunctions against federal rules on identical legal grounds. One such case prevented the implementation of a Department of Education rule that sought to limit the enforcement of "bathroom bills" such as the one enacted in North Carolina. Another prevented the implementation of a Department of Labor rule that would have required employers to disclose when they seek advice to prevent unionization (see generally Hertel-Fernandez 2016).

The 2016 injunctions against such rules are further evidence that the vague promise of special solicitude has solidified into an expanded state claim of standing to bring suits. Yet these same rulings also rejected many arguments derived from a traditional language of states' rights. In the cases about the Obama administration immigration orders, the courts rejected claims that the orders were intrinsically unlawful on constitutional grounds or that states were free on similar grounds to exempt themselves from the rule. In the Overtime Rule case, the opinion brushed aside a request for summary judgment (effectively, a claim that the rule was illegal on its face) and also declined to give consideration to state arguments grounded in the Tenth Amendment, the constitutional

provision at the heart of traditional states' rights arguments. In many
of the cases discussed thus far, successful arguments rooted in administrative procedure were initially put forward alongside unsuccessful arguments that directly invoked constitutional provisions about the powers of different levels of American government. Such arguments often
amount to little more than a legally sophisticated form of nullification
(see Sunstein and Vermeule 2016).

Although the starting point for this activity was a court ruling that
sought to compel the EPA to take positive action to limit climate change,
the administrative procedural arguments advanced in the following decade have yielded a rather different outcome. States' claims about their
own government interests have been used successfully to delay, weaken,
or entirely prevent the implementation of a range of major policies of the
federal executive. States have also succeeded in securing a lateral application of rulings from EPA policies to a range of other cases. The result
here is a curious one: these cases have yielded a markedly more favorable legal environment for state claims against the federal government
and also prevented the implementation of policies of genuinely large importance. Yet it has been a successful campaign that produced no conventional landmark legal victory. The cases have been decided almost
strictly in terms of the judiciary's own doctrines on administrative behavior. They have not reached more classically constitutional questions—a
contrast to the "New Federalism" of the late twentieth century—and,
even in the restricted domain of administrative procedure, none of them
appear to make a clear, important restatement about the judiciary's relation to the executive or the federal relation to the states.

This is not to say that successful state challenges to federal authority
have been confined to basically negative arguments about limits on federal power, such as those functionally advanced in APA-centered litigation. States have also had considerable success devising (and defending)
their own immigration enforcement strategies and have begun to explore
new states' rights arguments grounded in the "equal sovereignty" reasoning enunciated in *Shelby County v. Holder*. States have also challenged federal authority through new state guarantees of individual
rights. The following sections examine these developments. These positive arguments about state power are not yet well proved legally, but they
have met with some notable initial successes. They also establish that
state litigation seeks legal outcomes that go well beyond the disposition
of specific federal policies.

An Administrative Grammar of States' Rights:
Self-Deportation and Land Transfer

Traditional states' rights arguments grounded directly in features of the
Constitution such as the Tenth Amendment have stirred little judicial
interest in recent years. However, states have had notable success fashioning immigration enforcement policies without federal consent or direction. Both the model versions of the policies and the underlying legal
theory have been attributed to Kris Kobach, a conservative policy en-
trepreneur who has moved from a role as a law professor to head of the
Kansas Republican Party, Kansas secretary of state, and a Trump administration adviser on immigration and voting policy. In a series of law
review articles, Kobach set forth the view that state and local entities inherently possess the authority to enforce federal immigration law (Kobach 2005), that state immigration enforcement can gradually remove
undocumented immigrants from an area by attrition (Kobach 2007), and
that there exists "wide latitude for states and municipalities to act without being preempted, provided that the statutes are drafted correctly"
(Kobach 2008, 464). The policies he projected in these articles were intended to induce self-deportation by making it economically impossible
for undocumented immigrants to remain within a state and by rendering
immigration status visible in a wide range of routine interactions with
government. This policy was controversially incorporated into the national GOP platform in 2012 (Preston 2012) and was later endorsed by
the Trump administration, a matter discussed in the book's final chapter.

In addition to laying out a theoretical statement, Kobach has been
credited as the author of two important measures supporting an attrition
approach to state immigration enforcement. One, enacted in Arizona
as S.B. 1070 and commonly called the *show-your-papers law*, sought to
allow state and local law enforcement officials to inquire into individuals' immigration status during routine interactions and perhaps to initiate interactions for that purpose. Arizona's expansive implementation of
this law was partially rejected in *Arizona v. United States*. A revised version of the law, tailored in response to the Court's reasoning, was subsequently developed and enacted in a number of states (see Jones and
Brown 2017). The second policy makes use of states' authority to charter
businesses. This policy requires that all businesses within a state confirm
the employment eligibility of potential hires using the E-Verify data-

base, whose application was originally restricted to federal contractors.[8] By this means, administrators authorized to maintain state business records can seek to exert indirect legal pressure on undocumented immigrants. This policy was recognized as generally lawful in *Chamber of Commerce v. Whiting.* These employment-related policies were adopted in Alabama, Arizona, Georgia, Indiana, Mississippi, South Carolina, Tennessee, and Utah.[9]

The legal rationale for these strongly restrictionist state policies has developed during a period of greatly increased cooperation between federal, state, and local authorities. Since the 1990s, federal immigration policy has been intertwined with routine practices of law enforcement, a nexus often termed *crimmigration* law (Johnson 2016; see also Macías-Rojas 2016). Immigration enforcement is an intergovernmental patchwork (Provine et al. 2016), one that is highly dependent on state and local activity that is, technically, voluntary (Menjívar, Gómez Cervantes, and Alvord 2018). Yet the regulation of immigration has always been recognized as a federal prerogative—indeed, immigration is a policy domain where the federal executive historically enjoyed special and particularly expansive authority. It is only more recently that features of immigration law have begun to be subjected to more ordinary forms of judicial review (Johnson 2015). Self-deportation laws therefore challenged exclusive federal authority in immigration law at a moment when this authority was already regarded with increasing suspicion by the judiciary and when the federal government had become especially reliant on lower levels of government to handle the practical business of enforcement. These restrictive measures have been carefully crafted to provide a legal rationale rooted in existing, routinely exercised state powers. Though it is a bold foray onto federal turf, this practical assertion of states' rights is fashioned in administrative rather than overtly federalist language.

This period has also seen the development of a new states' rights argument. Since 2011, western states have quietly revived the political goals of the Sagebrush Rebellion, which began in 1979 and demanded the privatization or transfer of federal lands; in many states, federal agencies own or manage the great majority of all land. The rebellion was initially an intergovernmental lobbying effort, but it quickly escalated to overt intergovernmental conflict. In its first year, nine states passed measures demanding the privatization or transfer of all or most federal land (Titus 1981, 263–64). At the time, experts were largely dismissive of the legal claims advanced in support of these demands, which were variously grounded in the equal footing doctrine, the trustee doctrine, and readings of the enabling acts that authorized statehood (Leshy 1980). These claims were never put to a legal test. President Reagan, who embraced the rebels during his campaign, adopted policies that responded to many of the less radical demands of the movement (Babbitt 1982; Coggins and Nagel 1990), thereby prompting rapid abeyance (Popper 1984).

In 2012, Utah passed the Transfer of Public Lands Act, which demanded the transfer of virtually all federal land in Utah to state control. In the following years, similar bills have been introduced in every western state except California and Hawaii. Arizona, Nevada, Utah, and Wyoming have created bodies to study the legal and economic facets of large-scale federal land transfers; the lengthy, dry reports produced by these bodies may be understood as the first step in preparing a serious legal argument in favor of transfer. Utah also created an interstate compact in an effort to pool and coordinate these resources. The Arizona legislature voted in 2015 to join the compact, though this action was vetoed by the governor.

The land-transfer movement reprises all the legal arguments of the Sagebrush Rebellion; these arguments have met with similar dismissals from legal scholars (Keiter and Ruple 2014). However, the transfer movement has also presented a new legal rationale for its demands: equal sovereignty (Huffman 2016). Supporters contend that extensive federal control of land in western states violates their entitlement to a power of self-government that is equal to that of the rest of the states, a claim distinct from equal footing, which provides that new states enter the Union on the same terms as older states. The development of the equal sovereignty claim is significant for two reasons.

First, this claim has some basis in current judicial reasoning and is an attempt at a lateral application of a precedent such as that seen in the state challenges to the EPA discussed above. The majority opinion in *Shelby County v. Holder*, which invalidated the existing preclearance provisions of the Voting Rights Act, relied on the view that such oversight affronted a state's interest in equal sovereignty (see Molitor 2014). Scholars have noted that the doctrine may potentially affect many other questions of law; the legal academy's reception of *Shelby County* has generally been extremely unfavorable, but some conservative scholars have noted that the same sort of argument might be offered to challenge federal regulatory authority in areas such as environmental protection and gambling (see Colby 2016; Schmitt 2016). Whatever the view, it is agreed that much about the notion of equal sovereignty is yet to be elaborated and that equal sovereignty may have unpredictable effects on many questions of federalism (Davis 2015). Recent precedent, then, provides the transfer movement with a legal argument unavailable a generation ago; what is relevant here is not the probability that this claim would succeed but the readiness to seize on a new sort of argument.

In addition, the possible uses of an expanded equal sovereignty doctrine have induced many other states, mostly in the South, to make common cause with the land-transfer movement. The Arkansas, South Carolina, and Tennessee legislatures have passed resolutions in support of the movement, and such resolutions were introduced in Mississippi, New Hampshire, Ohio, and Virginia in 2016. Because so much of the practical success of recent state litigation against the federal government has occurred in the context of administrative law and cooperative federalism, some scholars have viewed the older rhetoric and goals of state sovereignty as otiose (see Gerken 2013b). The land-transfer movement—and extraregional sympathy for its claims—is an important suggestion that this dismissal may be premature: it is a much bolder assertion of state interests than is to be found in the procedural challenges to agency rules discussed above. Though the movement has not advanced far, its very existence, along with the persistent invocation of states' rights arguments in administrative procedure cases, suggests that many conservative state officials have retained aspirations that reach beyond securing injunctions against Obama administration policies.

From States' Rights to State-Guaranteed Rights

Over the course of the twentieth century, guarantees of positive rights under state constitutions and statutes figured significantly in the realization of progressive policy goals (Zackin 2013). Such state guarantees may often afford protections that go well beyond what could be achieved through rights claiming in the federal judiciary; the use of state constitutions to secure greater funding for public education is a notable example. This success has not been lost on conservative legal thinkers. Kris Kobach's first piece of published legal scholarship was an appreciation of the state-based activity of the Progressives (see Kobach 1994). Clint Bolick, the main litigator for the libertarian Goldwater Institute, has likewise written about the role of state-based rights provisions in the advancement of the civil rights era (Bolick 2012). Both authors identify state positive rights guarantees as a device worthy of study and emulation by conservatives. And, in recent years, states have extended new guarantees of positive rights to citizens as a means of challenging federal authority in place of direct claims of states' rights. Such newly guaranteed rights often conflict with existing federal policy and may thereby provide new avenues for producing legal controversies or new arguments to be used in ongoing controversies.

One example of such positive rights guarantees can be observed in challenges to federal gun regulations. One variant of this is the "battering ram" approach, in which gun rights organizations lobby for the passage of state gun law, allowing them to induce the development of Commerce Clause–based litigation that they could not have pressed directly as private actors (Orbach, Callahan, and Lindemenn 2010). Another variant is the adoption of a state constitutional guarantee of citizens' right to hunt, fish, and trap—these rights have been widely incorporated into state constitutions over the last decade. A constitutionally guaranteed right to hunt could, in theory, provide a basis for challenging a variety of gun control and environmental protection policies. Two other measures illustrate the further elaboration of the idea of using the state-guaranteed rights of residents as a means to challenge federal authority: secret ballot laws and right-to-try laws.[10]

"Save our secret ballot" measures guarantee the right to secret balloting in all elections, including union elections; the Goldwater Institute figured centrally in the development of this policy idea and campaign (see Bolick 2011). This proposal, framed by an appeal to the defense of voting rights and democracy, was popular enough to secure easy passage in many states through ballot initiatives in 2010 and 2012 (Beienberg 2014); other states have adopted the policy legislatively. Secret ballot provisions have been adopted in at least ten states since 2010: Alabama, Arizona, Indiana, Kansas, Maryland, South Carolina, South Dakota, Tennessee, Utah, and Virginia. Secret ballot laws are, proximately, an antiunion measure (see Milkman 2013): compared to secret ballot elections, it is generally faster and easier for unions to be certified by "card check," a method that results in certification if the majority of employees indicate in writing their desire to be represented by a given union in collective bargaining (Riddell 2004). Elections slow the unionization process and provide management with a formal opportunity to make an argument against unionization.

But secret ballot measures are also a challenge to federal labor law and associated judicial precedent. Since the New Deal, federal law has held that card check and other methods are valid ways of demonstrating employee support for collective bargaining, and many federal judicial decisions have upheld this view. Although federal law provides for specific procedures resulting in union recognition, it is a persuasive showing of workers' sentiment, rather than a fixed procedure, that is crucial to collective bargaining. Secret ballot measures seek to impose strict procedures on all unionization efforts, effectively closing off other, less formal avenues for initiating the collective-bargaining process. Arizona successfully defended its secret ballot law against a challenge in *NLRB v. Arizona*.

Right-to-try laws, which have diffused rapidly since 2014, entitle terminally ill patients to use experimental treatments and devices that have not been approved by the FDA, provided that a physician recommends them. In addition to creating a new positively guaranteed right, the measures represent an imaginative appropriation of progressive social movement tactics and legal strategies. The radical AIDS activist group ACT UP provides the inspiration for the bills, which have been called "Buyers Club" laws, in reference to the 2013 film *Dallas Buyers Club*, set during the AIDS crisis in the mid-1980s. The practical effect of these laws on access to useful treatments is likely to be very limited for the simple reason that very few experimental treatments—especially those in early phases of development—have any beneficial effect (Zettler and Greely 2014). The lifesaving antiretroviral therapies developed in response to the spread of HIV are, of course, an enormously important exception. Right-to-try laws create a clear conflict between state and federal law: federal courts have previously rejected the claim that patients have a fundamental right to experimental treatments (Shah and Zettler 2010), but not in a case in which states purported to guarantee that right. At present, these rights claims have not yet received a serious test in court. However, the recognition of the ability of states to guarantee such a right could be employed to challenge many other forms of federal regulation of biomedical research and clinical practice.

State-guaranteed positive rights, state assertions of administrative interests, and state challenges to federal administrative procedure combine to create a capacious, flexible set of legal arguments that can be employed to challenge particular policies and larger patterns in the exercise of federal authority. The adoption of these arguments—and a shift away

from direct assertions of states' rights under the constitutional allocation of powers—signifies both a readiness of conservative states to adapt
their claims to what the judiciary is prepared to entertain and a willingness to study and emulate both the legal form and the organizational
structure of earlier progressive legal activity.

The Control of State Attorney General Offices: Ready-Made Support Structures and Institutional Activism

In recent years, conservatives have used their control of state offices, especially state attorney general offices, as a ready-made support structure for significant judicial mobilization. In doing so, they have functionally surmounted some well-studied obstacles to the pursuit of major
legal and social change through the federal judiciary: resource limitations that hamper the attainment or consolidation of legal victories and
standing and controversy rules that make it difficult for movement actors to pursue major new rights claims. These constraints have, in turn,
generally made it very difficult for social movements to secure basic
changes in government structure: in the American context, such changes
require the imprimatur of the judiciary. Conservatives' successful control and use of state offices—as well as the special legal status of states
themselves—can therefore be understood as an unusual form of institutional activism, a phenomenon in which persons sympathetic to movement goals are embedded in the institutions the movement seeks to
change.

A large body of scholarship has engaged with Rosenberg's provoca-
tive claim that social movements generally commit a serious strategic er-
ror in seeking to use the federal judiciary to seek change (see Rosenberg
2008). The pursuit of major legal or political change through the courts
requires a robust and durable stock of legal resources. A successful program of litigation, first, requires the organizational capacity (and political will) to sustain large numbers of losses, a capacity that social movements frequently lack. Ab initio, movements may lack the legal resources
to generate a large enough volume of cases to set a legal agenda. Further,
private petitioners who have strong claims under existing law or who
have a material need to accept settlements tend not to shape doctrine
precisely because their cases are resolved quickly. Albiston's (2010) study
of the implementation of the Family Medical and Leave Act (FMLA)

provides a fine example of self-limiting legal success: strong claims by employees tended to be resolved out of court or through federal agency action, while employers sought in-court resolutions—and written decisions—in cases they were most likely to win, producing a body of case law that generally favored employers and thereby weakened the remedial rights protections afforded by FMLA. In addition, the funding structures of public interest law firms, which frequently litigate on behalf of movement organizations, often oblige such firms to accept settlements, thereby preventing them from seeking doctrinally significant outcomes (Albiston and Nielsen 2014). Serious legal setbacks can prompt the end of a judicial mobilization. Likewise, a landmark success can also result in premature demobilization. Extensive litigation is required to consolidate the apparent gains of a major case (Epp 2008), and it has long been understood that repeat players in the courts are successful not only in generally securing their desired outcome but also in blunting the effect of a significant adverse ruling (see, classically, Galanter 1974).

Conservative control of state attorney general offices has enabled a resolution of some of these common resource problems. As this chapter has shown, the litigation resources available to states have expanded substantially over the past twenty years. Given that the kinds of litigation activity examined here suppose a lengthy time horizon, it is significant that both the supply and the control of these resources are stable. Philanthropic support for public interest litigation may wax and wane; state budgets are, by comparison, extraordinarily reliable. Further, those appropriations may greatly exceed the support available for public interest litigators. Southworth (2008, 64) found that, through 2005, major foundation support for conservative public interest litigation, across all important conservative issue areas, came to about $30 million annually. Michigan, a notably active state in the suits discussed here, allocated $71.7 million to the state attorney general in fiscal year 2011, a sum that had grown to $93.8 million by fiscal year 2015 (Michigan State Budget Office 2018, C-76) and was to exceed $100 million by fiscal year 2019 (Michigan State Budget Office 2018, B-3).[11] These funds, of course, must be used to support a wide range of activities, and Michigan's office is unusually large, but it should also be noted that attorneys general have considerable discretion over how such resources are used (Provost 2010) and exercise that control over terms in office generally no less than four years in length and often much longer. With time and money on their side, state attorneys general have shown themselves quite ready to engage in a distributed search of the space of legal arguments even when this necessitates the pursuit of many losing cases and losing arguments. Further, the ongoing supply of resources for litigation is not contingent on legal success. Indeed, given that state attorneys general have the legal resources to sustain these losses, it is entirely possible that judicial setbacks may be politically valuable (see Beckwith 2015). The key contention of conservative critics of the administrative state is that an overweening federal executive, suborned by an activist federal judiciary, is trampling on the Constitution and the sovereign interests of state governments. Whatever the legal facts may be, within this worldview it is rhetorically simple to present lost court cases as evidence in support of the movement's basic claim and reason for mobilization. Control of state attorney general offices, then, positions conservatives to make politically productive use of judicial defeats.

In addition to the range of resource constraints just discussed, there is a second limitation on the use of courts by movements. Movement actors are limited in the kinds of legal claims that can be advanced: the matter must be one that judges will countenance as a genuine controversy, and the interested party must have standing to bring a suit. The grievances and goals of movements often fit awkwardly with the modes of legal argument available at a given moment (Burstein 1991). When a suitable controversy does arise, movements are generally constrained to litigate within a previously existing rights framework. These constraints on standing and the scope of legal claims that can be put forward by private actors have therefore placed certain classes of goals—especially those related to fundamental government structure—out of the reach of movements (Amenta et al. 2002; Meyer and Minkoff 2004). In the United States, such basic transformations are effectively subject to judicial ratification, and mass movement actors cannot seek such transformations, precisely because they are not part of the state. Such successes as can be attained by private petitioners are often narrow in their scope, and, if the success involves acknowledgment of a right, the new protection is often not directly enforceable (Kolb 2007, 97–114). Indeed, except in cases that are highly visible to the public, constitutional court decisions that require the nonsanctioned compliance of other government actors are ordinarily quite constrained in their effects (Hall 2011, 97–98; see also Krehbiel 2016).

Enforcement-related limitations also make judicial mobilization strategies generally reliant on sympathy from elite actors in other branches of government (for a review, see NeJaime [2012]). These sympathizers are often referred to as *institutional activists*. The study of institutional activism commonly examines progressive mass movements, such as movements for gender equality (Banaszak 2005), racial equality (Santoro and McGuire 1997), or environmental protection (Stearns and Almeida 2004). Further, Epp (2010) has argued that the post-1960s expansion of rights *in general* arises from lawlike behavior of bureaucratic activists. There is also a strong case to be made that concerted southern opposition to the expansion of civil rights—the politics of "massive resistance"—hinged not on white popular support for segregation but on the procedural and constitutional mastery of a handful of senators (Katznelson, Geiger, and Kryder 1993; Finley 2008, 4–10; Ward 2011, 5). This activity delayed civil rights reform for nearly thirty years after national sentiment had shifted against the South and undoubtedly weakened the reforms that were eventually adopted.

State actors in the "litigation state" era are well equipped to surmount both standing and compliance problems. As the series of cases against the EPA suggested, states have benefited from a relaxing of standing requirements and are also prepared to engage in extensive follow-up litigation to consolidate or expand on a shift in doctrine. Further, states are not necessarily obliged to wait for a suitable legal controversy to evolve—new state policy or new rights guarantees can be calculated to produce a controversy on demand.[12]

Control of state offices does not merely provide movement actors with broadened standing or ability to generate controversies; it also functions as a complement to earlier structural successes of the movement. Given that the conservative legal movement has diffused from the academy into the judiciary, the control of state attorney general offices by figures sympathetic to the basic vision of the conservative legal movement also creates the possibility of larger legal change by furnishing sympathetic judges with suitable cases and arguments. Strategic approaches to the study of judicial decision-making have long taken the view that court rulings are informed by judges' underlying policy preferences and awareness of structural constraints on enforceability (see such major statements as Posner [2008] and Epstein, Landes, and Posner [2013]). Yet studies of judges' subjective understanding of their mission as well as patterns of rulings indicate that judges are rarely so direct in their pursuit of desired policy outcomes: their first priority is nearly always to render what they understand to be the legally correct decision (see Cross 2007; Edwards and Livermore 2009; and Tamanaha 2009). Setting aside Supreme Court cases, which are unusually complex and thorny, the facts of a case are often clearly conducive to a consensus understanding of the correct outcome. Given that federal courts are small, stable groups, the norm of collegiality further promotes such consensus. This is to say that even judges with relatively strong or immoderate political leanings in one direction or the other will tend not to issue opinions on the basis of preferences for which there are not reasonably strong supporting legal arguments. The extensive, legally sophisticated pattern of state litigation against the Obama administration has furnished conservative judges with facts and arguments of this kind.

The expansion of the conservative legal movement's ideas and personnel into state elected offices can, then, be viewed as creating circumstances in which movement sympathizers occupy two of the three key positions in adversarial proceedings. This configuration helps account for another unusual feature of state litigation: conservative states have met with great success, but they have done so without a landmark victory—*Shelby County* possibly excepted—or a major shift in the way judges approach law. This strategy, which has involved a high volume of litigation reliant on relatively narrow procedural and administrative claims, stands in pronounced contrast to important legal developments of the civil rights era, in which judges adopted a much wider view of the kinds of questions deemed justiciable as well as the scope of application of key constitutional protections. Chapter 6 will consider in detail how these trends might continue under the Trump administration and what use progressive state officeholders might make of the expanded legal opportunity structure produced by conservative state resistance to the Obama administration.

This chapter has examined three legal patterns used by conservative state officeholders to challenge federal regulatory power: challenges to major agency rules based in evolving judicial interpretations of the APA; assertions of the states' right to use their existing administrative powers to fashion policy in areas, such as immigration, that have historically been federal prerogatives; and the use of state-level guarantees of individual rights to challenge the regulatory powers of important federal agencies. The judicial response to these modes of argument continues to evolve, but this litigation strategy has undoubtedly been a success for conservatives: state litigation has succeeded in weakening or entirely blocking major federal policies and regulations and has also consolidated an expanded claim of standing in suits against federal agencies. When states have lost on major claims, they have often succeeded in salvaging some victory from the case—this is true of states' adaptive response to the Supreme Court's ruling on show-your-papers laws in *Arizona v. United States* as well as the extensive set of legal and administrative controversies initiated by states after *National Federation of Independent Businesses v. Sebelius,* the ruling that recognized the legality of the core mandate of the ACA. State-led litigation has served as a direct means of achieving policy goals and expanding the legal scope for state activity. The ability to make successful use of the courts also creates the possibility for a dynamic interplay of state legal and administrative behavior—all other facets of intergovernmental relations occur in the shadow of the courts. This intertwined strategic behavior figures prominently in the activity discussed in the next two chapters.

CHAPTER THREE

Formalizing Defiance

Interstate Compacts in the State Challenge to Fiscal Federalism

The preceding chapter examined litigation ranging over many matters where the nature and practical exercise of federal power is both complex and open to various lines of legal attack. This litigation has exposed the places where federal administrative power has never been entirely formalized. But the dramatic twentieth-century expansion in federal power also built on a simpler and more legally solid foundation: the federal government controls enormous sums of money. Federal power to raise revenue began to grow during the American Civil War; by the ratification of the Sixteenth Amendment in 1913, Congress had enormous and constitutionally unassailable power to raise revenues through income taxes. Well before the constitutional and practical details about the operation of a federal administrative and welfare state had been worked out, federal tax power was being used to build this capacity through fiscal transfers to state governments. Where a vigorously exercised power of taxation has been deemed insufficient to meet government's needs, Congress may raise more by borrowing—a prerogative it has routinely exercised in most years since the New Deal, over which time the federal budget deficit has often been 3 or 4 percent of GDP and has run as high as 10 percent of GDP immediately after the 2008 economic crisis. As a proportion of GDP, federal spending increased by an order of magnitude over the course of the twentieth century (Harrison 1997, 3).[1]

With so much revenue to be disbursed, it is unsurprising that federal money has been a great persuader and a critical means of promoting reasonably harmonious intergovernmental relations. The latter part of the twentieth century has been acknowledged as a more or less distinct epoch of American federalism in which the defining questions of intergovernmental relations were, How much money? and, How many strings attached? As chapter 1 argued, the large-scale transfer of federal funds greatly changed the basic structure of state governments: large state executives have grown up, in part, to spend federal funds and administer federal programs. By the early twenty-first century, states had become highly adept at getting the most of this system—and had done so, to a great degree, by cooperative or persuasive means like intergovernmental lobbying or through forms of resistance to federal mandates that were often defensive or symbolic in character. In this period, intergovernmental conflicts tended to be sharpest on matters of policy where relatively little money was available to sweeten a mandate. Whether they were in sympathy with federal objectives or not, states were generally unwilling to leave money on the table even if they had always retained the legal right to do so.

During the Obama administration, important features of this pattern shifted. Many state governments refused large sums of federal money. Many of these same states also declined to use their administrative capacity to cooperate with federal policy goals or used administrative devices to seek further federal concessions. This pattern of partisan, uncooperative federalism is relatively well studied, particularly in the case of state resistance to the implementation of the ACA. This resistance showed, among other things, that a state government prepared to forgo money is in a strong position to frustrate federal policy.

This chapter begins with a brief overview of that body of research. It then discusses another dimension of recent state behavior: many states, in addition to using administrative devices to quarrel singly with the federal government, have also looked to the device of the interstate compact to coordinate their efforts, often in ways that are meaningfully associated with ongoing state litigation strategies. The use of interstate compacts to advance a position in a plainly partisan intergovernmental conflict is new—it is practically unproved and, in consequence, not yet an object of scholarly attention. This chapter will examine several proposed interstate compacts whose design would have allowed them to function as an administrative fallback in matters in which litigation was the primary state strategy as well as compacts that would have served to generate new litigation and compacts whose function would be to simplify interstate coordination to challenge existing federal policy. These proposed compacts vary widely in their sophistication and political and legal plausibility. However, in aggregate, they are an important suggestion of growth in interstate cooperation for political ends and in the interplay of administrative and litigation-based strategies to achieve these ends.

The chapter then gives extended consideration to the Compact for a Balanced Budget, an agreement that makes innovative and notably full use of the administrative and legal characteristics of interstate compacts. The compact seeks an outcome that would radically rearrange both fiscal federalism and the distribution of power in American government more generally: a state-initiated constitutional convention to enact an amendment requiring Congress to pass balanced budgets. Just as the passage of the ACA prompted the development of an uncooperative model of administrative intergovernmental relations, the early policy of the Obama administration prompted the spontaneous revival of calls for a constitutional convention. This, in turn, led to the emergence of three rival campaigns to promote a convention. The compact was the most successful of these. It was notably efficient in securing favorable consideration in states and succeeded in turning episodic state anger about federal spending and policy into a permanent, public administrative structure. As the language of its architects suggests, the proposal drives at something larger than a particular shift in policy: it is an endorsement of the idea that, working in cooperation, states can be—and, in the view of the architects, should be—more powerful than the national government. By focusing on a crucial source of national power—taxation and deficit spending—it seeks to make this vision a reality.

Administrative Behavior in the Growth of Uncooperative Federalism

Federal reliance on states to implement policy and programs—particularly social welfare programs—has always created a latent potential for conflict (Gerken 2014). The argument developed thus far has suggested that this potential had been tempered by the provision of funds on terms that afforded states some flexibility or discretion in their use (on which, see Nicholson-Crotty [2015]). That argument itself proceeds on the tacit assumption that elected officials would ordinarily allow these fiscal considerations to supersede ideological objections they might hold.[2] The process of sharper ideological polarization between parties as well as geographic alignment that has made state governments more stably partisan altered that calculus. The resulting pattern of more contentious intergovernmental relations under the Obama administration has been termed *uncooperative* or *partisan federalism* (see Bulman-Pozen and Gerken 2009; and Bulman-Pozen 2014). State noncooperation has become more pointed and proactive—as Burke (2014) argues, a significant shift from the mode of intergovernmental relations so aptly described by workhorse models such as that in Wright (1982). In this pattern, state opposition was often made manifest by rather more symbolic than material means (see Shelley 2008; and Jochim and Lavery 2015), and disagreements tended to be most pointed in the case of unfunded mandates—federal directives that came without fiscal assistance (Gormley 2006).

A simple but important break from this pattern has been the increased willingness of state executives to refuse federal funds. For instance, many governors made very public refusals of grants connected to the American Reinvestment and Recovery Act, commonly known as the *stimulus bill* (Nicholson-Crotty 2012). Similarly, the first major court ruling on the ACA—in *National Federation of Independent Businesses v. Sebelius*—held that states could not be compelled to adopt a key provision of the bill, that is, the expansion of Medicaid eligibility. Medicaid is a health insurance program for people with low incomes; it is substantially federally funded but primarily administered by states. States retain significant discretion in defining eligibility for the program and others like it—discretion that has widened with the growth of the "big waiver" approach, in which federal administrators are often willing to allow states to undertake considerable experimentation (Barron and Rakoff 2013). After the ruling, many Republican governors refused the Medicaid expansion (Barrilleaux and Rainey 2014), though the entire initial cost would have been paid by the federal government and some 90 percent of the cost thereafter (Gosling 2015, 216). Many states persisted in that refusal.

Outright refusal to implement a federal policy—and to forgo associated money available with few strings—is an important but extreme example of uncooperative federalism. There are also many other devices by which states can seek to redirect (or weaken) the thrust of federal activity by purely administrative means (Gerken 2013a). Again, the ACA is relevant; the initial refusal of Medicaid expansion resulted, in many states, in protracted political battles (Hertel-Fernandez, Skocpol, and

Lynch 2016). States sought to narrow or delay implementation by declin-
ing to establish health insurance exchanges, renewed rounds of intergovernmental bargaining, and simple foot-dragging (see, e.g., Leonard
2012; Haeder and Weimer 2013; Dinan 2014; Jones, Bradley, and Oberlander 2014; and Thompson and Gusmano 2014). It can be added that
the Obama administration's turn toward an executive model of intergovernmental relations—whose bypassing of Congress and state legislatures yielded some successes (Rose and Bowling 2015; Bulman-Pozen
and Metzger 2016)—is also an approach that is particularly vulnerable to
uncooperative state administrations.

As the preceding chapter suggested, uncooperative administrative activity also possesses a reciprocal relationship with state-initiated litigation. Suits may create delays in implementation that provide state governments time to devise policies and administrative practices that they
might have invoked if litigation had ultimately failed—the many home-
brewed plans for resisting the Clean Power Plan are one example. Similarly, litigation can also strengthen states' administrative position relative to federal agencies: the opening or reopening of rulemaking, in
which states can seek changes in policy or lay the groundwork for further suits, is a common remedy in administrative procedure cases. The
following discusses states' increased interest in using interstate compacts
as a means of coordinating opposition to many aspects of federal policy. Although there is ample research on states' individual resistance—
behavior with obvious, readily observable consequences for policy—
there is a lack of existing work on unproved but suggestive repurposing
of the interstate compact device.

The Uses of Interstate Compacts to Coordinate
State Opposition

Interstate compacts are formal agreements between two or more of
the states. Although the Constitution has always permitted such agreements, the development of the interstate compact as a form of horizontal federalism was slow. Until the twentieth century, compacts were ordinarily one-time agreements that served to clarify the borders between
states. Their use has expanded considerably in the past century. Of the
180 compacts that had received congressional consent through 2009,
154 were created after 1900 (Zimmerman 2012, 45). The function of

compacts has also become more complex. Beginning with the Colorado River Compact, a series of major agreements were developed to manage water systems that traverse multiple states. Water compacts are the most numerous kind of interstate compact (Zimmerman 2012, 46) and among the most administratively sophisticated—indeed, the Colorado River Compact is at the core of a legal corpus of truly byzantine complexity known as the Law of the River. In many cases, these compacts provide for allocations of water between states but also create standing administrative commissions to address more complex management issues and disputes.

Following some important initial successes with water compacts, this administrative form came to be used for many other purposes. Compacts are frequently used to facilitate the flow of information or to achieve regulatory uniformity across states. Compacts serve, for instance, as the administrative basis for matters such as the sharing of information about driving violations and arrest warrants, coordinating responses to emergencies and disasters, reciprocally recognizing professional licensures and qualifications, and arranging the adoption of children. A precise count of the number of compacts in effect will depend on the criteria used, but at a conservative count there were at least 155 in effect in 2003 (Bowman 2004), with several more having become effective in the following years.

In general, interstate compacts lack an overtly partisan character, though this is not to say that, as some of the benign usages just mentioned might suggest, they are all a strictly neutral or apolitical administrative form. A number of water compacts have been the object of significant political and legal disputes (Schlager and Heikkila 2009), some of which have been extraordinarily protracted (see Griggs 2017). The development of interstate compacts is also frequently responsive to federal policy activity, sometimes seeking to protect state prerogatives, and sometimes addressing pressing policy concerns in the face of federal inactivity (Bowman and Woods 2007; Woods and Bowman 2011). Many compacts represent experiments in policy, and the adoption of interstate compacts is thus more common in state legislatures inclined to engage in policy innovation (Nicholson-Crotty et al. 2014). Certain important proposed compacts, such as the National Popular Vote Interstate Compact (Muller 2007), seek a substantial change in the procedures of American democracy—in this case, nothing less than a circumvention of the Constitution's specified mechanism for electing the president (Drake

2014). Although these matters are plainly political, they are not obviously partisan.

However, since 2011, a number of proposed interstate compacts, adopted exclusively in Republican-controlled state governments, have sought to coordinate or augment the forms of state resistance to federal policy discussed throughout this book. The remainder of this section presents an overview of nine such proposed compacts. Although the matters of policy addressed by the compacts vary widely, their proposed functions represent three basic strategies. In the first strategy, the compacts seek to resist federal policies that were also directly challenged through state litigation; they amount to a fallback structure by which states could attempt to selectively opt out of federal requirements in the event that litigation did not result in an outright defeat of the policy. In the second strategy, the compacts serve directly as a means of developing state litigation or pressing a legal advantage. In the third strategy, they serve as a means of addressing coordination problems arising from individual state resistance to aspects of federal policy—they can, in this usage, reduce the number of actors whose behavior must be coordinated and centralize and standardize the collection and circulation of information.

Compacts as Litigation Fallback

This first group of proposed compacts can be understood as auxiliaries to state litigation against the ACA, the Clean Power Plan, and the Waters of the United States Rule. These compacts would allow states, with congressional consent, to opt out of federal requirements.[3] Under conditions of divided government such as those that obtained during the Obama administration, these compacts would therefore also have functioned indirectly as a legislative veto on the activity of the federal executive.

The Health Care Compact (HCC), developed in 2011, saw very wide introduction in state legislatures and was adopted by nine states (Alabama, Georgia, Indiana, Kansas, Missouri, Oklahoma, South Carolina, Texas, and Utah). It provided that members would, in effect, be exempted from the provisions of the ACA and instead provide health care services at the state level with the help of large block transfers of federal funds. The text of the compact acknowledges that congressional consent would be required for it to take effect; a major congressional appropriation would also have been required for it to have practical import.

The HCC can be understood as part of a larger ecology of strategies employed by opponents of the ACA. The initial ruling in *National Federation of Independent Businesses v. Sebelius* allowed for a wider range of state administrative resistance to the ACA and also prompted successive rounds of litigation. Had litigation proved less successful for state opponents, the HCC would have provided a fallback by which states could, in effect, individually opt out of the ACA. Because implementation of the HCC would have required much more than pro forma congressional consent, it did not enjoy serious prospects of enactment absent active, strong support at the national level. This was not forthcoming, for the simple reason that, by seeking voluntary, state-specific exemption from ACA provisions, the HCC is also a tacit acknowledgment of the law's validity. Republican congressional leadership, however, remained committed to outright repeal throughout the Obama administration and indeed passed such repeal measures many times.

In 2015, a compact structurally similar to the HCC—the Interstate Power Compact—was introduced as a putative means of shielding states from the regulatory requirements of the EPA's Clean Power Plan. The Interstate Power Compact would have provided that member states immediately refuse to submit compliance plans to the EPA. This noncooperation would, in itself, certainly have admitted of legal challenge by federal actors. The Interstate Power Compact also provided that congressional consent would guarantee that member states would not face adverse federal action for refusing to submit a plan. This compact can, like the HCC, be understood as a fallback to a preferred strategy of state litigation and as a means of allowing states to opt out of a major federal regulation individually without the repeal of the regulation itself. The Multistate Non-Navigable Waters Compact sought to allow states to reject the geographically expanded application of the Clean Water Act set forth in the Waters of the United States Rule. States adopting the compact would have declared nonnavigable waters to be under exclusive state jurisdiction, effectively shielding them from federal clean water regulations following congressional consent. Neither the Interstate Power Compact nor the Multistate Non-Navigable Waters Compact received serious state legislative consideration, perhaps owing to how far litigation had advanced by the time these compacts were first proposed.

This first group of proposed compacts did not have the function of producing arguments that states could put forward in litigation against the federal government. Rather, the compacts served as a fallback in the event that a primary strategy of litigation did not succeed. Provided that the compacts themselves survived legal scrutiny—certainly a debatable question—they would have enabled states, at their own discretion, to decide whether to comply with federal policy. Because such exemption from regulation would plainly favor member states vis-à-vis nonmembers, this group of compacts therefore undoubtedly requires congressional consent, thus making consent functionally an indirect legislative veto of federal executive action. In the case of the HCC, this strategy garnered little interest from a congressional leadership fully committed to outright repeal of the ACA; in the case of compacts addressing EPA regulation, litigation was already far along, making the adoption of a fallback compact structure unnecessary.

Compacts as a Means of Producing Litigation

Another group of proposed compacts would have served much more directly as a means of providing states with a basis for initiating litigation or exploring a legal avenue opened by other cases. By design, then, the provisions of this group of compacts are open to legal doubt: they are best understood as proposed devices for testing arguments in unsettled areas of law.

The Interstate Birth Certificate Compact was considered by the Arizona legislature in 2011 but never enacted in any state. Compact members would have adopted a dual system of birth certificates: one certificate for children of US citizens and one for children of parents who owed vaguely defined "allegiance" to other governments. The more radical (and legally dubious) thrust of this proposal would be to reopen the question of automatic birthright citizenship in the United States. The compact's implied suggestion that birth in the United States does not automatically confer citizenship is contrary to well-established interpretations of the Fourteenth Amendment. This view would have far-reaching and unpredictable effects on American law, particularly because American law cannot control how other countries confer citizenship on people who also have a claim to American citizenship (Stock 2016). It is difficult to imagine the abandonment of this doctrine.

However, a birth certificate is an important and much-used official document. Even if it proved legally irrelevant to the citizenship status of the certificate holder, a dual system of documentation would have the effect of calling attention to parental immigration or citizenship status during a variety of routine interactions (see also Wong 2013).[4] The requirement of maintaining separate types of certificates might also have had the effect of authorizing or requiring hospitals in member states to inquire into new parents' immigration status. If enacted, the compact would therefore have created not only a basis for pressing a radical challenge to the legal definition of citizenship but also an assertion that routine state administrative and record-keeping activity is a setting in which citizenship and immigration status can be legitimately investigated or made visible. The proposal was recognizably of a piece with other self-deportation approaches to immigration enforcement, which is no coincidence—Kris Kobach has been acknowledged as the author of the compact (Schumaker-Matos 2011).

The previous chapter discussed the development of the land-transfer movement and the prospect that states might seek a lateral application of *Shelby County v. Holder*'s equal sovereignty doctrine to the context of federal land management. In addition to considering (and in several cases passing) resolutions on federal land transfer, several states have also created groups to study the relevant legal and economic issues. In 2014, Utah enacted the Interstate Compact on the Transfer of Public Lands, which would seek to pool those resources for the express purpose of devising legal arguments and coordinating future litigation. The Arizona legislature voted to join the compact in 2015, but this measure was vetoed by the governor. The primary function of the compact would be to facilitate a test of the land-transfer movement's theories.

The Uniform Firearms Transfer Compact, devised in Arizona but not adopted elsewhere, would require that member states not enact any rules regulating gun sales that impose requirements or restrictions that exceed those specified by federal law. The compact represents itself as providing an affirmative defense for violators of state rules. This proposal is closely related to other state techniques for challenging federal regulations of gun sales (see Orbach, Callahan, and Lindemenn 2010). The proposal is open to serious doubt on the grounds of legal soundness and bears similarities to recent state-level measures on firearms that have endorsed a pure nullificationist position (see Read 2016). The provision that the compact provides an affirmative defense is, in effect, a means of deputing to private individuals the authority to challenge gun regulations on behalf of a state; a similar deputation of state standing to individuals was later rejected in the Supreme Court's 2013 ruling in *Hollingsworth v. Perry*. Setting these provisions aside, the assertion that the compact prospectively requires that member states maintain uniform laws on gun sales invokes another unsettled question of law, namely, whether the provisions of a compact legally supersede the provisions of individual state law. Recent cases about water compacts, such as *Tarrant Regional Water District v. Herrmann*, have shown this to be a complex and incompletely resolved question (see Larson 2015). Though its prospects of legal success would have been doubtful, the proposed compact would provide a basis for probing judicial doctrines on the Commerce Clause, the Tenth Amendment, standing, and horizontal federalism.

The group of compacts considered in this subsection were proposed with the clear aim of facilitating litigation in policy areas—immigration, land management, and gun control, respectively—where friction between states and the federal government is common. In each instance, the legal viability of the proposed compacts would rest on questions about federalism that remain, or have become, unsettled. Indeed, it is perhaps not in keeping with the spirit of these proposals to attempt to decide, a priori, whether the proposed compacts would have been legally viable: they would have been vehicles for producing cases that might settle some of these questions in a way favorable to the interested states. As the preceding chapter noted, many state-initiated suits and particular legal theories advanced in those cases are bound to fail, but this does not detract from the overall success of the strategy.

Compacts as a Device for Coordinating State Resistance

The third group of compacts seek to use the form in a way that is similar to familiar uses, with the exception that the substantive purpose of each of these compacts is a direct challenge to federal policy or practice. These compacts are conceived primarily as a means of resolving coordination problems. They do not broach actively contested matters of law and administrative practice in the same fashion as the compacts discussed above.

The Daylight Savings Time Preservation Pact was first introduced in the Oklahoma State legislature in 2016. Measures to cease the observation of daylight savings unilaterally had been introduced in twenty-two state legislatures since the beginning of 2015, but single-state proposals created a potentially confusing first mover problem—time standardization is clearly desirable even to actors who disapprove of seasonal time changes. The pact would attempt to resolve this first mover problem by providing for the simultaneous, multistate elimination of seasonal time change once a ratification threshold had been met. With few exceptions, the states that have contemplated an end to seasonal time change are also the states that have been most involved in litigation and other conflict with the Obama administration. The connection between time change and these larger policy issues is not immediately apparent from the limited legislative record surrounding proposals of this kind. (Part of the consideration, no doubt, is simple annoyance at the inconvenience of seasonal time changes, though the change is an irritant irrespective of party affiliation.) However, a link may be sought in the federal rationale for introducing and retaining daylight savings, namely, to regulate energy use. Similarly, the Interstate Compact to Build a Border Fence was proposed in Arizona as a device by which states sharing a border with Mexico could pool funds and coordinate rights issues arising in efforts to build a fence. Unlike the Interstate Birth Certificate Compact mentioned above, which was tailored to invoke questions about administration and immigration federalism, this proposed compact can be understood as a simple coordination device.

Finally, the Compact for a Balanced Budget seeks to coordinate the revival of efforts to call a state-initiated constitutional convention to enact a federal balanced-budget amendment; this demand, like the Sagebrush Rebellion, first arose in the West in the late 1970s and spread quickly through the United States. State legislatures began reintroducing petitions of this kind following the federal debt-ceiling crisis; by 2016, they had been introduced in almost all state legislatures and have been adopted in at least fourteen. For such measures to be more than a symbolic show of dissatisfaction with federal budgeting practices, a variety of complex legal, informational, and administrative matters must be worked out. The following discussion will suggest that the Compact for a Balanced Budget is a remarkably clever approach to addressing these issues.

The Compact for a Balanced Budget:
The Tax Revolt Reimagined

The compacts discussed in the preceding section were unrealized proposals or, in the more notable case of the HCC, legal placeholders whose possible effects were contingent on developments in Congress or the federal judiciary. They are evidence that many officials have begun to regard interstate compacts as one of a large array of strategies and devices that can be brought to bear in conflicts between states and the federal government. However, those proposed compacts do not attempt to make much use of administrative capacities—although some interstate compacts are little more than highly formal memoranda of understanding, others create permanent public agencies. This section examines the revival of state efforts to call a constitutional convention to enact a federal balanced-budget amendment, including the emergence of the Compact for a Balanced Budget, which is one of three recent, coordinated efforts to do so. It will show that the use of the interstate compact form simplifies informational and political challenges faced by state-led constitutional convention efforts. The compact's design allowed advocates to secure serious consideration of the proposal in state legislatures with a minimal investment of resources; having met with initial success, the compact has laid the administrative groundwork for a long-term campaign that may avoid many of the issues that commonly hinder similar movements for policy change.

The 2011 debt-ceiling crisis, coupled with significant discontent in many states over the ACA, prompted the revival of a long-dormant policy proposal: a state-initiated constitutional convention to enact a federal balanced-budget amendment. Although a state-initiated convention has never occurred, Article V of the Constitution provides that such a convention can be called by the petition of two-thirds of the states and that amendments can be ratified with the approval of three-fourths of the states. In the twentieth century, there were two serious movements for a state-initiated convention. The first, for the direct election of senators, spurred very begrudging congressional passage of the Seventeenth Amendment (see Schiller and Stewart 2015). The second was a state campaign for a federal balanced-budget amendment. This proposal spread rapidly following the tax revolt in California in the 1970s (Sears and Citrin 1985), and, by the early 1980s, thirty-two of the necessary thirty-four states had passed resolutions for a convention. The campaign was halted by a number of factors: coordinated opposition by progressive groups (Martin 2013); the opposition of constitutional conservative groups, most notably Phyllis Schlafly's Eagle Forum; and the 1980 election of Ronald Reagan, who placed tax limitation at the center of his campaign platform. The threat of a constitutional convention also figured in the passage of the Gramm-Rudman-Hollings Act, which sought to placate antitax activists by imposing deficit limitations on the congressional budgeting process.[5]

Between the early 1980s and 2010, no state enacted a new resolution for a federal balanced-budget amendment, and introductions of such resolutions in state legislatures nearly ceased. However, an immediate precursor to new state convention petitions is apparent in the widespread introduction of nonbinding resolutions affirming state sovereignty. The first state sovereignty resolution appears to have been introduced in Oklahoma in 2008; similar resolutions were passed in fourteen other state legislatures by 2010. The key assertion of those resolutions—"today the states are demonstrably treated as agents of the federal government"—is of a piece with larger patterns of state resistance to the structure of cooperative federalism. In these resolutions, one can discern long-standing objections to unfunded mandates as well as more immediate grievances about the national response to the financial crisis and recession and the development of the ACA.

The revived constitutional convention proposal spread rapidly. Between 2010 and 2015, fourteen states passed some form of petition for a constitutional convention to enact a balanced-budget amendment. During this same period, petitions were approved by one legislative chamber, but not formally adopted, in another fourteen states.[6] Although the initial revival of the constitutional convention movement appears to have been a spontaneous state response to the debt-ceiling crisis, several organizations thereafter arose to coordinate and build on this existing support for a federal balanced-budget amendment to achieve a uniform, binding policy outcome. By 2014, three different groups—the Balanced Budget Amendment Task Force, the Convention of States Project, and the Compact for a Balanced Budget—were concurrently pursuing a limited constitutional convention. These groups provide a useful opportunity for comparison as they seek the same policy outcome within the same structure of political opportunity using three different organizational approaches. A summary of these organizations appears in table 3.1.

The Balanced Budget Amendment Task Force is a traditional lobbying operation; in fact, it is an umbrella for a number of organizations, such as the National Taxpayers Union, that coordinated the original convention campaign in the 1970s. The task force picked up where this previous campaign left off. Its resolutions use language similar to that of petitions adopted during the tax revolt. The task force also includes un-

TABLE 3.1. **Characteristics of groups seeking a limited constitutional convention**

	Related organizations	Organization type	Key resource	Mechanism
BBA Task Force	ALEC, National Taxpayers Union, National Tax Limitation Committee	Traditional lobby	Money	Petition to Congress
Convention of States	Tea Party Patriots, Home School Legal Defense Association	Grassroots	Volunteers	Petition to Congress
Compact for a Balanced Budget	Goldwater Institute, Heartland Institute, CATO Institute, Heritage Foundation	Policy entrepreneur	Legislative ties	Interstate compact

rescinded state resolutions from 1970s in its count toward the requisite thirty-four petitions, a choice that has attracted significant criticism from rival campaigns (see Dranias 2014, 49–51); at the start of 2016, the task force claimed that it needed only seven additional ratifications to call a convention. As an effort by well-established organizations and activists, it appeared to enjoy a substantial advantage in fund-raising as well as early adoption of its resolution as a model bill by ALEC. The Convention of States Project is a grassroots organization. Its two cofounders also founded the Tea Party Patriots—the largest Tea Party movement organization—and conservative Protestant educational groups. The architects of the Compact for a Balanced Budget are mostly lawyers and are without exception fellows at conservative think tanks. Their approach makes innovative use of the interstate compact.

In the period when all three groups were active, they secured adoption of a comparable number of state petitions. In some cases, state legislatures have passed two or three of these measures. However, the strategy for managing the introduction and passage of petitions differs markedly. Through citizen activity, the Convention of States Project secured very wide introduction of petitions, but with relatively low rates of subsequent action or final adoption. The Balanced Budget Amendment Task Force and the Compact for a Balanced Budget have seen greater legislative efficiency. Through 2016, the Compact for a Balanced Budget had been voted out of committee two-thirds of the time and secured approval of at least one state legislative chamber in more than half its introductions.[7]

At first blush, this pattern is surprising. Public support for a balanced federal budget is very high in many states, and the Convention of States Project, with its strong ties to the Tea Party movement, was favorably positioned to mobilize this support. Indeed, the project could honestly claim at least half a million supporters, and, in less than two years, it built a national organization that secured the introduction of its petition in no fewer than forty-two state legislatures. Yet, despite limited financial resources and almost no public presence, the Compact for a Balanced Budget has had the greatest legislative efficiency, almost certainly for informational reasons. In states where public opinion is generally favorable, it is procedural uncertainty, and the tendency of such uncertainty to attract conservative opposition, that has been particularly significant. The interstate compact approach was tailored to address those concerns.

Any effort to call a constitutional convention faces a major organizational problem: no convention has ever been called before. While Article V of the Constitution clearly permits a convention, it offers no guidance at all on how this would be done. Setting aside entirely the prudence of a convention or the desirability of the particular amendments that might be considered, there are a host of practical issues to be resolved: What constitutes a valid state petition? How similar must petitions from various states be in order to count them together? How long does a petition remain valid? Who can certify the petitions and call the convention? When and where would a convention be held, and how would it be organized? How are delegates to be appointed? For many conservative groups, one other question is relevant: Can a convention, once called, be prevented from undertaking radical constitutional change?

The available records strongly suggest that such organizational questions are of central concern in legislative hearings on convention petitions.[8] In such hearings, legislators have rarely expressed concerns about the desirability of a balanced-budget amendment—entirely aside from the popularity of the proposal, state legislators pass balanced budgets every year (Rose and Smith 2015). Rather, legislators wish to know what other states are considering petitions or have already filed them, who maintains records of these petitions, what a convention would cost, and how it would be managed. They are particularly concerned that their state not be the first mover, pass a measure that will prove legally unworkable, or be saddled with burdensome administrative obligations.

Research increasingly demonstrates the importance of such informational concerns in the legislative process (see Baumgartner and Jones 2015). These concerns are especially salient for state legislators, who often lack the policy resources to produce such information independently—this is, indeed, a major reason why state administrative behavior is so important. Informational factors have been shown to be especially significant in the early phases of the adoption of interstate compacts (Karch et al. 2016). A constitutional convention is a complex and unproved policy mechanism, and, while public opinion is generally favorable in the states where petitions have been seriously considered, it provides little guidance about how legislators should address technical questions. Burstein (2014) argues that one of the most important arguments for the informational account of legislative activity is that public opinion provides little guidance for legislators, for the simple reason that the public does not have a manifest opinion on many matters, especially technical matters of this kind.

The Compact for a Balanced Budget provides a more thorough response to these questions than does the Balanced Budget Amendment Task Force or the Convention of States Project. The latter two include only a petition for a convention and a general description of the topic to be addressed. States that pass these petitions must therefore separately introduce a set of auxiliary bills to specify procedures for appointing, paying, and sanctioning convention delegates. The state petition method is also reliant on Congress to keep the petitions in order. No official recording system for Article V petitions existed until 2015, when an amendment to House rules required the chair of the House Judiciary Committee to track petitions. Because new House rules are adopted biennially, continued tabulation of such petitions is not certain. This approach also affords Congress considerable discretion in how petitions are collated. Given that a successful convention would impose substantial constraints on congressional activity, it is readily conceivable that Congress would prove to be a reluctant record keeper, just as it has tended to take little notice of episodic increases in popular support for congressional term limits.[9]

By contrast, the compact provides a specific amendment text. It also includes procedures for appointing delegates and specifies the time and place for a convention to be held. Because the amendment is "preratified" with the passage of the compact, in theory the sole responsibility of delegates would be to appear at the convention to vote yea. Further, the petition is not submitted to Congress when a state passes the compact. Rather, the state joins an interstate compact commission, a public entity that maintains the records and would submit them to Congress en masse only when the requisite number of passages had been secured. The simultaneous presentation of identical petitions seeks to eliminate uncertainties about timing and congressional discretion—a matter of significant concern to the compact's architects (Dranias 2014, 18). The matter of timing and collation is also a murky legal question as well as an information and coordination problem. There are hundreds of open state petitions for constitutional conventions on many subjects, some of them centuries old (see Paulsen 2011, 862–72). The Equal Rights Amendment campaign established a de facto seven-year time limit for ratification of a proposed constitutional amendment (Vile 2010), though the Twenty-Seventh Amendment, which was proposed during the original convention, was unexpectedly ratified after a period of more than two hundred years (Bernstein 1992).[10]

The compact also proved more effective at minimizing political opposition to its proposal during the short period when many legislatures were considering such petitions. Many major progressive organizations are opposed to a federal balanced-budget amendment. In addition, a number of conservative groups strongly oppose a constitutional convention even though they support tax and expenditure limitations (see Hawley 2016). "Paleoconservative" organizations such as the John Birch Society, the Eagle Forum, and the American Independent Party have always viewed a new constitutional convention as a serious threat to the American polity (Brennan 2014). Indeed, there is evidence that these groups remained wary of a possible convention well after the end of the tax revolt. Fifteen of the thirty-two states that passed petitions in the 1970s and 1980s have subsequently rescinded them, evidently at the prompting of conservative opponents of a constitutional convention, not progressive opponents of a mandatory balanced budget. Between the 1990s and 2010, twenty state legislatures considered bills rescinding previous petitions for a balanced-budget amendment convention. Each of these bills was sponsored by a Republican, typically a conservative Republican.[11] The revived convention movement has also attracted the opposition of gun rights and militia groups such as the Minutemen and the National Association for Gun Rights. Both paleoconservative and gun

TABLE 3.2. **Notable organizations testifying against convention petitions**

	Opponents
BBA Task Force	Conservative: Eagle Forum, John Birch Society, Tea Party, Farm Bureau Progressive: Common Cause
Convention of States	Conservative: Eagle Forum, John Birch Society, Tea Party, American Independent Party, Patriot Coalition, Minutemen, National Association for Gun Rights Progressive: American Civil Liberties Union, Sierra Club
Compact for America	None

rights groups fear a runaway convention in which delegates abridge the Second Amendment or other individual rights protections. In some instances, progressive groups have also testified against convention petitions. Table 3.2 lists major organizations appearing in opposition to convention petitions in public hearings.

The absence of opponents in public hearings on the Compact for a Balanced Budget is striking. This may be due, in part, to a successful effort at allaying the concerns of some conservative groups: the Eagle Forum participated in the design of the compact and deemed it secure from the threat of a runaway convention (DeMoss 2015). The absence of opponents also derives from the low visibility of the compact, which has a limited grassroots organization and social media presence and did not seek wide publicity in advance of hearings. In the modal hearing on the compact, the only witness was Nick Dranias, the compact's main designer. By contrast, the Convention of States Project, which relied on social and traditional conservative media to exert pressure on legislators and raise awareness of upcoming hearings, could not avoid attracting opposition, given that fiscal conservatives and libertarians are, to a large extent, embedded in the same political networks as paleoconservatives and gun rights advocates. At a Texas hearing, different Tea Party chapters testified for and against the Convention of States Project.

The preceding has argued that the Compact for a Balanced Budget's high legislative efficiency, relative to other convention campaigns, arises from its reliance on the organizational structure of the compact commission; administrative centralization may reduce uncertainty and simplify the task of coordinating the submission of petitions from multiple states. The use of the compact commission structure also provides the campaign with a durable organization that scales up in size with addi-

tional ratifications. The administrative capacities of the compact commission serve political and legal functions beyond simple record keeping. States that have adopted the Compact for a Balanced Budget name
a commissioner to the compact commission; to date, all the appointed
commissioners are elected officials in their respective states. The first
meeting of the compact commission in 2014 delegated the practical business of administration to a special purpose nonprofit organization with
strong ties to the Goldwater Institute. The primary responsibility of
compact commissioners, then, is to promote the adoption of the compact elsewhere, and in several cases the commissioners have served as
witnesses in hearings or submitted written testimony. Such commissioners may be able to draw on existing ties to legislators in other states and
are also well equipped to speak to the informational concerns likely to
arise in hearings.

By analogy to intergovernmental lobbying, in which representatives
of a government lobby up to a higher level of government (Cammisa
1995), the compact's diffusion model might be termed *cross-government
lobbying*, in which commissioners engage in political advocacy for a
form of horizontal federalism. However, because the compact commission is a public agency, both its appointed commissioners and the foundation charged with administering the compact are exempt from some
regulations on lobbying and political activity. In a memorandum published in 2017, the compact lays out its legal view that, as appointees of
a public agency, compact commissioners are not lobbyists and that the
foundation's formal role as administrator of the compact exempts it from
some rules constraining the political activity of 501(c)3 nonprofit organizations (Treadwell 2017).

Similarly, the compact's status as a public agency may render it less
vulnerable to the ebb and flow of interest in its goals. Under the Obama
administration, sentiment in many state legislatures favored efforts to
call a constitutional convention—the matter of who was spending federal money and to what purpose plainly increased concerns about federal deficit spending. Interest has since waned. Although the compact
has not secured any new ratifications since 2015, its commission remains
operational and continues to meet regularly; its published records show
continued efforts to garner interest in its proposal in other state legislatures and to secure action on a congressional resolution enabling a
convention.

In this respect, the compact commission can, as a public agency, also function as a heavily fortified abeyance structure for the underlying movement goal. Social movements scholars have long studied how movements survive during unfavorable political periods as well as what this survival costs: movements often lose significant ground in policy during periods when public opinion is unfavorable or attention merely dwindles (Sawyers and Meyer 1999); the quiet rescinding of earlier convention petitions can serve as an example. Taylor's (1989, 765) classic formulation of the abeyance problem identifies five relevant factors affecting the survival of a movement during periods unfavorable to the realization of the movement's goals: the temporality, purposive commitment, exclusivity, centralization, and culture of the abeyance structure. For a movement that primarily seeks the adoption of a particular policy, a compact commission is a nearly ideal abeyance organization along most of these dimensions. Interstate compacts persist indefinitely and are highly resilient to legal challenges. State withdrawal from the Compact for a Balanced Budget would be more difficult than rescinding a convention petition, not only because compact withdrawal would be subject to gubernatorial veto, but also because a state's appointed commissioner at any given moment is likely to be an elected official positioned to advocate for continued membership. The Compact for a Balanced Budget exists for the sole purpose of enacting a balanced-budget amendment. Participation in the compact organization is highly exclusive and incorporates only individuals appointed to advance its specific policy goal. The organization is highly centralized and enjoys the status of a government entity. It is difficult to venture guesses about how legal issues related to a convention would be resolved or when the proposal might regain renewed visibility. The use of the compact structure would, however, appear likely to increase the prospects of such a proposal's success, either politically or constitutionally.

Conclusion

Income taxation and fiscal transfers to states have served as pillars of modern federal power. However solid the legal basis for this pattern of federal activity, the practical workability of making federal policy through fiscal transfers and state implementation has supposed that states will be prepared to cooperate, either from sympathy with federal goals or from a desire to have the use of the associated funds. Through

the latter part of the twentieth century, states often succeeded in securing discretion and favorable terms under this arrangement by various cooperative and symbolically oppositional behaviors. Under the Obama
administration, many states adopted a less cooperative position, demonstrated most dramatically by refusals of large sums of federal funds as
well as less dramatic administrative practices that limited the implementation of the ACA.

In addition to these single-state behaviors, hostility to the ACA
prompted wide consideration and meaningful rates of adoption of the
HCC. The HCC is an early and notable example of many proposed
interstate compacts fashioned to advance state interests in overt disagreements with the federal government. Many of these proposed compacts are adjuncts to strategies of state litigation discussed in the previous chapter. Others—most notably the Compact for a Balanced
Budget—represent new efforts to use administrative means to simplify
and strengthen state coordination in opposition to federal objectives.
The compact has succeeded in creating a public agency whose sole purpose is to mount a direct challenge to one of the most important features of federal power: the use of deficit spending to underwrite an
enormous range of government activity, including large social welfare
programs. A balanced-budget amendment does not, of course, directly
speak to the matter of what Congress chooses to support; nor, in theory, does it preclude large tax increases as a means of balancing the budget. However, the timing of the proposals and partisan patterns of support strongly suggest a view that the appropriate means of achieving a
balanced budget would be cuts in spending, particularly spending on the
creation of public goods such as that encouraged in the American Recovery and Reinvestment Act of 2009 and on social welfare programs
such as the health insurance efforts at the center of the ACA—that is,
the same kinds of public spending that states supporting a balanced-
budget amendment have also opposed by a variety of other devices.

The compact does not simply envision a shift in congressional budgeting practices. It imagines a basic restructuring of the relations between
the states and the federal government, just as state litigants have effectively questioned the scope of federal administrative power as well as
particular exercises of that power. The compact's architects understand
it as a means of "attacking the problem of concentrated power in Washington" (DeMoss 2015). It confronts this concentration by seeking to el-
evate the several states to a position above that of the federal govern-

ment: "The Compact begins a process to reinsert the states back into the [formation of federal policy] by placing them in a 'Board of Directors' oversight capacity over Congress" (DeMoss 2015). As the board of directors metaphor suggests, the conception of good government here is one that bears some analogy to the activity of private firms. This chapter has made little effort to account for the motivations of government officials, which has proved to be an expedient means of describing how they have fashioned new practices to achieve goals that have been taken as given. However, by way of conclusion, it is worthwhile to touch indirectly on a point about one such matter: individuals and governments regularly understand taxation and public spending morally as well as economically, and the dynamics discussed here are not distinctively American.

Federal budgeting has a geographically redistributive character. Many of the states that have been most enthusiastic in their support of a federal balanced-budget amendment are also states that receive substantially more money from the federal government than their residents contribute in federal taxes. A balanced federal budget achieved through spending cuts, then, would almost certainly reduce revenue transfers to these states and likely result in limitation on the social goods available to their citizens. (And, of course, the refusal of a federally funded Medicaid expansion is, itself, a decision that directly limits the availability of such a good.) This would appear to be, in strict economic terms, an irrational decision, though those making such a judgment will also generally be expressing certain of their own views about how the funds in question are to be used.

This pattern is a common one in federated polities. Region-level political units regularly seek more power by broadened discretion, devolution of certain powers, or a negotiated process of autonomization. Securing such power often involves forfeiting the benefit of some geographic mechanism of redistribution mediated by the national government. Whether this is ultimately judged to be a good trade or not, it is worthwhile not to confine the assessment purely to the American context and to consider that Arizona might be usefully compared to Catalonia as well as to California. (As chapter 1 noted, region-scale capacity for coordination is an important determinant of the relative allocation of powers in many federated political systems.)

Likewise, the metaphor of states as America's board of directors ought to be taken seriously. Konings (2015) has noted that contemporary critics of capitalism—particularly those who couch their criticism in the vocabulary of neoliberalism—have tended to overlook or actively discredit the emotional and moral valences of economic relations. Thus one meets with a curious paradox: progressive critics of American conservatism like Frank (2004), who are firmly committed to a view that government should spend aggressively on social welfare, are apt argue that political behavior ought to be informed by rational economic self-interest. Conservatives who favor government behavior modeled on market relations and firm structures make their case in terms of reform and good government, a view that possesses an overtly moral dimension—a point developed further in chapter 5. This view is prevalent among individuals as well as policy makers. Debt is widely looked on by Americans as a moral responsibility just as much as it is a contractual arrangement (see Prasad, Hoffman, and Bezila 2016). Likewise, self-awareness as a taxpayer is often an important dimension of civic identity (Wenzel 2007), particularly in the United States, where taxpaying is complexly bound up in ideas of citizenship and attitudes about the public good. The association of tax with community membership is apparent in the Tea Party movement and other currents of modern conservatism (see Martin 2008; McVeigh et al. 2014; and Kincaid 2016). Yet it is hardly new: it figures in the myth of the American Revolution and became a major feature of American politics immediately after the Civil War (Walsh 2018)—contemporaneous with the first manifestation of a strong federal state, the "Yankee leviathan" (Bensel 1990). Taxation and fiscal transfers are, in sum, matters that speak directly to core questions about the meaning of citizenship in the United States. Contention within the framework of fiscal federalism thus goes beyond particular matters of policy to the foundational matter of who governs. The policy activity discussed in the following chapter takes up this same issue even more directly—contemporary conflicts over who can vote and which governments can define how America's electoral system is administered.

The Failure of Federal Electoral Oversight and the Emergence of a State Administrative Paradigm of Voter Restriction

Outside the case of pure, local democracy, the working of any participatory form of government relies on some degree of administration: a set of practices for deciding who may participate and what form that participation takes as well as how participation is reckoned to produce an outcome. However much a polity strives to make the administration of elections an objective process, these practices can never be far removed from the matters central to the very nature of politics—who counts, who governs, and what government can do. Answers to such questions will, almost by definition, favor some interests and injure others. The Constitution, as originally conceived, left it mainly within the power of the states to settle these questions according to their respective views about the appropriate form and extent of participation. States' control over the operation of elections was at the start and has remained a particularly important feature of state power within the system of American federalism. In practice, the exercise of that power has generally reflected partisan values—it is no surprise that, when given control over the basic procedures of participation, political parties have tended to refashion those procedures to their own advantage.

For most of their history, the federal courts viewed the administration of elections as being such an essentially political matter that the law could not intervene. This view accurately diagnosed the politically value-laden quality of election administration, but the abstentionist conclusion drawn from this understanding allowed egregiously unfair practices to flourish. Federal protections of the right to vote, which took shape in the 1960s, have therefore been justly celebrated. At that time, the Supreme Court, aided by other federal actions, concluded that there could be no lawful basis for administering elections in ways that promoted invidious discrimination—a line of reasoning that sought to end the disenfranchisement of African American voters in the South. Likewise, the Court concluded that individuals' participation in the electoral process should be accorded equal weight in deciding outcomes, a basic principle of equity that changed electoral practices throughout the nation.

The specification of certain objective requirements for elections administration, however, preserved important features of the original constitutional order. Although some federal standards and regulations now exist, the administration of elections is still primarily the business of the states. And the courts have continued to view election administration as possessing intrinsically political features that are not within the purview of the law. Provided it does not transgress certain specified boundaries, partisanship is still recognized as a legitimate motive for defining the ground rules for the electoral process.

This chapter examines a range of new state practices in registration, voter roll maintenance, and balloting that share an important feature: they impose procedural or documentary burdens on voters. Those burdens have a differential impact on the electorate—most notably, they are particularly likely to affect the participation of members of racial and ethnic minority groups, poorer voters, and older voters. (Voter identification laws, which are particularly well studied, are only one of a class of policies of this kind and also have important similarities to state administrative practices that limit the uptake of other public services and benefits.) Despite evidence of this differential effect, such policies regularly survive judicial review, and federal courts have accepted a variety of rationales as valid bases for enacting such policies. The first is a state interest in making elections more honest and credible, a rationale that is judged sufficient despite very little evidence that American elections are plagued by dishonest behavior. Further, a piece of federal legislation—HAVA—served as the starting point for this new moment of more restrictive voting by requiring states to develop a more robust and regular electoral administrative capacity.

This chapter argues that modern voter restriction is a result of two notable weaknesses in the federal voting rights regime. First, that regime has sought to maintain a legal distinction between legitimate partisan and illegitimate discriminatory objectives—a distinction far removed from the realities of political life and one that overly prizes administrative uniformity. Second, it has produced few federal administrative powers and left the federal judiciary to oversee state administrations, an arrangement that is awkward in many of the same ways as judicial oversight of federal administrative practice discussed throughout this book. The chapter begins with a historical overview. It then examines more recent legislative and judicial developments that were enabling conditions for restrictive state policies, then describes a range of these policies, including how they operate and where they have been adopted. It concludes with a detailed examination of the Interstate Voter Registration Crosscheck Program, an important record-sharing agreement that neatly exemplifies the complex, probabilistic character of contemporary voter restriction, as well as the reasons why federal judicial guardianship of voting rights has failed to curb the development of such practices.

Federal Election Oversight: A New and Incomplete Power

As ratified, the Constitution did not envision a sizable role for the federal government in the conduct of elections. Article I grants the states broad authority to regulate the "Times, Places, and Manner of holding Elections." The Constitution also provided for many structures that served to limit the direct influence of voters (see Dahl 2003). The most notable of these are the Electoral College, which continues to provide for the indirect election of the president, and the Senate, whose representation is not proportional to the size of state populations and whose composition was not determined by direct election until the twentieth century. The active involvement of the federal judiciary in deciding a wide range of questions about the conduct of elections in the twenty-first century therefore reflects a remarkable break from a deep historical pattern. This involvement relied on new powers of oversight asserted in the 1960s, partly through enabling legislation and constitutional amendments, but also to a great degree through judicial reinterpretations that set aside doctrines under which many election-related matters were not considered by the courts. This asserted authority has a enjoyed great deal of public legitimacy but little supporting administrative capacity;

in consequence, federal oversight has been weak and reflects a predominantly legal rather than bureaucratic mode of activity.

In the eighteenth century, the state-defined qualifications for suffrage in the United States effectively limited electoral participation to a very small number of property-owning white men. The franchise expanded over time. Throughout the early nineteenth century, states extended the right to vote to most white men, irrespective of their property, a development connected to the rise of Jacksonian democracy and mass parties—the proportion of Americans eligible to vote increased by well over an order of magnitude between Jefferson's time and Jackson's. The Fifteenth Amendment, ratified in 1870, extended suffrage to all men irrespective of "race, color, or previous condition of servitude"—at the time, a measure intended to guarantee the vote to former slaves. The complex legal status of Native Americans made their rights as electors uncertain during the nineteenth century, but a series of laws gradually established that all Native Americans were US citizens and on these grounds entitled to vote in theory—through often not in practice (Keyssar 2000, 202–4). The Nineteenth Amendment, ratified in 1920, guaranteed women the right to vote nationally. The Twenty-Sixth Amendment, ratified in 1971, lowered the voting age to eighteen. In principle, these measures have created an electorate in which all adult citizens are entitled to vote. Some of the expansions in suffrage—most notably the Fifteenth Amendment and the enfranchisement of Native Americans—were clearly the result of federal activity. In other cases, the franchise was directly expanded by the states or expanded by the federal government in response to state political agitation.

Expansions in suffrage have never been accepted without resistance, and patterns of class, racial, and regional support for parties have meant that there is almost always, in any given moment, a major party that stands to benefit from lower rates of electoral participation and one that stands to benefit from higher rates. Whenever the franchise has been expanded in law, it has been common for states to introduce new electoral administrative practices that have served to limit the practical expansion of participation.

The best-known instance of this is, of course, the "Redemption" of the South and the construction of the edifice of Jim Crow after the collapse of Reconstruction (for lucid historical accounts, see Franklin [1980] and Foner [2014]). Without directly revoking their franchise, southern states devised a complex system of racial domination that functionally prevented the great majority of African Americans from voting. This system relied heavily on the racially discriminatory exercise of administrative discretion at the local level, the involvement of nonstate actors, especially the Democratic Party, in the conduct of elections, and the use of intimidation and violence to deter voting. This approach was, by nature, highly reliant on local, informal activity (see Kousser 1974; and Cunningham 1991).

The latter part of the nineteenth century also saw the introduction of practices that limited the practical exercise of the franchise in other parts of the country. As Keyssar (2000, 122–31) recounts, the wide introduction of voter registration systems plainly operated to the disadvantage of poorer voters, especially those living in cities; indeed, in many states, voter registration rules initially applied only to cities, with the avowed purpose of disrupting the operation of political machines by disenfranchising the population likely to vote for their candidates. Features of ballot design and language, including the introduction of the secret ballot itself (Heckelman 1995), lowered electoral participation by serving as a functional literacy test. Similarly, states steadily abolished the alien franchise over this period (Aylsworth 1931).

State governments also engaged in districting practices at the state and congressional levels that resulted in remarkably skewed patterns of representation. Rapid urbanization, combined with county-based seat-allocation schemes, steadily eroded the electoral power of urban constituencies in both state and national elections from the late nineteenth century onward. This was exacerbated by many legislatures' simple refusal to redraw legislative districts decennially, justified in part through efforts to discredit the data produced by the census (see Anderson 2015). This behavior was long abetted by the federal judiciary, which declined to intervene on the grounds that key constitutional provisions protected individuals only from federal infringements of rights or that the conduct of elections was a political matter that fell outside the judiciary's purview.

In the 1960s, supported by popular sentiment and major acts of Congress, the federal judiciary successfully asserted authority to regulate two features of the state conduct of elections: the construction of electoral districts and representation schemes and individual voter registration. In both instances, federal intervention resulted in an electoral process that was, for its many remaining faults, much more inclusive and fair than American elections had ever been before. Although these two transformations were contemporaneous, they rested on different legal rationales and varied significantly in their immediate and subsequent geographic scope. The reapportionment revolution was national in its effects; malapportionment was a problem everywhere and was severest in the Northeast and the West. The protection of individual voting rights had the most pronounced effect in the South, in large part because these federal protections were devised to dismantle the specific model of disenfranchisement in place there.

In the 1960s, the Supreme Court handed down a series of decisions, beginning with *Baker v. Carr*, that came to be known as the *apportionment cases*. These cases yielded two important new legal doctrines. First, the Court reversed its prior view, clearly elaborated in *Colegrove v. Green*, that state districting practices were a political issue not to be handled by the judiciary—that is, it proclaimed its readiness to venture into what Justice Frankfurter had termed the *political thicket*. Second, in *Reynolds v. Sims*, it set forth the principle of one person, one vote, a doctrine that held that individual votes should have comparable political value. This doctrine has retained a persistent ambiguity—it has never been entirely clear whether it is meant to protect an equal interest in a vote's power to decide an election or an equal interest in representation, interests that are for demographic reasons often in a certain state of tension (Cowan 2015). However, the basic requirements of the doctrine are plain enough: one person, one vote requires that legislative districts be compact, contiguous, and of equal populations, with a variety of factors allowing for modest permissible deviations.

During this same decade, a number of federal measures effectively dismantled the legal regime that had been used in the South to deny African Americans the vote. The Twenty-Fourth Amendment, ratified in 1964, banned the use of poll taxes in federal elections; in *Harper v. Virginia Board of Elections*, the Supreme Court ruled poll taxes to be categorically unconstitutional. The Voting Rights Act of 1965 (VRA), as well as its related amendments and subsequent renewals, banned a wide range of discriminatory voting practices. Section 5 of the VRA subjected a number of jurisdictions with a history of voter discrimination—primarily southern states—to preclearance on the basis of a coverage formula set out in Section 4. Jurisdictions subjected to preclearance could not implement changes to their voting or election laws without securing approval from the Justice Department.

This paired set of legal developments produced rapid changes in participation, representation, and electoral competitiveness in the United States. Reapportionment yielded dramatic improvements in the representativeness of districting schemes. Prior to the apportionment cases, it had been common for the populations of congressional districts within a given state to vary by 50 percent or more; within a decade, congressional districts had nearly reached population equality (Hall 2011, 99–100). The effect was more dramatic in state legislatures. In 1955, there were five state legislative chambers—the Connecticut House, the California Senate, the Nevada Senate, the Vermont House, and the Rhode Island Senate—whose malapportionment was so severe that less than 14 percent of the state population could elect a majority of the representatives (Bullock 2010, 30–31). The most extreme districts closely resembled the "rotten boroughs" present in the United Kingdom before its nineteenth-century reforms. For instance, in the Vermont House, the smallest district had only twenty-four residents—the largest district was fifteen hundred times more populous (Ansolabehere and Snyder 2008, 27). Malapportionment was a serious problem in most states, and districting schemes tended to confer heavy electoral advantage on a particular party, hindering electoral competitiveness.[1] As equal apportionment has become the norm, the beneficial effect of redistricting on representation and electoral competitiveness has weakened (La Roja 2009). Redistricting has become a well-elaborated form of protection for incumbents, and sophisticated, computer-aided redrawing of districts has made it possible to create districting schemes that confer substantial, persistent partisan advantages without violating basic judicial requirements about the construction of districts.

Active federal protection of individual voting rights and oversight of polities with a history of voter discrimination resulted in similarly rapid increases in the electoral participation of minority groups. In the South, African American voter registration rates increased from 3 percent in 1940 to 62 percent in 1968 (Kolb 2007, 109). The minority language provisions of the VRA, which assure voters in many jurisdictions access to a ballot written in their preferred language, continue to have positive effects on electoral participation (Fraga and Merseth 2016). In addition to directly enabling individual participation, the VRA has also had important effects on election outcomes as well as on the behavior of elected representatives. In 1960, the lower legislative chambers of the eleven former Confederate states had 21 African American members. That figure increased to 246 by 2007 (Bullock 2010, 64). The reemergence of an active African American electorate likely contributed to the softening of southern senators' extreme, destructive positions on race and civil rights issues (Hood, Kidd, and Morris 2001) and figured substantially in the decline of Democratic Party machines, a development of national importance: "A newly competitive South mean[t] a newly competitive America" (Black and Black 2002, 369).

The developments of the 1960s yielded important successes but did not sufficiently provide individuals the opportunity to register to vote; in many localities, the continued limitations on places, times, and procedures for registering continued to make it difficult for many to place their names on the voter rolls. The 1993 National Voter Registration Act (NVRA) further expanded the practical ability of citizens to vote by circumscribing state and local administrative discretion in the registration process. The NVRA subjected states to strict requirements about the removal of registered voters from the rolls and required that completion of a federal registration form would also entitle a voter to participate in state elections. It mandated that individuals be able to register to vote when obtaining a driver's license or certain other public services, giving rise to the colloquial name Motor-Voter to refer to the NVRA. By the late 1990s, nearly half of new voter registrations were completed by methods provided for in the NVRA. In general, election policy at that moment favored the opportunity to participate in elections even if rates of participation were at a notable low. In addition to greater ease in registration and the continued federal oversight of jurisdictions with a history of discriminatory election practices, it was also relatively easy for voters to cast absentee ballots. Further, many states had begun to liberalize felon disenfranchisement laws.[2] Other onerous policies, such as extended residency requirements, had been eliminated, and many states adopted no-excuse absentee voting, early voting, and same-day voter registration (Biggers and Hanmer 2015). This period represents the present high-water mark in the legal right to vote.

The Emergence of a New Paradigm of Voter Restriction

This pattern of relative ease in electoral participation has been reversed. It is now generally harder to vote in the United States than it was in 2000, sometimes much harder. A range of new state laws and practices have generally survived judicial review despite extensive scrutiny and the existence of a rapidly expanding body of empirical evidence that they have the most marked effects on the poor and members of racial and ethnic minority groups. This section will argue that this approach to voter restriction has succeeded because federal protections of individual voting rights were weakly institutionalized and particularly oriented to the model of disenfranchisement developed in the South, one that combined overt racial animus with administrative informality. Contemporary restrictive laws, by contrast, are facially race neutral, limit discretion and interpretation, and are in many cases administered by states rather than local officials. This reliance on rationalized state administration has been particularly important because the legal transformations of the 1960s did not produce significant new federal administrative powers. This has made voting rights an unusual case, one in which important federal policy has been minimally reliant on the administrative state and state administrative capacity exceeds that of the federal government. The legal opportunity structure for this new approach is, to a great degree, the result of federal legislation and judicial reasoning that was probably not intended to produce the present outcome.

The 2000 presidential election was the precipitating event for the current period of restrictive voter policy. Some 37 percent of respondents in the American National Election Study viewed the 2000 election as somewhat unfair or very unfair (National Commission on Federal Election Reform 2002, 126). The election exposed systematic weaknesses in the American electoral system, including archaic physical infrastructure, bloated and inaccurate voter rolls, and ill-defined procedures for conducting elections and reckoning the results. This controversy centered on Florida: the state's electoral votes were decisive in the presidential election, and a wide range of procedural irregularities effectively compelled the Supreme Court to decide the outcome in *Bush v. Gore*. However, technical and procedural errors were ubiquitous in the 2000 election, and the rules imposed by the NVRA had created serious voter roll maintenance problems in many states. In Alaska, the District of Columbia, and Maine, to cite the most extreme cases, the number of registered voters on the rolls in 2000 greatly exceeded the number of adult residents (National Commission on Federal Election Reform 2002, 136–37).

In 2002, HAVA was enacted with enormous bipartisan support. It provided for the modernization of the physical infrastructure for casting and counting ballots. It also mandated minimal requirements to verify the identity of voters, revised the federal voter registration form, required states to maintain centralized, electronic voter rolls, and created a standard mechanism for voters to cast provisional ballots when their registration status was in doubt. HAVA created a new agency, the US Election Assistance Commission, to oversee the implementation of these provisions. The expert report and legislative record establish rather clearly that HAVA was intended to make elections more accurate and credible but not to make voting more difficult.

Yet HAVA has undoubtedly been a key enabling condition for the recent wave of restrictive voting laws. Its provisions have, by a number of direct and indirect means, provided states with legal justifications for more restrictive policies. The first means was the simple disruption of policy inertia: in 2002, very few states' election systems met the standards dictated by HAVA. This required that states take major positive action to create central, state-controlled administrative and record-keeping systems. As in many other policy domains, there is a well-documented status quo bias in state election policy (see, e.g., Burden et al. 2011; and Moynihan and Lavertu 2012). Absent a federal mandate, it is likely that many states would not have made reforms after the 2000 general election, despite recognized problems with their election systems. The federal mandate in HAVA thus resulted in a dramatic, temporary increase in passage rates for election-related bills: 19.3 percent of all election-related state bills introduced in 2003 were enacted; this rate dropped to 10 percent in the following year (National Conference of State Legislatures Elections Legislation Database). Many state legislators viewed the necessity of enacting new regulations as an opportunity to make those laws more stringent (Langholz 2008, 747–48). States have also interpreted HAVA as providing either a right or a positive requirement to make registration and voting more difficult. Voter identification laws and proof of citizenship laws, both discussed in greater detail in the following section, rely partially on state interpretations of HAVA.

The enactment of HAVA and subsequent state adoption of new procedural requirements to register to vote or cast a ballot have produced an ongoing series of court cases in which states have to a great extent succeeded in defending restrictive laws and also effectively curtailed federal oversight and regulation of voter registration and the conduct of elections. This phenomenon has involved three interrelated legal developments of recent years: the recognition of fraud prevention as a compelling state interest, the narrow judicial definition of persuasive evidence of discriminatory intent in the enactment of restrictive voting

laws, and the limitation on federal administrative authority in the regulation of elections.

Chapter 2 argued that *Massachusetts v. EPA* was an accidental landmark: there, the Court's legal reasoning interacted with political developments to create an avenue for states to initiate litigation contesting
a wide range of federal policies. *Crawford v. Marion County Election
Board*, decided in 2008, has had a similarly important role in elections
and voting rights. In *Crawford*, the Court considered a facial challenge
to Indiana's voter identification law that would require voters to present
photo identification when appearing at their polling place. The petitioners argued that the measure would impose an unreasonable burden on
the subset of eligible voters who lacked acceptable forms of identification
and noted that in Indiana such voters were likely to be disproportionately poor or older. The alternative voting provisions for people without
acceptable identification would impose a far greater time cost than securing identification itself. The petitioners also noted, by way of suggestion that patterned depression of electoral participation along these lines
was precisely the intention of the law, that the measure had been passed
on a strict party line vote. Indiana presented what the court would evalu-
ate as four rationales in defense of the voter identification measure: compliance with HAVA's electoral modernization requirements, maintaining more accurate and current voter rolls (a particular administrative
problem in Indiana that was partially distinct from HAVA), prevention
of in-person voter fraud, and protection of the perceived credibility of
the electoral process.

The opinion of the Court—written by Justice Stevens, joined by Justices Rehnquist and Kennedy—upheld the law and endorsed all Indiana's proffered rationales. It also dismissed the suggestion that partisan
polarization in legislative support for a measure was, in itself, a relevant
consideration for assessing the intention and legality of the measure.
The opinion recognized a compelling state interest in preventing fraud
and safeguarding the perceived integrity of elections, whether fraud was
a demonstrably serious problem or not, and found that, on balance, this
interest was sufficient to justify what the Court recognized as a genuine
but modest burden on a subset of voters. A concurrence written by Justice Scalia, joined by Justices Thomas and Alito, took the stronger position that no judicial reckoning of the balance of interests needed to
be considered, on the view that the burden of the identification requirement was too minimal to merit consideration. Dissenting opinions from

Souter (joined by Ginsburg) and Breyer drew different conclusions but proceeded in more or less the same spirit of applying a variety of existing doctrines for balancing individual interests in voting and state interests in conducting orderly elections. The possibility that the law might produce specifically racialized effects received relatively minimal consideration; Souter's dissent considered the poor and old to be the notably burdened groups. None of the opinions possesses the stylistic qualities that would be so pronounced in *Shelby County v. Holder* five years later. There are no quotations from Shakespeare or the Founders and very little in the way of either high rhetoric or quotable aphorism—in short, none of the compositional characteristics that tend to accompany opinions that the Court expects to be especially visible or divisive (see Hume 2006; Black et al. 2016).

Yet *Crawford* has been an important ruling. It provided states with what has become a most reliable formula for defending measures that make voting more difficult and also set forth a line of reasoning that effectively disqualifies from judicial consideration the most compelling forms of empirical evidence that can be marshaled against such measures. Almost uniformly, the prevention of voting fraud has been offered as a prime rationale for subsequent state enactments of restrictive laws of various kinds. There is essentially no evidence of widespread, deliberate voter-initiated fraud in contemporary American elections (Ahlquist, Mayer, and Jackman 2014). Indeed, there is strong evidence from both scholarly and government research that voter fraud is rare and typically inadvertent. Systematic state efforts to detect and prosecute voter fraud have similarly found it to be extremely rare. Further, state laws devised to prevent fraud generally do not address the largest source of fraud: election officials themselves (Benson 2009). These measures are also poorly designed to detect fraud if it does occur (Christensen and Schultz 2014), and there are various ways to deter or detect fraud effectively that do not impose additional burdens on individual voters (Perez 2017).[3]

Yet the legally recognized interest in fraud prevention and electoral integrity provides a permissible, neutral rationale for enacting restrictive laws, thereby affording them meaningful protection against facial challenges. This is doubly significant. A successful challenge to an electoral policy based on its demonstrable effects cannot unwork the harm already done. Further, federal courts apply very different standards for laws that are judged to be discriminatory in their intent, as distinct from facially neutral laws that are discriminatory in their effect. A law whose judicially recognized intent is to discriminate is presumptively illegal in its entirety. By contrast, laws that produce a discriminatory effect but also advance a legitimate state interest may be upheld in part or be subject to modification rather than revocation.

Moreover, the Court's dismissal in *Crawford* of partisanship as a relevant consideration also effectively turns judicial attention away from important findings about the interaction between race and partisanship.[4] In consequence, the judiciary has not been receptive to probabilistic evidence of such discriminatory leanings among elected officials (see generally Stoughton 2013; and Douglas 2015). But, in political practice, the empirical link between race and partisanship is clear for this class of policies. The clearest determinant of legislative support for restrictive voter policies is electoral competitiveness. At the state level, these policies are more likely to be enacted in Republican-controlled states that have competitive elections (Hale and McNeal 2010; Bentele and O'Brien 2013; Hicks et al. 2015). At the individual level, party affiliation and the racial composition of legislative districts strongly predict state legislators' support for restrictive laws (McKee 2015; Hicks, McKee, and Smith 2016). Similarly, audit studies have found strong evidence that many officials are differentially responsive in their interactions on the basis of the implied race or ethnicity of the member of the public in question (see Burstein 2014; White, Nathan, and Faller 2015; and Mendez and Grose 2018). Such evidence has been rejected as a means of demonstrating that voting laws were enacted with a discriminatory intent—on this point, see most notably the Fifth Circuit's ruling in *Veasey v. Abbott*, a 2015 voter identification case.[5]

A further obstacle to mounting effective legal challenges to new restrictive voting laws is their highly fragmented character. Measures targeting undocumented immigrants were generally adopted during a wave of omnibus state immigration reform (see Steil and Vasi 2014). By contrast, policies dealing with voter identification, election crimes, voter roll maintenance practices, and similar issues are generally dealt with in separate bills. In many cases, state reforms of a single aspect of election law, such as absentee voting, will be dispersed across several bills. Identifying either a strong intention or a strong effect in narrow measures of this kind would be no simple matter, and, as will be argued below, contemporary voter restriction is often an effect arising from the concatenation of burdens, any one of which can be plausibly construed as minimal when considered in isolation. An exception to this pattern is North Carolina, whose legislature enacted an omnibus election reform bill immediately after *Shelby County v. Holder* freed the state from the preclearance requirements of the VRA. Court challenges to provisions of this reform have been notably successful.[6]

It has proved difficult to devise successful challenges to election laws on the basis of their application. Standing-related doctrine, which had formerly been very permissive in voting rights cases (Zipkin 2010), has been abbreviated in recent years. The difficulty of making facial challenges to new measures also creates a curious outcome: behaviors that courts would deem to be compelling evidence of discriminatory application may be more likely to arise in states with less restrictive laws. For instance, weaker voter identification policies under which identification is requested but not required do not appear to have a statistically measurable effect on minority participation in elections (Hajnal, Lajevardi, and Nielson 2017, 374). Yet identification-requested measures give local election officials discretion, where strict identification-required measures do not. The same discretion that makes the aggregate effects of these laws less severe can also increase the chance that there will be some evidence of discriminatory application. Note the geographic distribution of cases discussed in Ross (2014) as well as evidence in Burden et al. (2016) on the connection between task complexity (which arises to some degree from local poll worker discretion) and rates of polling place incidents.

Finally, states defending restrictive voting laws have benefited from the larger shift in administrative law doctrines discussed in chapter 2. Court decisions on voting rights issues have turned on many of these same considerations of federal agency regulatory power (Nou 2013; Pildes 2013). For instance, HAVA created the Election Assistance Commission to facilitate the implementation of the bill's key goals, but it does not provide the commission any binding rulemaking power (Tokaji 2008, 474), and there have been lengthy periods during which the commission lacked the necessary quorum to make decisions.

The remarkable success of the VRA also depended mainly on its clear legislative intention and its moral authority, not subsequent agency activity—the VRA does not empower any agency or executive actor to make rules about key questions of enforcement. Most significantly, though it left the oversight of Section 5's preclearance regime to the Department of Justice, it did not create any administrative powers to modify the preclearance coverage formula set out in Section 4 (Elmendorf 2015). This absence of agency power may have contributed to the Court's reasoning in *Shelby County v. Holder*, which ended the enforcement of the preclearance provisions of the VRA. Crucially, the ruling upheld Section 5 and thus recognized preclearance as a permissible practice. Rather, the majority held that there was not a compelling rationale for the existing requirements—which had covered the same jurisdictions for nearly fifty years on the basis of an unmodified coverage formula—to continue to be applied. A number of new preclearance formulas have been suggested (Bullock, Gaddie, and Wert 2016, 172–88), some of which would be more sensitive to the contemporary political geography of voter discrimination.[7] However, because no agency is authorized to produce a revised formula or set of standards, a new (and very unlikely) act of Congress would be required to reimpose preclearance requirements on states and localities.

In sum, facially race neutral, uniformly administered state voting laws have generally survived judicial review. The development and diffusion of such laws have been, to a great degree, enabled by federal action. HAVA provided both a spur to reform and a measure of justification for enacting restrictive measures. The ruling in *Crawford* provided states with a complete vocabulary of justification while also setting forth an approach—consistent with many other cases on election issues—that has made the Court mostly unwilling to scrutinize evidence that such justifications are either dubious or insufficiently compelling when weighed against their effects on electoral participation. Further, given that legal and political challenges to restrictive voting policies now treat the problem as foremost one of racial inequity, it is striking that one of the Court's crucial rulings hardly discusses race at all.

The survival of these laws is closely related to the history of federal voting rights protections. Those protections are primarily judge made, and federal agencies have very little formally specified power to intervene in the state administration of elections. Moreover, these protections arose in response to a form of disenfranchisement that was overtly racist and procedurally irregular. Federal courts have therefore imposed evidentiary standards for challenges to state laws that are very difficult to meet if the measures are procedurally uniform and rely on antifraud or electoral integrity arguments.

This is a significant contrast to federal courts' persistently high, active involvement in redistricting cases. (Whether that higher involvement has yielded more equitable results in those cases is, of course, a wholly different question.) This difference may arise from two factors. First, the federal courts have read the VRA as rendering them directly competent to rule on the legality of districting schemes, which has made many standing and administrative procedural considerations mostly irrelevant. Second, legislative apportionment is virtually the only area where, through its creation of the decennial census, the Constitution grants the federal government a definite role in the conduct of elections. This understanding of the census and the recognition of census data as uniquely valid and persuasive evidence produced rare unanimity on the Roberts Court, which has been sharply divided in most voting rights cases. *Evenwel v. Abbott*, which considered whether Texas could be compelled draw legislative districts on the basis of the number of eligible voters rather than the total population, was decided 8–0 in favor of continued apportionment solely on the basis of census population figures.[8]

How Do Restrictive Laws Restrict Voting?

The previous section examined legal developments that have made it difficult to challenge new, restrictive state voting laws. However, that discussion did very little to demonstrate that such measures do, in fact, restrict voting or the means by which this restrictive effect arises. This section will discuss the extent to which various states have enacted restrictive voting policies since the passage of HAVA and examine how those policies may actually prevent eligible electors from casting a ballot. The discussion covers two kinds of restrictive policies. The first kind of policy restricts voting by imposing an administrative burden on individuals when they attempt to register to vote or appear at the polls. In many states, burdensome regulations are complemented by administrative practices likely to create uncertainty as well as deterrence: many states that have adopted burdensome regulations have also enacted severe felony penalties for various individual election offenses. The second kind of policy makes use of centralized, electronic record-keeping systems to scrutinize voter registrations or engage in active maintenance of voter rolls. A detailed examination of the Interstate Voter Registration Crosscheck Program (Crosscheck) will illustrate how record keeping and record sharing may interact with other administrative practices in order to restrict voting.

It should be noted at the outset that it is difficult to measure the effects of such policies on registration rates or voting behavior. This is so for several reasons. First, there is considerable state-to-state and election-to-election variation in both voter registration rates and voter turnout. Some of this variation is clearly structured: for instance, voter turnout is generally higher in presidential elections than in midterm elections. However, there is also a great deal of variation that is random or associated with factors other than election law, such as the appeal of a candidate, the perceived competitiveness of an election, the weather, or the voting behavior of friends and family members. Next, the reliability of some data is open to doubt. In states with voter identification laws, official counts of provisional ballots exist, and this gives some measure of who is affected by those laws. However, such counts do not include people who are inappropriately turned away at the polls. The counts also do not include individuals who do not appear at the polls because they believe, rightly or wrongly, that they lack the appropriate qualifications to vote or individuals who do not attempt to register because of a right or wrong belief that they lack the necessary documentation. In recent surveys, many voters—particularly minority voters—cite a lack of necessary documentation as a reason for not voting; the number of surveyed individuals who report actually being turned away at the polls is much smaller (Stewart 2013, 49–50).

It is difficult to know how many of these self-reports come from likely voters who became discouraged and how many from unlikely voters who point to stringent requirements when prompted to offer a rationale for not voting. Although restrictive laws can be viewed as intrinsically objectionable on equity grounds, the overall voting propensity of individuals likely to be affected by stringent registration or identification requirements is important for estimating the electoral effect of such measures. It is likely that the voting propensity for this group is relatively low (see Hood and Bullock 2012). Felon disenfranchisement laws are a better-studied case of a similar form of restriction. These laws have a much smaller effect on election outcomes than the total number of persons affected would suggest; for a variety of reasons, former offenders are, as a population, unlikely to vote even if legally entitled to do so (Burch 2011). However, even taking this very low turnout into consideration, it is likely that the felon disenfranchisement laws have had a decisive effect in many important elections (Uggen and Manza 2002). The matter is further complicated because election law is a highly salient topic in many states: the enactment of stringent laws with a perceived discriminatory intent may make minority voters more likely to vote (Citrin, Green, and Levy 2014), and changes in election laws often have unexpected effects (Burden et al. 2014). Yet the available evidence does strongly suggest that measures such as voter identification laws do meaningfully depress electoral participation of minority groups (Hajnal, Lajevardi, and Nielson 2017).

It is very plausible that these measures may sometimes affect the outcome of elections: close elections are common in the American states. Between 1948 and 2000, forty-one gubernatorial elections, thirty-two Senate elections, and thirty-one state-level presidential votes were decided by a margin of less than 1 percent (National Commission on Federal Election Reform 2002, 123–24). In the 2010, 2012, and 2014 general elections, four Senate races, four gubernatorial races, and the Florida presidential vote were decided by less than 1 percent; fourteen more gubernatorial and Senate races were decided by a margin greater than 1 percent but fewer than 50,000 total votes. In the 2016 general election, the states that tipped the balance in the Electoral College—Michigan, Wisconsin, and Pennsylvania—were, in aggregate, decided by little more than 100,000 votes, and the North Carolina gubernatorial election was decided by fewer than 5,000 votes. This is to say nothing of the great number of House races and state and local elections commonly decided by very small margins. It is very doubtful that current restrictive voting policies have electoral effects at all comparable in their magnitude to historical forms of mass disenfranchisement. However, it is readily conceivable that they could regularly have an effect of a couple of percentage points—enough, in many competitive states, to swing the outcome of an important election or determine party control of a legislative chamber.

The following discussion gives a brief treatment of a class of voting and election laws that make it more difficult for individuals to register to vote or cast a ballot. These include documentary requirements to register to vote; voter identification requirements; restrictions on voter registration drives; limitations on early voting, absentee voting, and voter registration periods; and felony penalties for individual voting offenses. These laws create difficulties by several means. They may impose time or financial costs on individuals who need to gather additional documents in order to register or vote.[9] They may impose cognitive costs by making voting regulations complex and intentionally dispersing necessary information across a number of sources. The effect of these laws may also be psychological: frustration, uncertainty, or fear may deter eligible electors from registering or voting, just as complexity does in other interactions between the populace and public bureaucracies (see generally Moynihan and Herd 2010; and Moynihan, Herd, and Harvey 2015). These laws can thus be a means of pursuing electoral goals through administrative practices.

A growing body of research in public administration examines the employment of administrative burdens to limit citizens' use of government benefits or to induce enrolled recipients to cease using those benefits. This form of administrative exclusion creates "nonparticipation attributable to organizational factors rather than claimant preferences or eligibility status" (Brodkin and Majmundar 2010, 827). Extensive questionnaires and lengthy and confusing applications and eligibility statements have, for instance, considerably limited the uptake of Medicaid and SNAP benefits in many states (Moynihan, Herd, and Rigby 2013; Herd 2015). Administrative burdens on benefits are much higher in states under Republican control, though there is not a clear relationship between states that have used administrative burdens in benefits and those that have used them in voting.

Indeed, aside from the obvious importance of Republican control, there are not particularly clear patterns in state adoption of restrictive registration and voting laws. Table 4.1 shows overall patterns of adoption for the five kinds of policies discussed in this subsection (the data are drawn from Biggers and Hanmer 2015 and the National Conference of State Legislatures Elections Legislation Database). There are thirty-five states that have at least one of these policies, but only four states— Alabama, Kansas, Texas, and Virginia—have enacted at least three. This table is not an exhaustive list of restrictive measures adopted in recent years: since the passage of HAVA, state legislatures have enacted more than three thousand bills modifying their election laws, many of which make very small abridgements to voting opportunities. The policies discussed below do, however, show that administrative burdens and uncertainty can limit electoral participation and will tend to have a disproportionate effect on minority voters.

The most restrictive of these measures, by far, is the documentary proof of citizenship registration requirement adopted in Kansas and Arizona; unimplemented versions of these provisions have been enacted in Alabama and Georgia. These laws require individuals to prove that they are US citizens to register to vote, meaning that prospective registrants must produce a birth certificate, naturalization papers, or a US passport.

TABLE 4.1. **Post-HAVA state adoption of restrictive voting policies**

Citizenship	Registration drives	Strict ID	New felonies	Voting limits
AL		AL	AL	AL
			AR	
AZ		AZ		
	CO		CO	
			CT	
				DE
			FL	
GA		GA	GA	
		IN	IN	
KS		KS	KS	
	KY			KY
	LA		LA	
				MA
	MI			MI
	MN			
	MO			MO
		MS		MS
	MT			
	NC		NC	
			NH	
	NV		NV	
				NY
	OH	OH		
			OK	
				PA
				RI
				SC
	SD			
		TN	TN	
	TX	TX	TX	
			UT	
	VA	VA	VA	VA
			WA	
		WI		
	WV		WV	

The stated rationale for this law is rooted in HAVA, which modified the federal voter registration form to include a check box asking prospective registrants to certify that they are US citizens. The record plainly indicates that this modification to the form was intended to save ineligible applicants from wasted time completing the form. However, some states have construed that change as providing a right (or a positive obligation) to inquire into the citizenship status of prospective voters.

Diffusion of this policy has been very limited. But, where it has been implemented, it has had a considerable effect. In Kansas, nearly 20 percent of new registrations were suspended for lack of proof of citizenship in the years after the requirement came into effect. In the 2014 general election, this provision affected a number of voters equal to 2.5 percent of the total turnout and did so in a very partisan fashion: Democrats were 1.55 times more likely than Republicans to have their registrations suspended. Unaffiliated voters were 3.8 times more likely than Republicans to have their registrations suspended.[10] The wide partisan variation in suspension rates is almost certainly not an indicator of any unfair exercise of discretion; rather, it likely points to different party preferences that are correlated with individuals' access to records such as birth certificates or marriage certificates. The high suspension rate for unaffiliated voters also suggests that individuals attempting to register without the assistance of an organization are likely to have more difficulty fulfilling the requirements.

The legal history of documentary proof of citizenship requirements has been a confused one. In *Arizona v. Inter Tribal Council of Arizona*, the Supreme Court considered whether Arizona could impose a registration requirement that exceeded what was requested on the federal voter registration form and also whether the Election Assistance Commission could be required to alter the form in a state that imposed an additional requirement; this question was made more difficult by the absence of a quorum on the commission and thus uncertainty about whether Arizona had actually exhausted its administrative remedies. After this decision, Arizona and Kansas requested modification of the federal form to include the states' documentary proof of citizenship requirements; in *Kobach v. US Election Assistance Commission*, the Tenth Circuit found in favor of the commission. A ruling in the DC Circuit, *League of Women Voters v. Newby*, barred the director from making state-requested modifications of the federal form without the approval of the chronically shorthanded commission. In Kansas, the list of registrations suspended for want of documentary proof of citizenship continued to grow, and, owing in part to the state's slow clearance of the backlog, the Tenth Circuit, in *Fish v. Kobach*, upheld an injunction against the enforcement of the documentary proof of citizenship requirement in the 2016 general election. The district-level trial on the matter was conducted in the spring of 2018; a range of administrative irregularities were central to the court's ruling against the continued imposition of the requirement.

Owing to the still ill-defined authority of the Election Assistance Commission, vagueness in the meaning and scope of the NVRA, and the contested process of the actual implementation of the proof of citizenship requirement in Kansas, no ruling to date has spoken unambiguously to the legality of the requirement. It appears that a state prepared to maintain a dual system of voter rolls could, in principle, impose the requirement (see Priest 2015).

Since 2005, at least fourteen states that have adopted laws that make it harder for organizations to assist individuals with voter registration. Most commonly, these laws impose requirements on individuals or organizations who intend to help others register to vote. Other laws restrict the compensation for workers in voter registration drives. These laws, too, have a likely partisan effect. Voter registration drives have a demonstrated effect on electoral participation (Nickerson 2015). Higher rates of voter registration and turnout generally benefit Democrats in elections, and minority voters are nearly twice as likely as white voters to register through a drive (Kasdan 2012). In addition, many progressive groups are reliant on private canvassing organizations whose usual employment practices may be contravened by new registration drive laws (see Fisher 2006). Many states have also adopted laws that impose more specific limitations on registration assistance. Most often, these laws prevent individuals from helping others apply for absentee or mail voting.[11] Restrictions on registration assistance leave more individuals to fend for themselves, which may make them less likely to vote and more likely to commit errors that will invalidate their attempted registration.

Such confusion is likely the most important effect of voter identification laws, and, to the extent that widespread public criticism of these laws increases their salience, it appears possible that opposition to them may have the paradoxical consequence of increasing the number of potential voters affected by them. Because this class of laws is well studied, the discussion here will be brief. Eleven states have adopted strict laws under which identification is required rather than requested in order to vote; eight of these states require photo identification.[12] The direct effect of voter identification laws can be measured from the number of provisional ballots cast by individuals who believe themselves to be qualified to vote but who appear at the polls without appropriate identification. Studies in Indiana and Kansas—states with strict photo identification laws—suggest that perhaps one voter in one thousand casts a provisional ballot that goes uncounted for want of identification (Pitts 2014;

Dobbs 2015). A larger number of voters stay away from the polls because they genuinely lack appropriate identification, though, as the preceding section noted, individuals who lack documents such as driver's licenses do not vote at very high rates. A much larger number of voters incorrectly believe that they lack appropriate identification. A detailed study of the Texas Twenty-Third Congressional District, where the 2014 House race was competitive, found that a substantial majority of individuals who claimed that a lack of acceptable identification was their reason for not voting did in fact possess an acceptable form of identification. About 80 percent of these individuals said that they would have voted for the Democratic candidate (Hobby et al. 2015, 7, 12).

Research has consistently suggested that many individuals are uncertain about their entitlement to vote. A class of laws that wants further empirical study may increase the deterrent effect of this uncertainty. Since the passage of HAVA, nineteen states have created new felony offenses for voting fraud committed by private individuals, though individual voting fraud is exceedingly rare and prosecutions for such fraud are rarer still. In at least three states, measures creating new crimes have also expanded the ability of state executive officers to initiate prosecutions. Local prosecutors generally decline to file charges for the most common form of fraud—inadvertent double voting by older voters who own property in multiple states (Hasen quoted in Lowry 2015). Secretary Kobach secured independent authority to prosecute election crimes; his initial canvass discovered only double voting of this kind.

At present, no evidence is available about the impact that such penalties might have on voting behavior, particularly when felony penalties are introduced concurrently with new registration or identification requirements. However, it can be noted that these penalties can give the appearance of criminalizing honest attempts at voter registration by individuals who do not have at hand the necessary documents to complete the registration.[13] One such felony law—in Iowa—was judged to be an illegal form of intimidation (Noble 2012). Many of these new felonies apply irrespective of an intention to commit fraud. Other laws would, for instance, impose felony penalties on an individual who placed a disabled neighbor's absentee ballot in the mailbox.[14] Some of these laws define new kinds of offenses—several states have, for instance, made it illegal for individuals to photograph their completed ballot or make that photograph public. The severity of the sanction may make individuals extremely reticent to create a case that will test the legality of a new restriction. It is notable that a case contesting a ban on ballot photographs—*Rideout v. Gardner*—stemmed from an act of civil disobedience in New Hampshire, where the penalties for the offense were much lighter.

The preceding class of policies may tend to limit voting by making it more difficult for individuals to register or cast a ballot and by making it harder for organizations to provide assistance to individuals who wish to vote. These policies are new and capitalize on HAVA's mandate that states create centralized election administrations. Though they are neutral on face, they are, on average, more likely to affect minority voters. A final set of policies does not make use of newly created authority but may heighten the effect of these other measures. Many states have limited opportunities to vote. The states included in the final column of table 4.1 do not permit early voting, no-excuse absentee voting, or same-day voter registration. Many other states have made narrower restrictions, such as shortening the registration period before elections, reducing early voting days, or shortening poll hours (for a summary, see Weiser and Opsal [2014]). Again, these are measures that are more likely to affect minority voters, who are more apt to make use of early voting, especially early voting on Sundays (Herron and Smith 2012). Such abbreviation of voting opportunities can also make for very long wait times on Election Day, an effect that is spatially concentrated in urban areas (Presidential Commission on Election Administration 2014, 13).[15] These limitations on voting periods can, in themselves, make voting inconvenient. They also afford voters fewer opportunities to discover and correct errors in their registrations or documents; in states where stringent laws are in place, it may be impossible to remedy these errors if voters become aware of them only on the day of an election.

The Crosscheck Program: Interstate Cooperation and Voter Purging

The preceding section considered several kinds of state policies that impose an administrative burden on individual voters, primarily in the form of documentary requirements and limitations on registration and voting assistance. These antifraud provisions may prevent large numbers of eligible electors from registering to vote or casting a ballot. Burdensome antifraud provisions make use of the centralization of state election administration following the passage of HAVA; these strictly applied rules stand in sharp contrast to historical discriminatory policies that relied on administrative discretion or simple denial of adequate opportunities to register. This subsection considers a similar bureaucratized permutation of a voter restriction practice that was formerly discretionary: challenging the eligibility of individuals who are already registered to vote. It was once common for individual voters to find their registrations challenged by nonofficial actors when they appeared at the polling place to vote; this was a core feature of the southern model of disenfranchisement and an enabling condition for voter intimidation. Prior to the introduction of voter registration requirements, party monitoring of polling places was also the primary guarantee of electoral integrity in other parts of the United States.

A more recent form of this practice is voter caging. In voter caging efforts, nonstate actors send nonforwardable mail to addresses of registered voters in areas with large minority populations, often asking the recipients to send the mail back. When mail is returned as undeliverable or does not receive a reply, vote cagers claim that the voter registration associated with that address is no longer valid (for more extensive treatments, see Davidson et al. [2008]; and Daniels [2010]). These techniques are of dubious legality. Immediately before the 2016 election, a ruling in *North Carolina State Conference of the NAACP v. North Carolina State Board of Elections* reversed the results of a voter caging effort. There, a private individual had sent nonforwardable mail to registered voters in predominantly African American areas in North Carolina. Mail returned as undeliverable was then presented to county election boards as evidence that the voters no longer resided at those addresses, resulting in the cancellation of their registrations. The court's ruling in that case dealt primarily with two matters: first, the registrations were canceled very shortly before the election, in violation of the NVRA. Second, and more significantly, the decision held that this behavior represented deliberate, selective targeting of African American voters.

Voter caging is a legally suspect practice because it allows nongovernment actors to play a large role in voter roll maintenance and because caging ordinarily targets minority populations. However, states may engage in highly active voter roll maintenance in a way that is lawful but has a similar effect. The prerequisite for this maintenance is the licit generation of a list of registrations to be scrutinized. The Interstate Voter Registration Crosscheck Program (Crosscheck) is an interstate record-sharing agreement organized by the Kansas secretary of state. The fol-

lowing discussion of Crosscheck is rather more thorough than the preceding discussion of restrictive voting laws. This is so for several reasons.
First, there is not yet any scholarly treatment of Crosscheck. It is also an
extensive and practically important program. Finally, it is a strong illustration of the role of state administrative behavior in modern conflicts
over the right to vote.

States that participate in Crosscheck send their complete electronic
voter rolls to the Office of the Kansas Secretary of State each year. The
office then makes state-by-state paired comparisons of individual enroll-
ments in search of duplicate registration records. Lists of possible duplicate registrations are then returned to participant states, which may
use these lists in voter roll maintenance. The avowed purposes of Crosscheck are to prevent fraud and promote the maintenance of current and
accurate voter rolls. These goals are both clearly permitted by HAVA.
Indeed, HAVA encourages states to engage in record sharing as it is not
legally practicable to create a centralized, federal voter registration system. However, Crosscheck generates large numbers of surplus matches
that can be used to purge state voter rolls of valid registrants. These spurious matches are disproportionately likely to affect African American
voters. These excess matches are perhaps the reason why Secretary Kobach has privately referred to the program as a means of "cag[ing] voters" (Lefler 2011).

Crosscheck began as a trial record-sharing program under Ron Thornburgh, Kris Kobach's predecessor as Kansas secretary of state. Under
Thornburgh, it included only four midwestern states. After Kobach assumed office, it grew into an extraordinarily large program. By 2015, it
included twenty-nine states encompassing some 65 percent of all registered voters in the United States. Widespread participation in Crosscheck undoubtedly owes to its low visibility and the ease with which
states can join. Although its existence and operation is a matter of public record, Crosscheck has received little attention. In distinction to laws
that may be burdensome on individual registrants and whose enactment
is often visible and divisive, no legislative authorization is necessary for
state election officials to join Crosscheck.[16] Bypassing state legislatures
has allowed executive officeholders to develop a program that may have
an extraordinarily large effect on the composition of the state electorate. Summary results of the 2015 Crosscheck were provided by the Office of the Kansas Secretary of State in response to an open records request; this request was fulfilled promptly and in full. Figure 4.1 shows

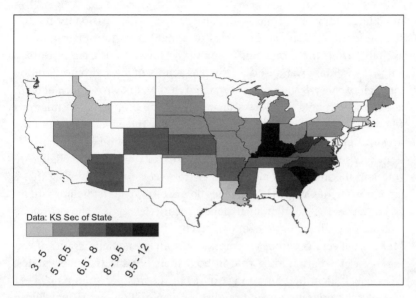

FIGURE 4.1. Percentage of voter registrations flagged as possible duplicates, 2015 Crosscheck

the percentage of voter registrations flagged as possible duplicates. In some states, more than 10 percent of all voter registrations were called into question.

The Crosscheck program compares voter registrations on the basis of first name, last name, and date of birth. A presumed duplicate arises when registered voters in two participant states share these pieces of data. In 2015, twenty-eight states participated; these state voter rolls together accounted for over 109 million voter registrations. The Crosscheck yielded 7.26 million record matches across 378 paired state comparisons. If all the matches were valid, they would represent 3.63 million individuals with duplicate registration records; if they were all invalid, they would erroneously call into question the legitimate registrations of 14.52 million distinct individuals who coincidentally share a name with other voters. The truth certainly lies somewhere in the middle.

Genuine record matches are created when a registered voter migrates and registers in a new state. Under these circumstances, the registration record in the sending state should be removed; it was the inability to make such deletions that caused state voter rolls to swell after the enactment of the NVRA. The evidence suggests that Crosscheck does identify a large number of genuine duplicate registrations arising from interstate migration. Reliable estimates of annual interstate migration are available from the American Community Survey (US Census Bureau 2015). These data were used to compile counts of in- and out-migration for each of the 378 state pairs compared in the 2015 Crosscheck and adjusted these counts to address the approximate proportion of migrants who are noncitizens or below voting age (adjustments derived from figures in Benetsky, Burd, and Rapino [2015, 4, 6]). The Pearson correlation between the estimated number of interstate migrants eligible to vote and the number of matched registrations is 0.83, suggesting that a large portion of Crosscheck matches do arise from interstate migration.

However, the number of matched records exceeded the estimated number of eligible migrants in 94 percent of paired state comparisons.[17] Making the very generous assumption that all interstate migrants of voting age were registered to vote in both their old and their new states, Crosscheck identified an average of 5,440 records per state pair in excess of what migration would predict, or 2.06 million excess matches in total. Figure 4.2 compares the number of Crosscheck matches and estimated registration-eligible migrants for each of the state pairs. The

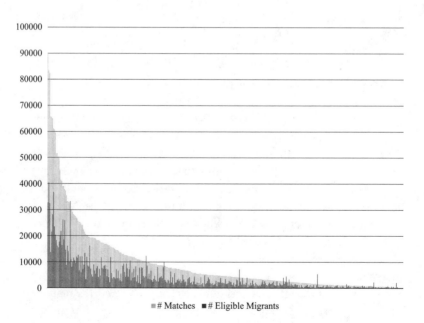

■ # Matches ■ # Eligible Migrants

FIGURE 4.2. Ranked excess matches in the 2015 Crosscheck, by state pair

excess matches could represent earlier interstate migrants who were not removed from the rolls or were slow to register in their new states. They could also represent spurious matches of the voter records of distinct individuals. Because twenty-one of the twenty-eight states had participated in Crosscheck at least twice before 2015, it is difficult to suppose that earlier migration accounts for the bulk of these excess matches.

A spurious Crosscheck match would arise from a relatively rare event: the birth on the same date of two people with the same first and last names. Though the event is rare, the 2015 Crosscheck made quadrillions of comparisons of record pairs, making possible a large number of uncommon spurious matches. A precise estimate cannot be made without complete voter rolls and Crosscheck matches, but there are reasons to suspect that spurious matches may be more likely to arise between two persons from the same racial or ethnic group, owing to differences in common given names and surnames across these groups. In addition, there are reasons to believe that such matches would arise more frequently among minority groups. These matches derive from underlying demographic features, and the matching method thus functions as an opening to an algorithmic mode of discrimination.

Patterns of immigration, fertility, and mortality have produced age structures that vary considerably across major racial and ethnic groups: the median age of non-Hispanic whites in the United States is 41.2 years; the median age of Asians is 35.3, of blacks and African Americans 31.3, and Americans of Hispanic origin 27.4 (US Census Bureau 2012b, 13). In consequence, larger proportions of these minority populations may share a given date of birth. Data on surname frequency from the 2000 Census show that large proportions of minority racial and ethnic groups in the United States share a small number of common surnames (US Census Bureau 2014). Table 4.2 summarizes the population distribution of major racial and ethnic groups by most common surnames.

The greater proportion of minority voters sharing a date of birth and

TABLE 4.2. **Cumulative percentage of population sharing most common surnames, by group, 2000**

Rank	Asian	Black	Hispanic	White
1	2.5	2.0	2.2	.8
10	11.5	11.8	13.8	4.1
25	17.5	18.1	23.3	6.4
50	20.4	23.8	32.0	9.7
100	21.9	31.4	40.7	13.5

a surname could make Crosscheck's matching method more likely to flag the valid registrations of distinct individuals within those groups. However, the frequency of these matches also depends on the number and proportion of within-group registrations being compared. These numbers differ considerably across racial and ethnic groups. In the 2012 data, the most recent prior data available, the twenty-eight states participating in Crosscheck accounted for 57.2 percent of all registered voters, which breaks down into 64.3 percent of all black voters, 60.5 percent of all non-Hispanic white voters, 33 percent of Asian voters, and 29.8 percent of Hispanic voters of any race (US Census Bureau 2013). In light of the very large proportion of the black electorate included in Crosscheck, spurious matches might arise at a particularly high rate within this group.

Table 4.3 shows the results of two regressions on the number of excess Crosscheck matches by state pair.[18] The geography measure takes states with a shared border as the reference group. The unit for record pairs is one trillion; substantively, this variable suggests the number of excess matches arising per million registrants in each half of a paired state comparison. The results of model 1 are as expected: geographically proximate state pairs (where higher rates of migration would be expected) and state pairs with large voter rolls both see more matches. Model 2 adds measures of the proportion of record comparisons involving within-race comparisons of black and white registered voters. The proportion of black voters in a state pair substantially increases the number of excess matches. This effect is smaller but still significant for white voters. This finding is consistent with the view that matches are more

TABLE 4.3. **Predictors of state pair record matches, net of interstate migration**

	Model 1 (N = 378)		Model 2 (N = 378)	
Geography				
1 state distant	−7,500.75***	(1,058.99)	−7,243.86***	(1,042.70)
2+ states distant	−8,211.25***	(898.74)	−7,544.73***	(907.53)
No. record pairs	335.96***	(18.59)	322.84***	(19.37)
Within-group pairs (%)				
Black			827.36***	(213.05)
White			68.82*	(39.69)
Constant	7,417.31		1,511.63	
Adjusted R^2	.532		.548	

Note: Standard errors are in parentheses.

***$p < .001$; **$p < .01$; *$p < .05$.

likely to arise between individuals from the same racial group and that the distribution of surnames makes such matches more likely to arise among black voters than among white voters. The inclusion of possible within-group matches for Asian and Hispanic voters did not improve the model: both groups represent very small proportions of possible matches for most state pairs. The relationship between the number of excess matches and the number of compared record pairs is linear: exponential functions did not produce a better fit between these two variables, and log transformations of the variables also produced very similar results. Regressions where the dependent variable is total matches rather than matches in excess of migration and the number of migrants is included as a control also yield very similar results.

The memorandum of understanding that governs Crosscheck provides states with considerable discretion over their use of matches; aside from agreeing to furnish additional information at the request of other participant states, officials can use lists of matches however they wish. Election officials in many states have evinced skepticism about Crosscheck results and used them with caution. Excess matches prompted Florida to withdraw from the program in 2014. Several participant states—Colorado, Louisiana, Nevada, and Virginia—have also joined the Electronic Registration Information Center, a rapidly growing program that employs a more rigorous method for matching voter registrations. Virginia summarily discarded nearly 100,000 Crosscheck matches in 2013 (Palmer, Riemer, and Davis 2014, 14).

However, state officials may also treat record matches as sufficient grounds for making further inquiries into a voter's registration, which may lead many valid registrants to be removed from voter rolls. North Carolina offers a clear example. The state has one of the largest African American populations in the United States, both in absolute numbers and as a proportion of the population. This may have contributed to the state's anomalously high match rate. The 2015 Crosscheck produced 331,000 record matches for North Carolina in excess of the number of eligible interstate migrants. As a proportion of registered voters, this number is nearly three times the average match rate for the 2015 Crosscheck. The 2014 Crosscheck yielded 35,750 exact name and date-of-birth matches between individuals who voted in the 2012 general election in both North Carolina and another state (Strach, Burris, and Degraffenreid 2014, 35). The North Carolina State Board of Elections has treated those registrations as particularly suspect, a seemingly reasonable view in light of the fact that these matches would appear suggestive of fraudulent double voting. However, such matches nearly always indicate two distinct individuals with the same name and date of birth. Kris Kobach's comprehensive canvass of records from several election cycles yielded only nine prosecutions for double voting (Kansas Secretary of State 2017).

North Carolina made it a policy to pursue Crosscheck matches by mailing nonforwardable address verification forms to registered voters. Formerly, nonresponse to such verification would have made a voter inactive, a status that was reversible if the inactive voter appeared in person on Election Day. After the Supreme Court decision in *Shelby County v. Holder* removed preclearance requirements, North Carolina adopted a number of major changes to its voting laws. In 2014, nonresponses to address verification mailings led registrations to be denied rather than declared inactive, making the registrants ineligible to vote without taking further action (Strach, Burris, and Degraffenreid 2014, 32). Voters removed from the rolls were not notified of this fact. Yet a substantial portion of nonrespondents would be persons still residing in North Carolina. Nonresponse could mean that the confirmation form was miscarried or that, if it was delivered, the voter failed to send it back. Previous research has found that nonresponse to such mail is especially high among minority populations and households with annual incomes below $35,000 (Perez 2008, 37–38). Nonresponse could also mean that the voter moved to a new address within the state: 18.1 percent of North Carolinians made an in-state move in 2013 (US Census Bureau 2014). Nationally, black annual migration rates are 39 percent higher than those for non-Hispanic whites (US Census Bureau 2012a). Evidence presented in *NAACP v. McCrory*, a court case that resulted in an injunction against several features of North Carolina's new election laws, shows that black North Carolinians have in-state migration and confirmation form nonresponse rates significantly above the state average.

In short, North Carolina's use of Crosscheck matches may substantially affect the racial composition of the state's voter rolls. It is likely that the initial set of Crosscheck matches is racially skewed in much the same way as are lists employed by actors engaged in voter caging. The state board of elections then uses a method for investigating these registrations that is both imprecise and particularly likely to affect a minority population already disproportionately represented on the initial list. In many states, erroneous record purges of this kind can be corrected, albeit at a significant cost of time to the affected voter. However, other changes in North Carolina's election laws make it very unlikely that voters dropped by this method would be able to cast a ballot: North Carolina has abolished same-day registration, restricted early voting, and eliminated the right of voters to cast a provisional ballot if they appear at the wrong polling place. As a result, erroneously denied registrants who learn of their removal on Election Day may have no means of voting.

The preceding has argued that underlying differences in the distributions of names and dates of birth across racial and ethnic groups make Crosscheck disproportionately likely to erroneously flag the valid registrations of black voters. The example of North Carolina has served as a demonstration of how states can employ lists of Crosscheck matches in a manner that will tend to remove valid registrations of poor and minority voters from the rolls.

To date, Crosscheck has not been the subject of any court ruling, though a case filed by the American Civil Liberties Union in 2018, *Moore v. Kobach*, raised legal challenges about the program's data-management practices. But, in view of the discussion of judicial reasoning developed in this chapter, it is instructive to consider the likely shape and result of a challenge grounded in voting rights law. There is certainly nothing in the public record of Crosscheck's development or implementation that a court would construe as persuasive evidence of racially discriminatory intent; indeed, as a multistate administrative agreement not subject to legislative authorization, there is little deliberative record of any kind. Crosscheck could nonetheless be challenged under Section 2 of the VRA, which remains in effect after *Shelby County* and allows for laws and practices to be challenged as discriminatory in effect even if they do not have a manifestly discriminatory intent (Elmendorf and Spencer 2015). A significant ruling that sets out the relevant standard is *Thornburg v. Gingles*, a legislative districting case. The Fourth, Fifth, and Sixth Circuits, which cover most of the states where Crosscheck is likely to have a particularly large effect on minority voting, have adopted a two-part test of discriminatory effect derived from the *Gingles* ruling. As presented in *Veasey v. Abbott*, a recent voter identification case, the test for discriminatory effects requires that a policy "impose[s] a discriminatory burden on members of a protected class" and that the "burden must in part be caused by or linked to social and historical conditions that have or currently produce discrimination against members of the protected class" (No. 14-41127 5th Cir., *20–*21).

The preceding evidence has suggested that Crosscheck produces spurious voter registration matches that are disproportionately concentrated among members of a protected class—African Americans. However, the mere fact of producing spurious matches does not produce a burden, as participating states have discretion over their use of Crosscheck matches—and, indeed, can decline to use them entirely. A plaintiff could take up the matter of the aggressive use of these matches in voter roll maintenance in states such as North Carolina; however, a ruling on this point would not directly touch the Crosscheck program itself. Further, voter roll maintenance informed by these matches would almost certainly not be regarded with the same judicial suspicion as third-party voter caging practices, given that Crosscheck is a means of pursuing state interests that have been recognized by federal courts through a practice encouraged by federal legislation.

Supposing that a court concluded that Crosscheck and associated voter roll maintenance practices did impose a discriminatory burden, it would also be necessary to connect that burden to historical or ongoing social mechanisms of discrimination. The argument presented above suggested that concentration of spurious registration matches among African Americans derives mainly from interracial differences in the distribution of surnames. One could argue that this distribution of surnames is itself the result of historical and ongoing processes of discrimination. The initial acquisition of surnames by African Americans in the United States is unambiguously a consequence of slavery. At the start of the Civil War, 89 percent of the census-defined black population was held in slavery (Haines 2006, 48). Slaveholders' surnames were commonly ascribed to the people they held in slavery, and, even when former slaves selected a different surname, they often selected names common among slaveholders (Laversuch 2011).

To a great extent, the current distribution of surnames among the African American population mirrors the distribution of surnames among the population immediately after emancipation. The stability of the surname distribution over this long period is no great surprise: for African Americans, endogamy has long been the norm and was until recently a legal compulsion. In many states, bans on interracial marriage persisted until such laws were declared unconstitutional in *Loving v. Virginia*. Although racial intermarriage rates increased considerably in the years following this ruling (Kalmijn 1993), in relative terms such mar-

riages and relationships are rare (Qian and Lichter 2007), and rates of
out-group dating and marriage for African Americans are substantially
constrained by persistent geographic segregation that limits opportunities for cross-racial interaction as well as the aversive preferences of
other groups (Yancey 2009; Robnett and Feliciano 2011). In short, the
initial distribution of surnames across the African American population—which this chapter has pointed to as a prime cause of high match
rates—was a clear consequence of racial domination, and the persistence
of that distribution across several generations derives to a substantial extent from a combination of overtly discriminatory laws and racially informed individual preferences.

Yet this is a historically and causally lengthy chain of reasoning and
one that relies on forms of statistical evidence (onomastics and historical
demography) that differ significantly from the smaller and less complex
class of social statistics, mainly derived from the census, commonly considered in cases tried under Section 2 of the VRA. Indeed, even such material as that is used sparingly and often begrudgingly: in oral arguments
in *Gill v. Whitford*, a case concerned with partisan legislative districting practices, Justice Roberts evinced considerable skepticism about the
adoption, as a legal standard, a statistically derived criterion for assessing the legality of a districting map. Justice Alito was no less skeptical of
the social statistical evidence at issue in another districting case, *Cooper
v. Harris*. This aversion is scarcely new—Justice Frankfurter warned that
taking up the matter of legislative districting at all would leave the judiciary mired in statistics. One person, one vote was a boldly progressive
doctrine but also, and not coincidentally, one that could be applied with
minimal engagement with quantitative data. A national reliance on judicial protections of voting rights, then, creates a disjunction between the
kinds of evidence produced by bureaucracies and those commonly used
in the courts—a tension also observed in other matters discussed in this
book and not strictly connected to the particular leanings of the justices
of a given moment. Basic features of legal training, temperament, and
reasoning have made judges leery of dealing with complex, probability-
based forms of evidence. This aversion, especially when coupled with
the persistent judicial distinction between partisan and racial motives,
has provided state administrators with a means of enacting and defending policies that reshape the electorate to the advantage of a given party.

The Failed Federal Administration of Electoral Politics

This chapter has examined the emergence of a new paradigm of voter restriction that relies on alterations in how states manage the voter registration process and administer elections. These changes include stricter
or more complex requirements to register to vote or cast a ballot; limitations on when, where, and how voters can cast a ballot; stricter regulations on the provision of assistance in registration or voting; the establishment of new election-related crimes carrying severe penalties; and
more aggressive voter roll maintenance practices. The elaboration of
these restrictive measures was enabled, in large part, by the procedurally troubled 2000 general election and the resulting mandate that states
modernize and centralize their election administration systems. Centralization is a necessary condition for many of the measures discussed here.
Centralized, uniform administration has also proved to be an effective
practical defense against legal charges of discrimination. There is a substantial and growing body of evidence that these new practices disproportionately affect minority groups that have historically suffered from
discrimination and disenfranchisement; when considered alongside the
strong Democratic Party identification of these groups, this fact does
much to predict which states have and have not adopted such measures.
Yet states have, in general, succeeded in defending new laws that make
it harder to vote.

This successful defense is a powerful illustration of the weak legal
and institutional foundations of federal electoral oversight. The assertion of federal authority in the 1960s resulted in dramatic improvements
in the fairness and openness of American elections and for a time also
prompted more vigorous electoral competition. However, this expanded
federal involvement relied heavily on judge-made law coupled with
strong public support for reform. The most significant congressional act
addressing this topic—the VRA—substantially reinforced the emerging
judicial view of voting as a fundamental right but did not create important federal agency powers. (Nor did HAVA, though it was also enacted
at a moment when there was nationwide bipartisan support for major reform to election administration.) Federal voting rights protections were
fashioned during the national confrontation with Jim Crow and therefore particularly disfavor electoral practices that involve intimidation, involvement by nongovernment actors, or the grant of extensive discretion

in the application of election law. The federal voting rights regime is thus, in practice, a set of doctrines offering voters strong protections against laws and administrative norms that are unambiguously informed by racial animus but very weak protections if they are adversely affected by facially neutral laws that produce a racially disparate effect by a series of intermediate causal steps. These protections have been furthered weakened by the larger shift in judicial doctrines on federal agency power.

The VRA, the NVRA, HAVA, and federal court doctrines all show a tendency to view uniformly administered elections as being fair; indeed, it is this view that, absent any strong evidence of fraud, has allowed voter fraud prevention to suffice as a valid reason for adopting restrictive new measures.[19] This body of law also makes an implied endorsement of the validity of the politics-administration distinction—that is to say, federal actors have proceeded as though it is possible to extend voting rights protections to minority groups in an objective manner that steers clear of partisan considerations. The view that uniform administration is fair is a sound presumption in relative but not in absolute terms. The imposition of procedural regularity on American elections has undoubtedly resulted in elections that are fairer than they were before. With population equality and geographic contiguity established as firm requirements, there is no currently legally cognizable method of drawing legislative districts, however extreme in its partisan motives, that can produce apportionments as unrepresentative and unfair as those that were the norm in nearly all state legislatures in the 1950s. Likewise, no currently permissible alteration of state voting procedures, however administratively burdensome, will result in mass disenfranchisement if voters are free of devices such as poll taxes and have a reasonable expectation of voting without being threatened by violence. Freedom from violence and intimidation is, emphatically, a matter of political culture that should not be taken for granted or entrusted to judicial guardianship.

Where deep racial and class inequalities persist in society as a whole, a uniform electoral rule may nonetheless produce a disparate outcome. Indeed, a uniform rule may be adopted precisely because it will produce this disparity predictably in a way that is obviously to the advantage of a given party. The federal voting rights regime therefore produced a significant legal blind spot: many states have proved themselves to be adept at submerging electoral and partisan politics within a particularly obscure domain of state administration.

CHAPTER FIVE

Conservatism in One State

The Kansas Experiment and the Logic of Reform

The preceding chapters examined a variety of legal and administrative behaviors by which Republican-controlled state governments resisted federal policy over the course of the Obama administration. This behavior is concordant with the familiar explanation of party polarization as a driver of change over the past decade: the major parties drifted further apart ideologically, and what remained of a pragmatic interest in cooperation in governing gave way to a commitment to ideological consistency and vigorous resistance even if this came at a high practical cost. Such is the common account of the behavior of congressional Republicans from the enactment of the ACA onward, and partisan motives were also, plainly, an important feature of the uncooperative state behavior examined in the preceding chapters—this was particularly evident in many states' flat refusal of federal funds.

But those chapters also made a case that this state-level activity is creative. It has involved the development of a variety of legal arguments that move past a traditional language of states' rights and the extensive use of litigation as a tool to explore the potential scope of application of new rulings. The preceding chapters also described the reimagination of existing administrative forms like interstate compacts as well as the use of new administrative practices to provide an indirect route for states to enforce federal immigration law and make voting more difficult without running afoul of federal protections of voting rights. In many cases, these actions were deliberate emulations of forms of political behavior and legal claims used successfully by liberals. Simple partisan hostility or a crude opposition to governing cannot exhaustively explain this complex, novel, and relatively successful combination of state government behaviors—this particular mode of resistance to federal authority and policy is also suggestive of a larger vision of state government.

Further, the more general phenomenon of partisan polarization and Republican convergence on a more sharply antigovernment position cannot fully account for the particular pattern of state involvement in those behaviors. There were twenty state governments wholly under Republican Party control after the 2010 general election (Balz 2010; Storey 2010), a figure that had grown to twenty-four by 2014; in many other states, the Republican Party clearly had the stronger position in state government even if it did not fully control the key elected positions. However, the states that have been especially active in litigation against the federal government, adopted a wide range of restrictive voting laws, and taken up policy proposals like the HCC number only around a dozen.

Thus, it remains to describe what larger conservative ideal of state government has informed this activity. This chapter will offer a description of that vision through an examination of Kansas. The state government of Kansas was involved in many of the intergovernmental matters considered here: it was one of the most frequent signers of briefs in multistate suits against federal agencies, refused the ACA Medicaid expansion and other federal funds, ratified the HCC, fashioned a notably restrictive set of election laws, and coordinated the operation of the Crosscheck Program. And it is plain from the preceding chapters that Kansas secretary of state Kris Kobach is a central figure in elections and immigration policy in conservative states.[1]

At the same time that the state was taking an active role in the larger conservative state conflict with the Obama administration, Governor Sam Brownback was using Kansas as a laboratory for a wide range of novel state policies. These policies included a phased abolition of the income tax and exemption from taxation of personal income from business sources, a move toward quasi-privatization of Medicaid, extensive restructuring of the state government, adoption of a new model for funding local education, and the creation of a new kind of executive agency meant to facilitate the contraction of government. Following Brownback's own description, this has come to be known as the "Kansas Experiment."

Kansas is a particularly useful case for understanding the more general vision of government at work in some of the particular forms of intergovernmental conflict examined in this book. First, the rest of the country has taken an interest in the findings coming from the Kansas laboratory: policy ideas originating there have, in fact, diffused to other states or become models for Trump administration policy. Second, Governor Brownback had unusual freedom in trying out his vision of government—Kansas is a state where executive powers are expansive and the legislature relatively weak, and, at the outset of his governorship, Brownback also enjoyed a legislature that was friendly to his ideas. Third, the political culture and institutions of the state make it a somewhat simpler case for analysis than states like Arizona or Michigan. At the time Brownback assumed office, the state's economy was in relatively good health, and government was not especially burdened by debt or fiscal problems. The reforms were thus undertaken on the view that they were a worthy approach to government, not in response to exigency. Brownback himself is not given to making particularly incendiary or loaded statements, and, though he and his policy experiment were to become extraordinarily unpopular by the time he left office in 2018, his tenure was not marred by personal or political scandal. Race and immigration have a less prominent role in the politics of the state than is the case for many others, and, contrary to the most superficial appearances, Kansas' political culture has been little affected by cultural or religious varieties of conservatism. The ascendant conservative wing of the state party thus closely approximated the form of small government conservatism that assumed a central position within Republican politics around the time of the Tea Party mobilization. Just as Kansas appeared to Brownback as a promising laboratory, Brownback's Kansas appears to the researcher as a neat basis for describing what a governor with a principled belief in market mechanisms and limited government—as well as a degree of administrative and legal sophistication—will do with a state.

This chapter begins with a brief overview of Kansas political history. It then turns to the core features of Brownback's executive-centered experiment in small government, which were put in place quickly after he took office, as well as the results of these reforms and the reaction. Although it is not the most substantively important of the reforms, the chapter gives particular consideration to the operation of the Office of the Repealer, which offers a particularly evocative view of this logic of government reform. The chapter concludes with a reflection on the approach to governing described in the body of this book and its similarities to the strategies and basic view of government found in Progressivism: an ends-oriented mode of reform relying on strong executive power, seeking to restructure government administration along lines emulating those of firms, and imposing significant restrictions on popular participation in government decision-making.

Kansas Politics from John Brown to Sam Brownback

To a greater extent than in almost any other state, the political life of Kansas has revolved around one group: the Republican Party. The extraordinary stability in nominal control of the state government belies the existence of three more or less distinct eras in the state's political life: a period of upheaval, radicalism, and experimentation running through the opening of the New Deal, a sedately moderate approach to functional, efficient government in the postwar period, and a shift toward small government conservatism in the twenty-first century.

The state was organized by abolitionist Republicans in the run-up to the Civil War, and, with very limited exceptions, the party has controlled the state ever since. The Kansas Senate is one of two legislative chambers in the United States that has been under the continuous control of a single party for at least one hundred years (see Dubin 2007, 68, 87). Republicans have also controlled the Kansas House for ninety-eight of those years. The state has not sent a Democrat to the US Senate since the 1930s and has not been carried by a Democratic presidential candidate since Lyndon Johnson. In recent elections, it has returned the country's largest all-Republican delegation, a recurrence of a pattern also observed at the height of the New Deal (see figure 5.1). An exception to this general pattern has been Kansas voters' willingness to elect moderate Democrats as governors.

The Populists mounted the first (and last) serious challenge to Republican dominance, winning very brief control of the state government in the 1890s. Although the state was an early adopter and ardent proponent of temperance and Prohibition (Bader 1986), its Populism was notable for its lack of xenophobia (Nugent 2013). The Populist Party's presence in government quickly gave way to the influence of Progressivism. The state was one of the first to have a recognizably Progressive Republican faction, and, unlike many other states where Progressives were upstarts, this faction's leaders were career politicians who already possessed considerable power (see La Forte 1974). Though the strength of this faction was evenly matched with the old guard for much of the period, the

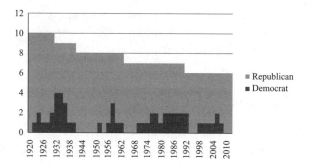

FIGURE 5.1. Party composition of Kansas congressional delegation, 1920–2012

state's policy during the early part of the twentieth century is unmistakably Progressive in tenor: it was strongly oriented toward government efficiency and integrity and made extensive, bold use of government power to temper class conflict in the state. Kansas adopted primary elections in 1904 and permitted city commissions in 1907 and the council-manager form of city government in 1917. It adopted the country's first comprehensive securities regulations in 1910 (Fleming 2011). It adopted further securities regulations in the 1920s that largely anticipated the mission of the SEC (Schruben 1969). It was the first state to establish an office of revisor of statutes (1929) and a legislative council (1933) (Fenton 1965), two nonpartisan government efficiency measures that have since become very widely diffused in the American states.

The state experimented freely with agency structure throughout the 1910s and 1920s. The most notable new agencies can be regarded as (failed) efforts to maintain social harmony through state intervention. The state's film censorship board, which later became a notorious tool for social conservatism, was established in 1915 with the immediate aim of preventing *The Birth of a Nation* from being screened in the state, on the grounds that it would promote racial hatred and sectional tension (Butters 2007, 85–86). The Court of Industrial Relations (1919–25) engaged in a form of compulsory arbitration that sought to moderate the disruptive effects of the state's labor movement. The court received considerable attention in national politics and in the pages of law reviews; it was disbanded after the US Supreme Court declared many of its key rulings—and, by implication, its core activity—unconstitutional. However, the approach to industrial relations embodied in the court anticipated many of the major labor policies of the New Deal. The strong agrarian movement in Kansas also succeeded in imposing new forms of regulation on the farm economy by creating cooperatives, subjecting boards of trade to state control, and further regulating the activity of banks (Schruben 1969).

This reform era came to a close in the 1930s. The Farm Bloc, a group of predominantly midwestern congressmen led by Kansas senator Arthur Capper, had for several elections succeeded in steering a middle course between the factional divisions in the national Republican Party (Hansen 1991). However, for partisan and policy reasons, the national strength of this group waned (Feinman 1981), and, at the state level, the reform era wound down, though Republicans continued to win elections: in 1934, Alf Landon was the only incumbent Republican in the United States to retain gubernatorial office.

From the Civil War to the New Deal, Kansas figured in the national imagination as a source of social radicalism, producing notable figures such as the abolitionist John Brown, the populist Mary Lease, the temperance crusader Carrie Nation, and the socialist publisher Emanuel Haldeman-Julius. The view of Kansas as a social and political backwater is a postwar development (Bader 1988), one in some respects justified. The more dramatic moral debates of the state's early life gave way to modest antialcohol and antigambling activity (Miner 2002). The dominant orientation in state politics was pragmatic, seeking to operate a functional, efficient state government while managing the effects of the dramatic urbanization of the state's population and the associated decline in rural populations. This balance has often been achieved by policies favorable to local control.

The state granted home rule to cities in 1961 and counties in 1974. The Unified School District Act consolidated the state's ten thousand school districts to about three hundred geographically delimited districts with elected school boards (Drury 1970, 222–26). A series of state constitutional changes greatly expanded the power of the governor to restructure state government through the mechanism of the executive reorganization order (ERO) and provided for a large state role in funding primary and secondary education. Major legislation allowed for the creation of public sector unions, recall elections, and relatively strong open meetings and open records laws. A new criminal code, fashioned in the late 1960s and adopted in 1970, was recognized at the time as modern (Meyer 1972) and took a liberal stance on abortion (Wilson 1968).

The signal political fact of Kansas life in the latter part of the twentieth century was the suburbanization of the populace.[2] Scarcely 20 percent of the state's residents lived in cities in 1900; now around 80 percent do. Owing to the large population around Kansas City, whose urban core is located primarily on the Missouri side of the state line, the population is also greatly suburbanized. Though the state's population has grown continuously, 75 of the state's 105 counties have declined in population since World War II. Demographic projections for 2040 predict further loss of population for 83 of 105 counties; by that time, the four most populous counties will constitute two-thirds of the state's population (Kansas Statistical Abstract 2014, 453–57). The shift in the distribution of the state's wealth has been even more pronounced. The overall balance of wealth has shifted closer to the Kansas City suburbs, whose income now nearly equals that of the rest of the state combined: suburban Johnson County, the most populous in Kansas, has a median household income in the ninety-seventh percentile nationally.

The emergence of "two states" with widely divergent needs for public services had become pronounced by the late 1980s and early 1990s (Frederickson 1994), posing increasing problems for the administration of the state. The divide was illustrated most dramatically in the short-lived secession movement in the western part of the state (McCormick 1995). However, the defining tension of this period has been over levels of state spending and the degree of geographic redistribution, manifest particularly in conflicts over public school finance. The reforms of the 1960s established a large state obligation in funding primary and secondary education, though the operation of schools was left to the unified school districts. A 1966 constitutional amendment mandated that the legislature provide fair and adequate school funding. Beginning in the 1960s, primary and secondary education has accounted for the majority of spending from the state's general fund (see Harder and Davis 1979, 141). By the 1980s, differential rates of spending for schools had emerged as the most significant legislative issue in the state (Loomis 1994). A court challenge from the Shawnee Mission school district, located in Johnson County, prompted the state to adopt a new school funding allocation formula in 1992 (Drury 1993).

That reform was a compromise: the state funding formula strongly advantaged small rural school districts, whose limited economies of scale make education an expensive undertaking. The new approach also created the device of the local option budget, which afforded the unified school districts significant power to levy property taxes to supplement state support. This power has been used most readily and effectively by suburban school districts with large tax bases and large proportions of households with school-aged children. For suburban communities, schooling and school quality are very significant political issues. For very small towns, they are a matter of survival: elected officials and residents view schools as the central social institution for rural Kansas communities and the key to their continued existence (Wood 2008, 31–34; Wuthnow 2011, 124–25).

A variety of small government conservatism moved from a marginal to a central role in the state Republican Party in the twenty-first century. That development must be understood primarily in the context of persistent contention in the state over public finance—a pattern also relevant for the advance of conservative views elsewhere (see Martin 2008). School funding contention was an important facet of Tea Party mobilization (McVeigh et al. 2014). The rightward drift of Texas Republicans—roughly contemporaneous with the development of the conservative faction in Kansas—was also driven to a considerable extent by contention over state allocation formulas for primary and secondary education (Kincaid 2016).

While this claim that the transformation of Kansas politics has been spurred mainly by school finance is plain enough to those who have watched the state's politics for some time, it is certainly not consistent with the image of the state in the national imagination. Cultural and religious currents of conservatism have, in fact, had a relatively limited role in the state's politics, though the national perception may be otherwise. This perception likely owes, in part, to two symbolically potent political episodes. Operation Rescue's 1991 Summer of Mercy initiated decades of contentious and sometimes violent conflict over abortion. But it should be noted that Kansas became a focal point for these efforts precisely because its abortion laws were considerably more permissive than those in neighboring states and remained so. In the late 1990s, high conservative turnout in primary elections shifted the balance of the elected state board of education. The new majority voted to remove evolution from the state school curriculum—a transient change in policy that attracted a great degree of national attention but was of little practical consequence in a state where nearly all important curricular decisions are made at the district level.

Such episodes, in turn, figured in Frank's (2004) placement of Kansas at the rhetorical core of his argument about the purportedly growing importance of cultural conservatism among working-class voters. That claim has shaped national conversation (see Willis 2006), but it has very little relationship to the empirical realities of voting behavior in the state (Bartels 2006; Young 2013). Currents of conservatism shaped by Evangelical adherents have had little influence in Kansas (Cigler, Joslyn, and Loomis 2003), where Roman Catholics are the most numerous group of adherents and Methodists have been political prime movers (Wuthnow 2005). Kansas Methodism had suppressed vice so thoroughly for so long that by the 1990s there was little to mobilize around, and, indeed, the trend in the last generation has been toward more permissive state laws on these issues (see Miner 2002).

Kansas is by most national measures a center-right state. Estimates of state ideology rank it as the twentieth most conservative state in the United States (Tausanovitch and Warshaw 2013, 337), and, in the middle of the period considered here, it was ranked eighteenth nationally in rates of self-identified conservatism (Newport 2013). Immediately before the 2010 election, party polarization in Kansas was below the national average (Shor and McCarthy 2011, 546). Consistent with the suggestion that sectional politics are significant in the state, an unusually large amount of this polarization derived from variation in sentiment across geographic areas (Shor and McCarthy 2011, 549). Many in the state have a self-consciously, purposively moderate political identification (Smith 2010, 2013).

Despite the relatively persistent moderation of the electorate itself, the Republican Party organization shifted notably to the right in the twenty-first century, a pattern carefully chronicled by Flentje and Aistrup (2010). A group of more conservative figures entered Kansas politics around the time of the Gingrich Revolution and rose steadily over time. They were swept into control of state government in the 2010 election. From that position of power, this group has "persisted in trying to govern to the right of its constituents" (McKee, Ostrander, and Hood 2017, 308). Sam Brownback, then a US senator, was elected governor of Kansas. Kris Kobach was elected secretary of state after a stint as a notably conservative chairman of the Kansas Republican Party (Carpenter 2007)—and after a primary election victory over long-serving secretary Ron Thornburgh's preferred successor. Derek Schmidt, then state Senate majority leader, was elected attorney general.[3] Brownback took office with the benefit of Republican supermajorities in both chambers of the state legislature, which shifted markedly toward a conservative bent after the Kansas Chamber of Commerce targeted eight moderate Republicans in the forty-seat state Senate for defeat in the 2012 primary election. Two of those targeted did not stand for reelection; four more were defeated in the primaries. The defeated incumbents had held leadership positions in the Senate and had chaired several committees at the center of important policy-making activity, including the Education, Judiciary, Reapportionment, Rules, and State-Federal Relations Committees—in short, the key legislative figures positioned to oppose the core features of Brownback's policy experiment, which was substantially in place after his first two years in office.

The Kansas Experiment

On assuming office, Governor Brownback was quick to set in motion an executive-centered program of reforms meant to reduce the size and increase the efficiency of state government; in pursuit of this goal, he made by far the most extensive use of executive powers in the state's history. This section describes the features of those reforms and their consequences for the state. Brownback issued forty-nine executive orders in his first year in office, a number that greatly exceeded the previous one-year high (twenty-seven, in 2007) and the annual average of ten (Kansas State Library n.d.). The first of these executive orders, which created the Office of the Repealer, is discussed in greater detail in the next section as it is a revealing glimpse into the logic of government contraction.

Brownback also made extensive use of EROs, a mechanism by which the governor can undertake the restructuring of the state administration. Executive reorganization powers in Kansas are among the strongest in the United States, maintaining difficult requirements for legislative veto and a very short time period for the legislature to exercise this veto power; only Michigan's governor, who enjoys nearly absolute powers in states of emergency, has obviously stronger reorganization power (Benjamin and Keck 2011, 1630). In 2011, Brownback issued nine effective EROs—a one-year total that exceeded the total number of EROs issued by any previous governor in the course an entire administration (Kansas Legislative Research Department 2013). Those orders resulted in significant agency consolidation and the elimination of many jobs in the state executive branch. At the same time, the state—like most others—undertook changes to the structure and governance of its pension system (Levine and Scorsone 2011, 211) and took steps to restrict the political power of public sector labor unions (see Dannin 2012, 503).

The most practically significant of these EROs led to the creation of KanCare, which converted the state's Medicaid system to a private cap-itated managed-care model. Medicaid, of course, is a program whose operation in most states involves some meaningful degree of collabo-ration between state government and managed-care organizations (see Kim and Jennings 2012). KanCare is notable, first, for being the most extreme example of a move in the direction of a managed-care model (Hall et al. 2015). More significantly, McCannon (2016) finds that Kan-Care was established out of a principled belief that markets should de-liver health care, rather than any strong objections to the quality of state-administered Medicaid on a fee-for-service model or lobbying from insurance companies or other interests. Indeed, the program was developed in a notably top-down fashion from within the state executive branch, with limited consultation with interested parties—including in-surers. The design of KanCare has thus produced no winners: managed-care organizations initially lost significant money on KanCare, while problems with implementation have adversely affected the quality of care and services available to recipients (Owen, Heller, and Bowers 2016; Williamson et al. 2017). A state audit of the program identified a wide range of issues with payments, service availability, case management, and data collection (Kansas Legislative Division of Post Audit 2018).

In 2011, Governor Brownback also developed a tax bill that was en-acted in 2012 by very narrow margins. The bill, which received the sup-port of Arthur Laffer (on whom, see Popp-Berman and Milanes-Reyes [2013]), contained a handful of important provisions. The state had pre-viously used a three-bracket income tax system. The top bracket was abolished, and the rates in the two lower brackets were reduced; the bill provided for these reduced rates to be drawn down further over time, with the abolition of the state income tax as an end result. These draw-down provisions remained in effect through 2017. The bill also com-pletely eliminated taxes on personal income derived from a variety of business sources, a provision whose applicability has proved to be much wider than previously estimated. This "LLC exemption" was the first of its kind in the American states. The tax bill also eliminated a number of deductions and credits; these included the elimination of a tax credit for renters, certain property-related deductions, and a reduction in the earned income tax credit. In its overall effect, it was strikingly regressive: models estimated that it would result in a net increase in income taxes for the poorest 20 percent of households in the state while more than 90 percent of the total reduction in taxes would benefit households with incomes above $165,000 (Institute on Taxation and Economic Policy 2012).

The effects of the tax plan on state revenue figured in the final significant piece of Governor Brownback's reforms: efforts toward a permanent resolution of litigation over school funding, which had been a constant feature of public life in Kansas for decades. In 2014, the state supreme court ruled in *Gannon v. State* that the state's funding provisions for education were inadequate. Given that litigation over school funding has been nearly continuous for decades, such rulings are not unusual and have ordinarily been resolved through tinkering with the allocation formulas. Brownback broke with this pattern, instead devising a block grant mechanism for state funding of school district operations—itself eventually rejected by the state supreme court. Thus, in a short period of time, the Brownback administration sought to change nearly all the important features of Kansas government—its basic tax model, state agency structure, level and method of support for public goods such as education, and approach to delivering key benefits. Brownback also attempted, mostly unsuccessfully, to modify the practices for the appointment and retention of members of the state judiciary. This occurred contemporaneously with the activity discussed in the preceding chapters. Brownback refused some federal grants as well as Medicaid expansion and urged the adoption of the HCC; Attorney General Schmidt was frequently taking part in suits that pitted states against the federal government; Secretary of State Kobach was developing a remarkably restrictive set of voter registration laws, expanding Crosscheck into a large national program, and seeking independent authority to investigate and prosecute election-related crimes.

This experiment has been notably unpopular. Contention has focused particularly on the effects of the tax bill. The initial revenue estimates from both the Kansas Department of Revenue and opponents of the plan proved to be too optimistic: some of the provisions, especially concerning business income, lowered the tax burden for high-income households much more than expected, creating dramatic revenue shortfalls. In 2014, the state saw a drop of 24.3 percent in receipts from individual income tax from the previous year, producing an 11.6 percent one-year decline in general fund revenue (Kansas Department of Revenue 2015,

19–20). Revenue shortfalls of similar magnitude recurred in the following years. Making good on these shortfalls has required other measures that are also regressive in character, including an increase in the state sales tax and the introduction or increase of fees to use many state services. The state legislature regularly broke records for session length as it dealt with school funding issues and continuously sought ways to rebalance the state's budget as revenues continued to decline.

Governor Brownback won reelection only narrowly in 2014 and with a plurality of the vote. His second term charted a path to extraordinary unpopularity. A Docking Institute of Public Affairs survey of Kansans found that a very large majority disagreed with his administration's positions on the major policy issues that have dominated states politics in recent years, including corporate taxation, economic development, school funding, Medicaid expansion, handguns on college campuses, same-sex marriage, and voter fraud (Docking Institute of Public Affairs 2015, 11, 14, 22, 30, 31, 27, 36). By 2016, polls showed that fewer than a quarter of Kansans approved of the governor, and serious efforts to dismantle his tax policy and significantly increase appropriations for public services were under way. A major tax increase was passed in 2017, aided by a concerted business mobilization in favor of increased taxes on businesses (Alvord 2018). The governor defended his experiment to the last, and a tax increase was adopted only when a veto-proof legislative majority—including a majority of legislative Republicans—voted to halt the experiment. Brownback resigned in 2018 to take up an ambassadorial post in the Trump administration, but other figures in the state—most notably Secretary Kobach, the 2018 Republican gubernatorial nominee—were committed to defending and restoring the key features of his policy.

The Office of the Repealer: Government Contraction and Quasi-Public Space

In its material and political effect, Brownback's tax plan was the most important measure enacted during his time in office. It created a budget crisis every fiscal year and forced cuts to all forms of state services. Closing the deficits created by the tax reform and contending with mandates to improve school funding in the midst of calamitous revenue shortfalls virtually monopolized political activity in the state for years. This section considers an initiative that is far less materially significant but offers a striking miniature example of the interrelated set of strategies of government contraction discussed in this work.

Brownback's first official act as governor was the creation of the Kansas Office of the Repealer, a novel agency charged with evaluating electronically submitted citizen suggestions for the repeal of state laws and regulations that are "unreasonable, unduly burdensome, duplicative, onerous, or in conflict" (Brownback 2011). Suggestions judged to have merit were to be forwarded to the state legislature with the office's recommendation. The state of Tennessee established a similar office that began operation in 2013, and other states have considered proposals to create repealer offices. In its form, the Kansas Office of the Repealer exemplifies a large class of measures—electronic government initiatives—meant to promote government transparency and facilitate citizen participation. However, the office differs from typical electronic government initiatives in that its activity is almost entirely shielded from public view and that it takes government efficiency as its sole purpose.[4] In addition, most forms of electronic government invite citizens to submit responses to proposals or actions originated by government; the wave of comments submitted on the EPA's Waters of the United States Rule is one example.[5] The Office of the Repealer, by contrast, invited citizens to propose government activity—or, rather, to propose abridgments of government activity.

The office possesses two structural features that illustrate a logic of government contraction. First, it is, in essence, a pseudo-public space that gives the appearance of soliciting public input on the activity of government while disregarding this input in practice. The appearance of public support, in turn, allows it to obscure the fact that nearly all the proposals it has presented to the legislature originate from actors within the state's executive branch. Second, the office functions as a ratchet: it can decrease the size of state government but cannot increase it, and citizens can effectively engage with it only on its own terms. That is, they must accept the premise that state government is by nature inefficient, overly expensive, and in need of reform. Such ratcheting techniques have been a key means for state-level conservative actors to limit the scope of government activity in the United States.

The ability of the office to achieve these goals depends on a particular balance of publicity. The agency must be visible enough to elicit the interest of citizens and trumpet successes. However, visibility can also provide a means for citizens and interest groups to gain publicity or seek to exercise control over the agenda. In other electronic government initiatives, visibility has also attracted waves of tendentious and low-quality participation. However, various structural characteristics of the office have made it very difficult for outside actors to influence its operation or use it to secure publicity.

In response to an open records request, the Kansas Department of Administration disclosed all proposals submitted to the office over a forty-two-month period. These records include 489 unique policy suggestions submitted through the office's online portal; the count does not include mass comments in support of specific repeal measures, a matter that will be discussed below. These records include the proposed action and, in some cases, the original text of the proposal as submitted. The records include proposals from private citizens as well as individuals within the Kansas government—in addition to notifying the public, the office solicited proposals from a number of state agencies. For 2011, 2013, and 2014, these two kinds of proposals are readily distinguished; for 2012 the records are ambiguous. The volume of suggestions indicates that initial public interest in the office tailed off quickly. The office received 170 citizen suggestions in nine months in 2011, 92 probable suggestions in 2012, 13 in 2013, and 8 through the first nine months of 2014. Approximately 200 additional suggestions originated from within the state government. The submissions from citizens vary widely in their topic and quality. They can be broken into four general categories, whose overall distribution is shown in table 5.1.

The most numerous group of suggestions fell outside the remit of the office. These expressed diffuse grievances with government or proposed actions that fell outside state jurisdiction. Such submissions included, for instance, proposals to repeal the ACA, abolish common law marriage, or eliminate billboards in the city of Wichita as well as general complaints about the governor, the legislature, the highway patrol, truck drivers, undocumented immigrants, the mail service, government sur-

TABLE 5.1. **Nature of citizen suggestions to Kansas Office of the Repealer**

Suggestion type	Count	% of total	Cumulative %
Grievance/no jurisdiction	79	41.4	41.4
Lobbying	43	22.8	63.9
Repeal (nonsubstantive)	31	16.2	80.1
Repeal (substantive)	38	19.9	100

veillance, and so on. Another class of citizen submissions advocated for the passage of bills under active consideration in the state legislature; these were, in essence, treating the office as an indirect means of lobbying state legislators. Some submissions proposed the repeal of a law but did not clearly identify the law or offer any substantive or legal reason for the repeal: for instance, one suggestion reads in its entirety, "Repeal seatbelt laws," and another reads, "Abolish daylight saving time." Only one citizen submission in five proposed the repeal of a recognizable state law or regulation and offered some justification, however limited, for the proposal. By contrast, nearly all the proposals submitted by members of government clearly identified a specific statute and presented a legal rationale for its repeal.

In addition, there were two coordinated efforts to submit large numbers of repeal suggestions along lines commonly employed in legislative advocacy. In 2011, the Kansas Equality Commission prompted a number of people to submit comments supporting the repeal of the state's sodomy laws. In that same year, Trust Women, a reproductive health organization, engaged in mass petitioning of the office to propose the repeal of a number of abortion laws. Trust Women employed a similar approach in subsequent years. This petitioning approach has been unsuccessful, for a rather simple structural reason: proposals submitted to the office are not publicly visible, the office's deliberations are not a matter of public record (K.S.A. 45-221), and the office does not comment on proposals it declines to forward to the legislature. It is therefore difficult to marshal evidence that the activity of the office has a partisan bent or that it is ignoring the input of a large number of citizens. This is an indication of unusual aspects of the publicity of the office. Because its inputs and deliberations are opaque—being covered by statutes that shield backstage forms of administrative behavior from public view—it was possible for Governor Brownback to represent the office as an apolitical, efficiency-oriented agency even while it exercised a great deal of political discretion. Similarly, the office may present itself as responsive to citizens and, in some sense, representing a public desire for smaller government, though the bulk of its proposals originated from within a government with an avowed commitment to reducing spending and support for public goods.

In the 2011–12 and 2013–14 legislative sessions, twenty-three bills were introduced in the Kansas legislature at the recommendation of the Office of the Repealer. These bills—many of which propose the repeal

of several statutes—included only seven suggestions submitted by citizens. The remainder came from government or the office itself. Each of
these bills passed the House with substantial majorities or unanimous
consent. Eighteen passed the Senate and became law, again with very
large majorities. The remaining five died in committee in the Senate,
evidently because of limited interest rather than political opposition. In
sum, these bills proposed the repeal of sixty-nine sections of the Kansas
Statutes, of which sixty-two sections were actually taken off the books.
Table 5.2 shows the policy domains covered by these repeal proposals.

The concentration of statutory repeal in a small number of areas is
largely an artifact of the postwar period of government reform discussed
above. Many of the repealed statutes had been long dormant as the result of these changes or subsequent EROs. Nearly all these changes were
technical in character and have had no effect on the state's revenue or
expenditures. To the extent that the repealed statutes did not bear on
the activity of government, the Office of the Repealer cannot be said to
have furthered the goal of government efficiency, though rationalized legal codes are arguably worthwhile in themselves.

The easy success of the office's bills during two extraordinarily fractious legislative sessions is a sign of the considerable discretion the office exercised in endorsing repeal proposals. The proposals did not include any statutes whose repeal would have an appreciable effect on
revenue, expense, or the daily activity of government; as matters of policy, these certainly would have elicited opposition from some quarter or
another.[6] More significantly, the office took no action on proposals to
repeal obsolete—and in many cases unconstitutional—provisions that
touched on issues of importance to social conservatives. For instance,
it took no action on the state's sodomy laws, another law on sexual conduct, or a ban on the Communist Party. All these statutes are dormant
and, according to the records provided by the office, clearly contra-

TABLE 5.2. **Repeal of Kansas statutes by policy area**

Legal area	Proposed	Repealed
Agriculture and natural resources	17	17
Corrections	27	26
Government operations	12	9
Professional regulation	9	8
Property and taxation	4	2
Total	69	62

vened by judicial precedent. They also touch on polarizing social issues on which the office, under the supervision of a conservative governor, might not wish to appear liberal. The same can be said for the office's inaction on obsolete statutes pertaining to alcohol and gambling, both of which were extraordinarily divisive issues in Kansas politics throughout the twentieth century, as well as an obsolete statute protecting intellectual property.

The office retains all the initiative about what issues are made salient. It can decline to introduce proposals that are politically inconvenient or likely to elicit opposition and can exercise its veto passively because suggestions are not visible to the public. Additionally, it need not clarify where its proposals originate. Though it is nominally an agency that is responsive to citizens and has been championed on this basis, private communication within state government has been the main source of its repeal proposals. This is not to say that it is engaged in any misleading behavior: the state readily provided records whose disclosure could have been resisted easily, those records offer clear indications of the sources of proposals, and the invitation for government officials to submit suggestions was itself public. Rather, this pattern calls attention to the narrow government efficiency rationale that informed the creation of the office.

The peculiar feature of the office is that it occupies no definite space in the public sphere, which makes it highly resistant to outside efforts to use it as a site from which to initiate controversy (Adut 2012). It is visible to the public only intermittently, when some other, more definitely located political actor such as the governor calls attention to it. It therefore provides the governor with something for nothing: free ideas that can be used if they advance the governor's goals and ignored without political risk if they do not advance those goals. However, this benefit is necessarily small and requires that the office remain at the margin of public awareness. If it becomes too visible, it may become embroiled in controversy. If it is not visible enough, it does not receive enough proposals to provide a political benefit.

Viewed in terms of its practical success, the Office of the Repealer is only an administrative curiosity. However, it is a notably clear typification of a large, important strategy for reducing the size of government. It is an agency that operates as a ratchet: in the execution of its functions, it can only diminish the size or scope of government, not broaden it. Ratcheting techniques of this kind have been used widely by groups

seeking to limit the size of state government and can be viewed as a special case of automatic lawmaking practices, which have become increasingly prevalent in recent years (Gluck, O'Connell, and Po 2015, 1812).

Beginning in the 1980s, many states adopted sunset review, a practice
by which state agencies are automatically abolished unless they survive
periodic scrutiny (Opheim, Curry, and Shields 1994). Through the 1990s,
states adopted tax and expenditure limitations, measures that trigger automatic tax cuts during periods of surplus and automatic spending cuts
during periods of deficit (Rose 2010); ballot initiative sequences during this period often displayed a similar iterative quality (Kousser and
McCubbins 2005). Governor Brownback's tax bill included automatic
spending cuts of this kind in addition to rate reductions that continued
to go into effect at prespecified times. Such restrictions—often enacted
during periods of undivided state government—may themselves be very
difficult to repeal at a later date (Hicks 2015). The rationale behind these
approaches is market-like—the suggestion is that, if it is not subject to
continuous pressure, administrative activity will drift into inefficiency.
Forms of review or automatic devices introduce a form of scrutiny meant
to function in some ways like competition.

These mechanisms have had a remarkable effect in Kansas. The state
has seen net tax cuts in every year from 2017 at least as far back as 1995;
cumulatively, in nonconstant dollars, this amounted to a net reduction in
state tax receipts of about $15 billion through 2013 (Kansas Department
of Revenue 2013). Nationally, state fiscal practices reflect a similarly patterned small government bias: states tend to cut taxes during periods of
economic growth and cut spending during periods of contraction (Kwak
2016). This tendency, when combined with the nearly universal adoption
of state balanced-budget requirements, effectively guarantees overall reductions in the scope of state government.

These techniques may have a quite limited immediate impact. However, they are important because of their durability. Tax and expenditure limitations, for instance, have had a much more pronounced effect
on state government during the recent recession and crisis of fiscal federalism than they did when originally passed during a period of steady
growth. More extreme ratcheting measures of this kind may also reliably produce fiscal crises; given that the projected revenue neutrality of
Brownback's tax plan relied on fantastic growth assumptions, the progressive phaseout of the income tax was virtually certain to create fiscal problems. As noted above, such crises may allow government actors

to use statutory requirements to reduce levels of state support for public goods.

These efforts aim to limit the scope of government, but they also attempt to make these efforts appear legitimate and politically desirable or, by displacing the activity in time, make politically unpopular actions appear inevitable or immediately necessary. The Office of the Repealer is a notable elaboration on this logic because it invites citizens to participate in this process while at the same time restricting the form that this participation can take; in this sense, it is a pseudo-public initiative. Structurally, this is quite similar to the involvement of states in the federal regulatory process. This involves intergovernmental lobbying groups that are "granted privileged access to the regulatory process" but are "insulated from public scrutiny" in such a way that "the groups can take a 'state' position even where state constituents or even group members do not agree" (Seifter 2014, 958). It is also in some ways analogous to the state grant of positive rights to citizens, which can in turn be invoked by states themselves in litigation. Practically speaking, an elected official like an attorney general does not represent the people in the direct way that a hired attorney represents a private client (see Lemos 2012), yet for legal purposes these relationships have been treated as equivalent.

The Echo of Progressivism

This chapter, like the ones preceding it, has accepted officials' own representations of their values and goals more or less on face. There is a double stamp of sincerity in this behavior. These officeholders do approximately what they say they will do, and some, like Governor Brownback, stick doggedly to their approach even in the face of extraordinary unpopularity. In this work, they have been termed *conservative*, not only because this is the self-representation of officials, but also because the positions state officeholders have taken on matters such as immigration and voting rights often appear illiberal.

Although their activity is licit, it does not proceed through many of the typical channels for making policy. While the large, plain ends in view are familiar ideals of limited government, the pursuit of those ends involves a remarkably free, experimental combination of means. The untraditional character of this activity and its view of law and administrative power as flexible instruments rather than constraining rules may appear out of keeping with some commonsense understandings of *conservative*. These two facts could easily draw this argument toward discussion of what it really means to be conservative or whether it is a contradiction or hypocrisy to make extensive use of strong executive powers with the aim restricting the scope of government. Questions posed in that form tend to be answered according to the sentiments and preferences of the person asking (Kurzman 1991; Martin 2011). This is hardly an idle observation: a good deal of social science ultimately judges the coherence and worth of political activity in precisely this way. Rather than pursuing this sort of reflection, this chapter will conclude by noting that the basic approach to government described in this book has an important historical analogue: Progressivism. The point, simply, is that policy ideas and goals admit of being combined in a variety of ways (Skowronek 2006) and that the manner of combination is a useful dimension for understanding and comparing political episodes.

Progressivism has proved to be a slippery term to define, particularly because it was a political affinity or orientation toward government, rather than a phenomenon with a clearly shared credo or formal organizational basis (Hofstadter 1955; Filene 1970). It was a pronounced tendency in American political life in the early twentieth century and pursued two significant ends. First, it sought to transform the structure and workings of government administration. Second, it sought major reforms of the electoral process, with an eye toward limiting the influence of political party organizations—and the groups whose support made those party organizations powerful. Progressivism was strikingly ends oriented in its approach to politics and government; indeed, the constitutional conservatives who today oppose efforts to call a convention under Article V are directly descended from groups alarmed at Progressives' cavalier handling of law (Lienesch 2016). Viewed from the other side of the rights-based transformations of American life in the mid-twentieth century, Progressivism is a tendency that can seem paradoxical. Certain of its policy goals align with those of modern liberalism, but Progressives embraced government paternalism (Link 1992), had deeply antidemocratic views of government operation (Blum 1993; McCann 2012), and espoused a range of overtly racist and xenophobic views.

Progressives desired a government that would serve the people's interests but also had a decidedly narrow view of how the people should be and when they should have a say in the operation of government. Thus, they are responsible for the public primary election (McCormick 1986) and various modes of direct democracy (Cronin 1989) but also brought about the abolition of the alien franchise (Bloemraad 2006) and the introduction of voter registration. The two approaches represent a shared end: to create electoral devices that could define an electorate worthy of the right to vote (Smith and Tolbert 2004; Ansell 2011) and to limit the electoral power of cities, which is to say, of racial minority and immigrant groups. John R. Commons, a major architect of Wisconsin Progressivism, openly proclaimed this as a key goal of these election reforms (see Commons 1907).

This approach to elections reflected a larger anti-immigrant sentiment among Progressives. Main currents of political Progressivism treated almost all immigrants of the period as racial others (Fox and Guglielmo 2012; FitzGerald and Cook-Martin 2014). Progressive policy often sought to suppress "non-American" practices and traditions among those already in the United States (Stromquist 2006) and to avert differential patterns of fertility that could lead to white "race suicide" (Wilde and Danielsen 2014). They also pursued highly restrictionist federal immigration policies (Zeidel 2004; Petit 2010). When federal policy was adjudged insufficiently stringent, many states fashioned restrictive immigration practices of their own (Graham 1972; Tichenor and Filindra 2012).

The administrative agenda of the Progressives possessed a similar duality. They sought to serve the people but also to shield government from the people (McCann 2012). Reforms of the era sought to curb the power of elected partisans, yet the achievement of those reforms was reliant on the extraordinary exercise of state executive power (Tolbert and Zucker 1983; Barry 2009): the modern American presidency, in fact, took shape in the image of the most vigorous and powerful of the Progressive-aligned governors (Ambar 2012). And the Progressive vision of a public administration openly proclaimed the superiority of private enterprise as an administrative model (Weinstein 1968) and also accepted core orientations of firms and markets as guiding principles for government (see Waldo 1948). This fact may be obscured in the present, in part, because the structure of private enterprise itself has changed so dramatically in the past century, but also because of uneven patterns of organizational survival. Certain kinds of public bureaucracy of the period have proved remarkably persistent (Cremin 1961; McGerr 2003), but the activity of the period was often highly reliant on privatized models of administration (Lee 2008; Nackenoff 2014) and bodies of expertise from outside government (Eisenach 1994; Abbott 1999).

There are a number of remarkable similarities between the Progressive view of government and the activity examined in this book, which has also embraced strong state executive power and turned it against cities, taken a restrictionist approach to elections administration and in some cases immigration, and looked to private enterprise for models of government (an orientation that can be, as in the case of Kansas, something very different from making government policy with an eye toward what will benefit influential business interests). Figures like Brownback, Kobach, and Pruitt regard themselves as crusading reformers and are by no means shy about their ideas and achievements; like those of the Progressives, many of those important ideas had a long gestation in the academy before moving into the world of politics. At some points, the comparison is one drawn by conservatives themselves, as in Kobach's interest in the activity of the Progressive Era and in the critique of public sector unions, which makes an entirely explicit comparison with the anticorruption efforts of the Progressives (Krinsky 2013; DiSalvo 2015).

The comparison is offered here, in part, to show that there may often be a meaningful distinction to be maintained between the view of the basic function or purpose of government and a view about the appropriate methods for seeking to achieve that purpose and how much public support is needed to authorize a method. Many of the figures studied here take what appears to be, in effect, a plebiscitary view by which lawful installment in office also implies ample freedom to use any of the lawful powers the office confers.

But the comparison also serves as a suggestion that the present moment can be understood as a permutation of the relationship of partisan politics and administration similar to the one that existed at the opening of the Progressive Era and a reminder that this relationship is never a settled one. The Progressives sought to move aspects of the operation of government outside direct political control. They and their successors did achieve a measure of legitimacy for rule by experts as well as substantial expansion of America's administrative and regulatory apparatus. Progressivism also secured recognition that political parties are, in meaningful respects, public organs (Goodnow 2002) and should be legally controlled on that basis, rather than treated as little more than private clubs. Some thinkers, such as Woodrow Wilson, envisioned administration virtually cut off from politics.

Such a proposal is impossible for a society that, like the United States, is committed to some ideal of democratic participation and representative government. It is also very doubtful that, once established as the main coordinators of interests in a polity, political parties can ever subsequently be supplanted by nonviolent means (see Martin 2009, 283–320). Parties are "inevitable" (Masket 2016), and any apparent division of responsibility between administrators and politicians is a truce in what is destined to be a perpetual conflict over the nature of government. In America, that conflict has often been between intellectual and anti-intellectual orientations to government (Hofstadter 1963), one in which the anti-intellectual orientation is often, also, the conservative orientation. But this work has shown that this is not the only possible division: the partisans examined here have learned from progressive and liberal approaches to law and government and have found means to direct the powers of state administration against government itself.

CHAPTER SIX

Conservative Innovators and Liberal Emulators

The Future of American Federalism in the Trump Administration and Beyond

T he labor of writing this book coincided exactly with the media phenomenon of the Trump campaign and the opening of the Trump administration. So far as possible, this book has sought to provide an account of the conservative political response to the Obama administration without interpreting this activity retrospectively through the lens of the Trump presidency. The argument has proceeded on the view that there is much to learn from a primary focus on the official behavior of conservative officeholders. Matters of rhetoric and motivation have, in the main, been set aside, partly as an analytic decision, but partly because the behavior of the people being studied called for such an approach: many of the actors under study have been notably constant in their pursuit of a few large, plainly stated goals. Making ordinary allowances for the nature of politics, the key figures seem to intend roughly what they say and to do roughly what they say they will do. Using this approach, the body of this book discussed how conservative state officeholders have made use of a range of administrative and legal techniques to challenge Obama administration policy and chip away at the legal and political pillars of modern federal power.

The ends of that state activity represent familiar conservative ideals about government—limited taxation and regulation, reductions in the scope of the welfare state, and the expansion of states' power relative to that of the national government. The innovation of this book's titular conservative innovators is one of means, not ends. The preceding chapters have described activity involving a continuous interplay of new administrative activity and litigation. The success of that approach was made possible by the long-term growth in the relative power of both the federal and the state executive and the recognition that the office of state attorney general provides a ready-made support structure for extensive litigation against the federal executive. The book has also noted a growing degree of administrative and legal coordination between states. These activities follow an intelligible pattern and have identified and made use of a significant, latent structure of opportunity arising from the conjunction of partisan polarization and growth in executive power. However, the conservative state resistance to the Obama administration does not seem to have been a self-conscious or deliberately planned movement. And, indeed, among Republican-controlled states, there has been considerable variation in involvement in the kinds of challenges to federal power and policy discussed here. Of some thirty states wholly or substantially controlled by Republican officeholders over the past decade, perhaps ten have had an especially active role in most of the kinds of activity discussed in the preceding chapters; the backgrounds and dispositions of individual officeholders appear to matter as much as the prevailing political climate in a state.

The immediate policy consequences of this activity have been clear. What remains to be discussed is what long-term effect, if any, this activity will have on the structure of American government and the pattern of intergovernmental relations. The period spanning roughly from 2010 to 2016 could represent an important but transient episode—or it could represent the genesis of what could become a widely diffused, standard repertoire of political behaviors. If the pattern continued, it would yield a more antagonistic mode of intergovernmental relations and curtail the practical power of the federal government. This concluding chapter cannot settle that question. However, examining the first year of the Trump administration in the terms already laid out in this book offers a strong suggestion that intergovernmental disagreement—made manifest in administrative resistance and litigation against the federal executive—will be no less significant in the decade to come than the decade past. This could conceivably spur larger structural changes.

Extending this book's basic approach from the politics of the Obama administration to that of the Trump administration is, necessarily, to

ignore much of what is regularly considered to be the most important—
or, at least, obvious—consequence of Trump's entry into political life:
his overturning of uncodified norms about the conduct of the campaign
and the presidency.[1] The 2016 general election and the opening of the
Trump administration gave every indication of having set American political life on an even more polarized, conflictual course.

The dramatic change in the tenor of political life belies important
continuities. This chapter will show that the official actions of the Trump
administration in its first year hewed rather closely to the conservative
political commitments described to this point in the book. This is to say
not that the activity of the preceding years prefigured the Trump presidency but that, where many matters of domestic policy are concerned,
President Trump has governed as a conventional conservative. And, in
doing so, he has, like President Obama, relied heavily on unilateral executive action to pursue major objectives, in part because Democratic
congressional opposition has significantly limited his legislative success.
This has left those actions similarly vulnerable to legal challenges. Democratic state executive officeholders were quick to adopt many of the legal strategies and arguments used so successfully by conservative states.
Major litigation takes years, but the early indications suggested that the
judicial climate remained hospitable for state challenges to federal action; indeed, changes in the ideological composition of the federal judiciary could make the climate more favorable. While the partisan roles
have been reversed, the structure and substance of contention is similar,
and the next few years may, very plausibly, present a mirror image of the
patterns discussed in the body of this book.

The outcome of this pattern of partisan intergovernmental contention
is not yet determined, and this chapter will not venture very firm predictions. In place of a pronouncement, this book concludes with three questions whose significance is clearly suggested by the overall argument.
These are live questions for American politics and government as well as
questions that admit of social scientific study.

First, it remains to be seen to what degree the federal judiciary will remain receptive to state litigation against the federal executive. The current moment of doctrinal uncertainty produces an intellectual challenge
for judges. It is difficult to predict how this challenge will be resolved.

Second, a number of ongoing developments make it appear very likely
that states will have a widened scope for independent action in many areas of policy, irrespective of the disposition of open legal questions. But

it remains to be seen whether devolution will promote convergence or divergence in policies across states. And, just as significantly, it has yet to be seen whether states will be able to develop the fiscal or administrative capacity to pursue bold experiments in areas of policy where federal involvement or authority may wane.

Third, particular policy outcomes and the overall structure of intergovernmental relations will both depend, in part, on the extent to which the state conservative activity of recent years develops into a general model of political action. Such generalization will occur only if liberals come to recognize the conservative state activity of recent years as discovering to view an important structure of political opportunity and are able to envision a rival state-oriented policy agenda. The realization of that opportunity will depend on the ability of liberals to take conservative successes seriously. Just as the immediate patterns of contention under the Trump administration mirror those of the Obama administration, the larger situation in state government finds liberals in a position very similar to that faced by conservatives at the beginning of the conservative legal movement.

The Trump Administration's Conventional Conservatism

The scholarly and media attention paid to the Trump administration has rightly pointed up a host of things about it that are wholly unconventional. Much of the president's public conduct, relations with the other branches of government, and handling of the unofficial responsibilities of the office breaks markedly from prior presidencies. These are genuinely important changes that create significant uncertainty and merit the close attention they are receiving. However, a day-by-day focus on the administration's overturning of conventions—the tendency to view the campaign and the administration as an ongoing event or rupture in American political life (Wagner-Pacifici and Tavory 2017)—can obscure other patterns about the 2016 election and the first year of the Trump presidency.

The preceding chapters have attended mainly to administrative and legal dimensions of intergovernmental relations in key domestic policy areas. On these matters, the Trump administration's official actions have plainly advanced a set of goals strongly concordant with the vision of state-level conservatives. Those official actions are not markedly different from what one might expect from any very conservative Republican president. It can be added that, while public opinion is singularly polarized, it is nonetheless consistent with established partisan patterns. This section, in short, makes the first half of the case that the opening of the Trump administration marked a continuation of the patterns already discussed in this book. The following section, which will deal with liberal state opposition to the Trump administration, will serve to establish that the current situation is, in many important respects, symmetrical to the pattern of partisan intergovernmental contention that so shaped American government under the Obama administration.

The 2016 election was a powerful demonstration of the strength of partisan identification. The Republican primary elections were divisive, and core figures in the party were very slow to embrace Trump's candidacy; many never did so. Yet most voters who would have been expected to vote for a Republican did vote for Trump, whatever particular reservations they may have held. Voting behavior between the 2012 and the 2016 presidential elections differed little (figures here and below are drawn from Federal Elections Commission [2013, 2017]). Overall turnout was almost unchanged, and Trump's share of the national vote was less than 1 percent higher than Romney's in 2012. The national two-party vote share was also quite close to what polling had predicted, though polling (and interpretation of that polling) was well off the mark in the handful of states—Wisconsin, Michigan, and Pennsylvania—that determined the outcome of the Electoral College vote.

The Republican share of the vote in these decisive states also shifted little from 2012 to 2016: Trump outperformed Romney by 1.3 percent in Wisconsin, 1.6 percent in Pennsylvania, and 2.8 percent in Michigan. It is true—as suggested in numerous media accounts that sought to represent the electoral outcome as a major regional shift in partisan alignment—that Obama carried many of the nonmetropolitan areas of these states in 2008, including almost all Wisconsin's nonmetropolitan counties. However, Republicans have controlled both chambers of the legislature in all three of these states since 2010. At the time of the election, Wisconsin and Michigan both had two-term Republican governors. Viewed strictly in terms of demonstrated partisan leanings, the outcome, though consequential, is hardly shocking: a Republican presidential candidate narrowly won three states that had voted Republican in several preceding state-level elections. The media construction of an archetypal Trump voter who is white, older, less educated, and living in a nonmetropolitan area is therefore, at most, a story about a marginal shift in party sup-port—in the main, Trump voters were people who would, in other cir-cumstances, be considered Republican voters.

In office, Trump has been a notably unpopular president, and pub-lic opinion on his performance is extraordinarily divided. State by state, however, approval of his performance corresponds very closely to par-tisan leanings and political ideology: his approval ratings into 2018 had remained highest in Republican-leaning states with high levels of self-identified conservatism and lowest in Democratic-leaning states with low levels of self-identified conservatism. This is all to suggest that the public response to the Trump administration represents further amplifi-cation of geographic, demographic, and ideological patterns of partisan alignment and polarization that were already pronounced in American political life and became more intense in the years following the emer-gence of the Tea Party. Those sentiments also have a meaningful rela-tionship with the administration's tangible policies.

The Trump administration's official actions in domestic policy are readily understood in terms of the policy goals already discussed in this book. It is worth noting, as a preliminary, that those commitments were reflected, in part, in the staffing of important positions. Vice President Mike Pence was a leading figure in a congressional caucus, the Repub-lican Study Committee, that was a major precursor to the Tea Party–aligned groups in the House. As governor of Indiana, he advanced a conservative policy agenda, most notably in his endorsement of a strong religious freedom restoration act following Supreme Court rulings about same-sex marriage. Attorney General Jeff Sessions, though a senator, had long been an especially notable defender of state prerogatives.[2] Oklahoma attorney general Scott Pruitt, after building a reputation from his notably pugnacious opposition to the EPA, was appointed by Trump as administrator of the EPA; former Texas governor Rick Perry, who had previously pledged to abolish the Department of Energy dur-ing a presidential bid, was made secretary of energy. A similar pattern is also apparent in President Trump's judicial nominees. A major success of his first year was the confirmation of Neil Gorsuch to the Supreme Court; Justice Gorsuch is a member of the Federalist Society and a no-tably conservative judge in many areas of law.[3] Trump likewise secured the confirmation of a large number of federal appeals judges in his first year—a notably conservative group of jurists on the whole.

Chapter 1 identified seven objectives that seemed to cover most of the policy goals pursued by state conservative officeholders in recent years. There was nothing especially new or unusual about these goals; the rest of the book served to show that state officeholders identified a number of unconventional means to pursue certain of those goals. The president, who possesses enormous powers, can use more conventional devices to seek similar objectives. The following considers those seven goals in the order they were set out at the beginning of the book and examines what actions the Trump administration took toward those goals in its first year. It is worthwhile to structure a discussion of the Trump administration by reference to those points. Nearly all the significant achievements and actions of the Trump administration plausibly advance these goals, and, within the realm of domestic policy, those goals substantially account for the administration's key policy actions in its first year.

1. Continuously reduce taxation and government expenditure, preferably by automatic or compulsory mechanisms

The signal legislative achievement of the first year of the Trump administration was the passage of a major reform to the federal tax code, the Tax Cuts and Jobs Act. From the campaign onward, the Kansas tax plan had been noted as a potential national model. As the tax bill advanced rapidly through Congress in the latter months of 2017, media coverage also made frequent comparisons to Kansas. There are indeed important similarities, including a reduction in the top marginal income tax rate and in the number of brackets, the elimination of a wide range of exemptions, and markedly more favorable treatment of business income—in the national case, not only something similar to the pass-through provision from Kansas, but also large cuts in the corporate tax rate. Unlike the Kansas tax plan, the federal tax reform was not enacted with a serious expectation that it would be revenue neutral. In Kansas, initial projections relied on assumptions of extremely high rates of economic growth as well as an incorrect (and low) estimate of the number of earners who would benefit from the tax exemption on personal income from business sources.

The federal reform, by contrast, was passed with the acknowledgment that it would likely result in significant reductions in federal tax receipts—one reason why certain changes in personal income tax provisions are not permanent. The reform's potential effect on the deficit was a key concern of the few Republican holdouts. The magnitude of this reduction remains uncertain, for many of the same reasons as in Kansas: compared to sales or property taxes, income tax receipts are much more sensitive to economic conditions. Similarly, the effect of changes depends, in part, on the degree to which individuals respond to the code's creation of incentives to rearrange their affairs in ways that will reduce their tax burden.

In Kansas, revenue shortfalls—predicted by opponents of the plan but not officially anticipated by the government itself—came to monopolize legislative activity in the following years. Faced with a legal requirement to balance the budget, the state undertook major cuts in spending across all functions of government. Those cuts had an especially pronounced effect on education and social welfare provisioning, both because these areas accounted for much of the state's spending in the first place and because Governor Brownback had undertaken major changes to state activity in those areas, fiscal crisis aside.

Congress, of course, has no legal obligation to enact balanced budgets and routinely runs large deficits. Yet it is not hard to conceive that the fiscal effects of the tax code reforms may, in time, create political pressure to cut federal spending. Periodic votes to raise the federal debt ceiling have become more publicly salient and politically contentious than they had been in the past. It is also worth recalling the discussion in chapter 3 of state campaigns to impose legal restrictions on congressional budgeting activity. Remobilization of these campaigns would certainly be conceivable if the tax reforms contributed to significant increases in the deficit; constitutional questions held wholly aside, those campaigns might create significant political pressure for cuts very similar to the pattern seen in the years following the 1970s tax revolt. Changing the tax code itself is an enormous political labor, one not successfully undertaken since the Reagan administration (on which see Prasad [2006]). The change is therefore likely to persist and will undoubtedly figure in the crucial politics of budgeting for many years to come. As in Kansas, it is likely that funding of social welfare programs and entitlements and transfers to lower levels of government will be subject to particular pressure, both as a reflection of Republican policy priorities and because a significant component of federal spending is nondiscretionary. Whatever theoretical mechanisms are invoked to explain it, it is a reliable empirical pattern that fiscal problems cascade down federal systems.

The Trump administration has also made use of executive orders to seek continuous or automatic reductions in government activity. Most obviously, freezes or reductions in hiring, coupled with high rates of attrition from the federal civil service, will have the effect of diminishing the human capital and institutional knowledge on which public bureaucracies are reliant. Other orders have directly addressed the regulatory activity of agencies—major reductions in federal regulation have been another significant Trump administration goal. One early order mandated a continuous reduction in regulation by directing agencies to repeal two regulations for each new one adopted and directed that the new regulations from a given agency in a given year could not produce an aggregate increase in economic effects of regulation (Trump 2017m). This order was complemented by one directing a cooperative search for repealable regulations, informed by assumptions and language similar to that underlying the creation of the Office of the Repealer in Kansas (Trump 2017b). These orders have a simple ratcheting effect—they can result only in a net reduction in regulation.

Attrition in staffing, mandated reductions in regulation, and declines in revenue all have cumulative effects, particularly because rebuilding lost administrative capacity is economically and politically costly. It is not possible to say now what effect changes in staffing and regulatory practices in federal agencies will have, nor is it possible to say what fiscal effect the tax code will have or what political response it will engender. But it is clear that, while these actions are not among the most visible or divisive of President Trump's first year in office, they have the potential to produce constant, significant, and ultimately enduring effects on the operation of government.

2. Use private or market means to provide services currently delivered by government

Outright privatization of government functions was not a notable feature of Trump administration policy in its first year. But neither would this action have been expected. As discussions earlier in this book have suggested—and as the enormous literature on neoliberalism, public-private partnerships, and the new public management also suggests—moves toward privatization are particularly notable in programs where much of the routine activity of administration is delegated or carried out at lower levels of government. The overall federal policy environment under the Trump administration is, undoubtedly, one favorable to a market orientation to government service delivery.

3. Reduce federal agency discretion, particularly in environmental and regulatory matters

The issuing of orders meant to have a general effect on the scope of regulation has been discussed immediately above. In addition, the Trump administration was quick to begin rolling back key Obama administration policies, particularly concerning the environment and natural resources. By executive order, President Trump directed EPA administrator Pruitt to begin rescinding the Waters of the United States Rule (Trump 2017n) and the Clean Power Plan (Trump 2017j), both significant policies discussed at length in chapters 2 and 3. The order that initiated the review of the Clean Power Plan also brought new scrutiny on a number of other EPA rules. A Bureau of Land Management rule on fracking—ensnared in litigation whose pattern was nearly identical to that of these EPA rules—has also been reversed. President Trump also withdrew the United States from the Paris Climate Accords, making it virtually the only country not subscribing to this agreement.

In response to executive order (Trump 2017o), Interior Secretary Zinke began revisiting protections and designations of a wide range of federal lands. He recommended abbreviating or entirely eliminating many protections and designations. Although federal protections of many lands and waters are being revisited, the most notable and expansive recommendations concerned federal lands in Utah and Arizona. These can be viewed as efforts to meet some of the concerns of the land-transfer movement, which has been strongest in Utah, Arizona, and Zinke's home state of Montana. These actions recall the Reagan administration's accommodation of some of the demands of the Sagebrush Rebels.

These orders are mainly reversals of a predecessor's policies rather than genuine changes in the structure of operations. Other executive orders with less tangible, immediate effects are suggestive of a larger shift toward limited regulation of these matters. In several orders, President Trump has sought to create a dramatically streamlined environmental assessment and permitting process for mining (2017g), offshore drilling (2017h), and infrastructure projects, including oil and gas pipelines (2017d, 2017f). These infrastructure orders seek to impose a strict timeline on the evaluation process. More significantly, they seek to consolidate the permitting and environmental assessment process, which frequently touches on matters under the authority of many different federal agencies. They seek to place a single agency in charge of issuing a unified decision. In practice, then, the Trump campaign's professed priorities in infrastructure have, in office, mainly taken the form of limitations on the scope of agency regulatory power.

4. Resist implementation of the ACA; expand state discretion in implementation of federal programs

In the 2016 general election, repeal of the ACA was a key goal for both the Trump campaign and Republican congressional candidates. Representative Tom Price (R-GA) was appointed as secretary of health and human services, in no small part because he had been a leading advocate of ACA repeal and was the architect of a purported replacement. ACA repeal was the top legislative priority of the new year, and, over the course of 2017, Congress considered a wide array of models of repeal. These ranged from outright repeal of the law, to measures that preserved some of the more popular and successful features of the ACA such as the Medicaid expansion, to a pure block grant approach modeled on the provisions of the HCC. These repeal efforts were narrowly defeated in Congress; repeal of the individual mandate was later incorporated into the tax reforms.

By means of executive order and other executive actions, the Trump administration sought to limit the reach of the ACA. For instance, an early order sought to identify all the facets of the law in which action was placed at the discretion of the health and human services secretary rather than commanded (2017i). Other actions have signaled a readiness to recognize a wide range of religious and moral exemptions to the contraception mandate, a portion of the ACA subject to especially strong challenge in the courts, and another order has significantly relaxed rules about state insurance marketplaces (2017k). Actual or threatened changes in reimbursements and subsidies created significant uncertainty and instability in state insurance exchanges. The administration has also shown itself willing to grant states more control in other delegated programs. For instance, in early 2018, the agency charged with administering Medicare and Medicaid proclaimed itself willing to grant waivers to allow states to impose work requirements on some Medicaid recipients—a further extension of the big waiver model of exemption from federal requirements that has already produced remarkable state-level variation in the workings of the program (Barron and Rakoff 2013).

5. *Limit federal regulation and increase state regulation of elections*

As chapter 4 showed, the development of new, more restrictive requirements for voting has not relied on any directly professed intention to make voting more difficult—and, legally, could not have done so. Rather, those measures have rested on carefully crafted arguments about federalism and compelling government interest. States have successfully asserted that they possess a compelling interest in conducting elections with integrity and have pared away the already limited federal oversight powers in this area, in part by relying on the language of legislation such as HAVA.

In 2016, the Trump campaign frequently raised the specter of extensive fraudulent voting and the effect that such fraud might have on the outcome of the general election. Although Trump won the election with a majority of copartisans in both chambers of Congress, he nonetheless maintained that the election had been plagued by fraud and ordered the creation of a commission to study the integrity of the American electoral process (Trump 2017e). Secretary Kobach was made the de facto head of the commission and showed an interest in using the commission to address many of the same aspects of election administration that he had taken up during his tenure in Kansas. The commission requested voter rolls and related information from all states—a source of data that would enable, at least as a form of study, national voter roll comparison of the kind employed in Crosscheck. In a much-discussed opinion piece, Kobach also criticized electoral procedures in New Hampshire, focusing particularly on matters of residency requirements, personal identification documents, and length of registration periods—aspects of election administration concerning which many states have adopted more stringent policies in recent years and are on relatively firm legal ground in so doing.

The commission was dissolved early in 2018 without producing a report or recommendations; a number of liberal and Democratic-leaning states declined to disclose requested information, and many other states made minimal disclosures. Mississippi—always a vigorous defender of state prerogatives—likewise declined to disclose any information. It was always doubtful that the commission would have substantial effects on policy, precisely for the reasons laid out in this book—federal authority in this area of policy is limited. The ill-fated commission is nonetheless suggestive of the general disposition of the administration on these matters.

The administration also intervened on behalf of Ohio in *Husted v. A. Philip Randolph Institute*, a Supreme Court case concerning the legality of Ohio's voter roll maintenance practices. There, in effect, it argued that Ohio's practice of removing registered voters from the rolls for nonvoting and nonresponse to a piece of forwardable mail was permissible under the NVRA. The Court narrowly endorsed this view, but as Justice Sotomayor noted in oral arguments, this position reversed views on voter registration practices that had been advanced by solicitors general of both parties running back as far as the 1970s. This position, too, is a plausible signal that the administration will take a narrow view of the protections conferred by major federal election laws, which may be manifest in enforcement priorities and interventions in litigation.

6. Limit government oversight of commercial activity and labor markets

The first year of the Trump administration was undoubtedly one of deregulation. A very brief summary is sufficient. The Trump administration has delayed or reversed Obama-era rules respecting matters such as overtime pay and higher education. By executive order, a number of federal contracting rules have been loosened. The FCC has sought to repeal net neutrality regulations. Finance-related regulations have been repealed or loosened. Justice Department guidance on gender identity—which could have had important effects on the application of federal antidiscrimination law in employment—have been reversed. With the administration's support, Congress enacted a federal right-to-try law in 2018. Aside from such concrete regulatory changes, the administration's general outlook is certainly one that favors a smaller federal role in the oversight of economic activity. The discussion above mentioned important Trump appointees who are most noted for their vigorous defense of states relative to the federal government. It can be added that the initial appointees to important positions such as secretary of state, commerce, the Treasury, education, and agriculture had significant prior experience in the business world.

7. Strictly enforce immigration law by resisting federal efforts at liberalization, expanding state power to undertake enforcement independently, and curtailing local discretion

The body of this book noted that immigration is an area of policy where there was not consensus among state-level conservatives. As chapter 2 discussed, Republican attorneys general were unified in their opposition to the Obama administration's executive orders on immigration; the list of states participating as amici in *Texas v. United States* was extraordinarily long. Many states, likewise, began to develop policies restricting sanctuary jurisdictions in 2015 and 2016. However, measures providing for direct state enforcement of immigration law were adopted more sparingly, and the Supreme Court's Obama-era rulings on immigration matters did little to clarify core questions—in practice, immigration remained a legal, political, and intergovernmental tangle at the conclusion of the Obama administration.

The Trump administration has strongly embraced all the features of the restrictive approach to immigration outlined, for instance, in the academic writing of Secretary Kobach. Indeed, a restrictive immigration policy was the centerpiece of the Trump campaign and has been pursued actively in office. In 2017, the Trump administration announced a phase-out of Deferred Action for Childhood Arrivals (DACA), the most significant of the Obama administration's immigration policies. This move was preceded by a series of executive orders bearing on many aspects of immigration policy. A first order directed expansion in the capacity of the Border Patrol and Immigration and Customs Enforcement (Trump 2017a). A second dealt with immigration enforcement within the United States (Trump 2017c). That order directly endorsed the proposition that state and local law enforcement can independently enforce federal immigration laws. It also provided for the compilation of a list of sanctuary jurisdictions and the withholding of federal funds from such jurisdictions. A series of orders, commonly referred to as the *travel ban orders*, imposed restrictions on entry into the United States from a number of countries (the first such order is Trump [2017l]). In addition to these notable orders, federal immigration enforcement efforts have been more active under the Trump administration, and changes to other aspects of immigration policy, such as admission of refugees, rules about visas, family reunification practices, etc., have been tightened; the circumscription of grounds for asylum claims and the practice of family separation attracted particular attention in 2018. A year into the administration, the construction of an ocean-to-ocean wall on the southern border remained a professed but unrealized goal.

The Trump administration's immigration policies have attracted particularly strong opposition from Democratic officeholders at all levels of government. To a greater degree than in any other policy area, the response in immigration serves as an indication that the opening of the Trump administration has brought about a relatively direct reversal of roles. The following section examines how Democratic officeholders have responded to the Trump administration, noting that this opposition has taken a form remarkably similar to the Republican opposition that has been the central concern of this work.

The Liberal Response to the Trump Administration

The preceding section has shown that much of the Trump administration's domestic policy behavior is aligned with core commitments of state-level conservatives. The administration's tax reforms and immigration policies are recognizable adaptations or extensions of existing state policies. Trump has appointed many notable conservatives to national positions. A series of executive orders and rule changes have disposed of many specific policies that had elicited state litigation and administrative resistance during the Obama administration. Further, partisan polarization has been extremely pronounced, and Republican officeholders have, in the main, closed ranks in support of the Trump administration. After a year, then, it seemed plain that the shift in partisan control of the national executive had resulted in a significant deescalation of conservative state contention with the national government. The formal patterns of interbranch and intergovernmental contention, however, have not abated; in the first year of the Trump administration, Democratic officeholders resisted Trump administration policies in much the same way as Republican officeholders resisted Obama administration policies. This work has examined a few behaviors in varying levels of depth: congressional noncooperation, state-initiated litigation, and such uncooperative state administrative behavior as refusal of funds, actions calculated to provoke litigation, and interstate cooperation by means of compacts and other administrative agreements. In the first year of the Trump administration, all these techniques were put to use by opponents.

Democratic members of Congress proved capable of highly unified resistance to President Trump's key legislative priorities. Senate Democrats, for instance, mustered complete party line opposition to the variants of ACA repeal as well as the tax reforms—a level of unified opposition that is somewhat surprising, viewed in light of the relatively more diffuse, less ideological coalition on which the modern Democratic Party has been reliant (Grossman and Hopkins 2015). Democrats also showed themselves willing to provoke at least a brief government shutdown in pursuit of a permanent version of DACA, a maneuver very much reminiscent of the government shutdown in 2013. In these respects, Democrats appear to have learned well from Republicans' success in halting the Obama administration's legislative agenda through intransigence. The highly polarized political climate and President Trump's extraordinary unpopularity among Democratic supporters undoubtedly facilitated this.

State-level Democratic officeholders, likewise, have shown an initial readiness to draw from Republican successes. This has been most apparent in state litigation; Democratic state attorneys general have filed suits contesting most of the major orders and actions of the Trump administration. In many cases, these suits seek to preserve Obama administration rules or challenge the procedures by which rules have been rescinded, altered, or delayed. In such cases, fundamental matters of federal authority are not at issue, only the propriety of the Trump administration's early efforts to overturn rules—including, in some cases, those whose legal validity had not been firmly settled.

In other cases, Democratic litigants have relied more thoroughly on newer lines of reasoning that emerged from significant Obama-era rulings. In an important early case on the first travel ban order, *Washington v. Trump*, the state of Washington successfully asserted its ability to challenge the order on the grounds that it would affect the operations of its public universities. Here, the state relied on the very broad claim of interest analogous to that asserted in cases such as *Texas v. United States*. Similar arguments underpinned state-initiated suits seeking to preserve DACA; these claims were endorsed in some federal district courts, leaving the program in place pending the outcome of what appeared likely to be very protracted litigation.

President Trump's major domestic immigration enforcement order provided for the withholding of federal funds from jurisdictions that did not comply with federal immigration detainer requests. Judicial reasoning in those cases has turned in part on specific language in the order—notably, its reliance on the word *sanctuary*, a common political term for which there is no corresponding legal definition. Yet cases dealing with these provisions of the order also raise questions about the extent to which the federal government can use fiscal transfers to secure state and local compliance with preferred policies. Along the same lines as the ruling in *National Federation of Independent Businesses v. Sebelius*, which held that states could not be compelled to expand Medicaid under the ACA, courts in cases like *County of Santa Clara v. Trump* have held that funding contingencies can be drawn only narrowly; such limitations on the potential reach of punitive budgeting have also conceivably emboldened local government resistance to federal enforcement efforts. Weeks after the passage of the tax reforms, the states of New York, New Jersey, and Connecticut announced their intention to form a coalition to challenge the legality of the federal bill's cap on deductions of state and local tax payments. This case, too, bears important similarities to *National Federation of Independent Businesses*, which dealt not only with fiscal federalism but also with the uses of congressional tax powers—the individual mandate was, technically, a tax penalty.

Intransigence and litigation are easily emulable—the activity described above does not involve the pursuit of any new policy but only the attempt to preserve the policy conditions obtaining at the time Obama left office. Other behaviors discussed in this work are certainly emulable as well. This is true, for instance, of the use of positive rights guarantees by states with the specific aim of frustrating federal policy. As noted previously, this approach to rights provisioning had in fact been an important source of progressive success for quite some time (Zackin 2013) and itself served as a specific model for recent conservative activity. Orren (2012, 2014) argues that this approach to rights provisioning is in structure more favorable to progressives, both in the current issue environment in the United States and perhaps generally. California's S.B. 54, enacted in 2017, stands as an example of this approach. The bill not only directs law enforcement agencies in the state not to cooperate with federal immigration detainer requests; it also directs agencies not to dedicate any resources to investigations into immigration status. An elaboration of this approach that would extend to the conferral of a sort of "state citizenship" is readily conceivable according to existing law (Markowitz 2015) and might draw on practices already employed by some localities (see Villazor 2010; and Hayduk 2015).

The withdrawal from the Paris Climate Accords immediately prompted a number of liberal state governments to form the state-level US Climate Alliance, whose members pledged to fulfill the goals of the accords, share data, and support research and policy. Although there is not a formal compact undergirding the alliance, it possesses many of the same features. Aside from agreement to meet a set of well-defined objectives, the alliance has a standing administrative presence (in this case, located at the United Nations) whose operation is underwritten by member states as well as some private philanthropic sources. It remains to be seen whether such approaches to coordination will become a prospective strategy for pursuing new policy goals rather than one that is primarily reactive to federal action.[4]

Federalism 2028: Three Pertinent Questions about What Comes Next

The sections immediately above make an initial case for the persistence of partisan intergovernmental disagreement possessing a particular focus on executive power. This is partly evidence of continuity: in both form and substance, policy disagreements under the Trump administration closely resemble those observed in the preceding eight years. The same evidence also raises the possibility of larger change. Chapter 1 argued that evolution of a large, active national government in the United States was the product of a negotiated, bipartisan consensus. That claim also implied that it would be difficult for the action of a single party to disarrange that settlement entirely (see Bednar 2011, 281). The indications that more confrontational forms of intergovernmental disagreement are diffusing across party lines, then, do not simply promise still more years of heightened political disagreement. They also raise the possibility of larger structural shifts in American federalism. This concluding section considers three questions whose resolution will do much to dictate whether the persistence of intergovernmental disagreement will significantly alter the arrangement that produced a century of growth in federal power—and what a successor to this arrangement might look like.

American government structure generally evolves slowly. Stasis was an intended feature of the American constitutional order. Even in matters where constitutional and statutory provisions offer little guidance or constraint, other kinds of institutional arrangements tend to slow change and baffle its effects. Taking a broad view, the present structure of American government has resulted, to a great degree, from a handful of developments that are now relatively old: the creation of a permanent income tax and the consequent growth in federal fiscal capacity, the diffuse social welfare state arising from the New Deal, and the achievements of the civil rights era. With regard to this larger structure, the past decade has not brought about great changes. The dominant political parties still exist and still endorse roughly the same vision of government they did a decade ago. These parties are supported by roughly the same voters who supported them before. The branches of government still behave more or less as they did before.

From this vantage, the important events discussed in this work—elections won or lost, policies implemented or dismantled, cases decided—are only perturbations. They may be first signs of a gradual shift toward a different government arrangement, or they may be wobbles in an institutionalized settlement that will ultimately remain stable. That outcome will depend, in part, on the behavior of parties and partisans. Yet, beyond the simple observation that strengthened partisan identification and polarization have made coordinated opposition simpler, this work has offered no great claims about the nature of parties or the likely future of American's current partisan alignment. The discussion of the first year of the Trump administration has suggested that such allegiance is strong enough that even so unusual a figure as Trump has not appreciably disrupted the basic alignments and commitments. Indeed, the process of polarization and increased antipathy, which appeared to have an asymmetrical dimension around the time of the Tea Party mobilization, now appears to be mutual, and nothing in published scholarship, the news, or everyday experience suggests that this situation is likely to give way to an era of good feelings anytime soon.

Yet it is entirely possible that the near future will bring some dramatic change that the descriptive framework employed here could not anticipate. A major voter realignment, an irreparable rift in a major party, or a constitutional crisis could all occur, just as they have done in the past, but nothing written here offers meaningful guidance about the likelihood of any of these developments. What follows, then, is not a positive effort at prognostication; it is an exploration of key questions that will plausibly direct the future of American federalism, supposing that the partisan aspects of political life continue along something like their present course.

Proceeding according to the view that federalism is a joint institutional and partisan settlement, and supposing stability in the party system itself, a default assumption would be that the Trump administration will have no enduring effect on the structure of government. There are features of the first year of the Trump presidency that could counsel for this starting view: a year into his term, Trump was an unpopular president whose actions invariably attracted the scrutiny of a mobilized, staunch opposition. He was inexperienced in the conduct of government and had limited legislative successes despite the benefit of a majority of copartisans in both branches of Congress—a majority that, itself, appeared quite vulnerable heading into the midterm elections. It is with these sorts of factors in view that Callen (2017) suggests that, like a conventional modern Republican presidency, the Trump administration will alter the policy priorities of the administrative state while leaving its basic structure intact. After some flirtation with arguments about devolution, the Democratic opposition will likely seek to preserve American federalism more or less in its present form. This will arise both from an inclination to maintain the party's long-established policy goals, which are reliant on a large federal administrative role, and from the stickiness of the institutional arrangements themselves.

This view is a plausible starting point for thinking about potential changes in the structure of American federalism and is consistent with historical patterns. The major limitation of such an account is its primary focus on the president and Congress. This work has consistently argued that the judiciary and state governments play an increasingly important role and that unresolved questions about the courts and the states will be important for what the next decade will bring; with these processes in view, the Trump administration's pledge to deconstruct the federal administrative state seems a much more serious prospect (see Metzger 2017).

Will the Judiciary Remain Hospitable to Litigation against the Federal Executive?

The first year of the Trump administration left little doubt that Democratic states will make extensive use of litigation to contest the actions of the federal executive, and there appears to be approximate symmetry in party control of resources for litigation. In advance of the 2018 midterm elections, Democrats controlled fewer attorney general offices than did Republicans, but they did control the offices in a handful of very large states with notable records of success in the federal courts. It remains to be seen how receptive the federal judiciary will be to state-initiated challenges to the actions of the federal executive and what mode of reasoning, if any, the courts might use to stem the flow of cases.

Chapter 2 of this book described how the Court's ruling in *Massachusetts v. EPA* was an important legal enabling condition for the wave of state litigation against the Obama administration. That result, however, was probably not intended or foreseeable from the bench. It became an enabling condition only when considered alongside nonjudicial patterns that could not have directly informed the Court's reasoning: the consolidation of state attorney general offices into a large, effective litigation support structure, high partisan polarization, and a sharp presidential turn toward executive unilateralism. The drift of judicial reasoning on matters of standing and administrative procedure thereby landed the Court in the middle of a political problem, but judicial politics, in the simple sense, offers few hints of the likely resolution.

The post-*Massachusetts* era has made the solidity of federal agency and executive power seem doubtful mainly in the crude sense that states have become prolific litigators and have had some successes. States' vigorous exploration of possible lateral applications of decisions has heightened the practical effects of judicial scrutiny of executive activity over the past decade. Aside from the unusual fact that the relevant support structure is public, the pattern is a familiar one of a litigation structure pressing the Court to address issues it might otherwise be disinclined to take up (Epp 1998). Such mobilizations often conclude with a decision that can put an end to the percolation of cases up through the judicial hierarchy. However, the cases of the past decade have not yielded anything like a new *Chevron*—a coherent, more or less mechanically applicable statement of a doctrine setting forth the courts' relationship to the executive. Nor have they produced a cogent statement about the grounds on which states might seek to challenge federal action when their own administrative interests are conceivably affected; *United States v. Texas* appeared to be a case well suited to address this issue, but the shorthanded Court decided that case per curiam, leaving the larger issue, for the moment, open. *Shelby County v. Holder* offered bold words about state sovereignty but did not, in the following years, prompt serious revision of federalism doctrines beyond the specific context of voting rights.

A major decision that revisited core matters of judicial deference to agencies or clarified the scope of states' grounds for bringing suits could indirectly have large political effects by making litigation a significantly more or less attractive strategy for states to use in intergovernmental disagreements. However, settling those deeper questions is no simple matter, and it seems conceivable that the Court will endeavor, for as long as possible, to dispose of state-initiated suits against federal entities without settling these questions. Further, it is difficult to anticipate how the Court would resolve those questions, supposing it did seek to hand down a major statement: the questions closely approximate conditions where appellate judicial reasoning is particularly thorny and hard to predict. First, the questions are formidably difficult in strictly legal terms. Second, there are large bodies of nonlegal expertise that are relevant for the outcome and many interested parties that are likely to commend those expert findings to the Court's attention. Finally, and perhaps most significantly, the possible outcomes do not neatly map onto a simple left/right political ideology that so reliably predicts the results of many federal appellate cases (see Epstein, Landes, and Posner 2013). Both liberal and conservative state officeholders are pressing formally similar claims. Further, for judges of a conservative outlook, there is an additional dilemma—there are well-developed (though distinct) conservative legal arguments both for making it easier and for making it harder for states to sue federal agencies.

A ruling that circumscribed states' ability to bring suits grounded in administrative procedural objections or positive claims about states' own administrative practices would be consistent with a more general line of reasoning that has made litigation more difficult. The pattern is particularly well studied in the case of discrimination law (Edelman 2016) but is a wide-enough trend to have been characterized as a court-based "counterrevolution" against federal litigation (Burbank and Farhang 2017). Legal scholars have suggested a number of ways in which the lines of reasoning in those cases might also be used by federal courts to close (or narrow) the opening for state litigation created in *Massachusetts* (see Merriman 2018). Yet curtailing states' scope to sue federal agencies would cut off access to the courts for the litigants who have been most effective in challenging federal agency actions. In effect, this would enable less legally constrained exercise of federal agency power. This is hardly an outcome likely to be attractive to a conservative judge, particularly one inclined to view states' claims with particular sympathy.

Conversely, the Court probably cannot markedly increase its scrutiny of federal executive behavior—as conservative critics of the administrative state might wish—without pursuing a more direct engagement with the substance of the expertise that underpins agency actions. Deference to agencies is of course not, in any simple sense, a positive or political endorsement of the activity of the federal administrative state even if such may be the practical consequence. This is a major reason why many scholars have argued that the judiciary should confront the substance of agency decision-making much more directly, particularly on economic grounds (see Vermeule 2009; and DeMuth 2016).

Yet increased scrutiny of the substance of agency decision-making is likely to be an unpalatable proposition for many judges. Doctrines that shield some agency reasoning from direct examination also enable judges to decide cases on grounds that accord with their own training and expertise. Justices across the ideological spectrum have been reticent to make much direct use of nonlegal forms of evidence and expertise—and this is true even in some of the Court's boldest civil rights decisions (see Ansolabehere and Snyder 2008; and Moran 2010) and in original jurisdiction cases where the Court is obliged to produce rather than digest a body of facts (Sarine 2012). Aside from Justice Breyer, who has shown a persistently high interest in empirical scholarship, it seems doubtful that many justices, left or right, would look to remake doctrine in a way that would leave them afterward obliged to steep themselves in statistics or cost-benefit analysis—or hire economist clerks to do such work on their behalf.[5] This is particularly true for judges, such as Chief Justice Roberts, who have regularly expressed concern that the complexity of judicial reasoning, in itself, may harm the credibility of the Supreme Court. The first large wave of state-initiated cases against the Trump administration—which have arisen from his immigration orders—appeared unlikely to force a resolution of these questions. These cases, as they evolved, appeared to provide a means of resolving the cases based on First Amendment considerations, the president's public statements, or issues in the construction of the orders.

In short, political developments of the past decade created a practical problem for the courts. The federal appellate judiciary contended with an increased volume of state litigation against the federal executive, and, owing to the high policy stakes in the cases as well as circuit-to-circuit variation in how such challenges were received, these cases found their way onto the Supreme Court docket with remarkable frequency. Going on the very plausible assumption that the conjunction of partisan polarization and executive unilateralism will continue to make litigation an attractive option to some subset of state officeholders whose preferences diverge dramatically from those of the federal executive, the development of such cases is likely to continue.

The common view in law and society scholarship is that litigation of this kind is informed, in part, by play for a particular rule. A new rule, once clearly articulated, can provide a basis for such cases to be predictably soluble in lower courts and serves to bring a campaign or a mobilization to its conclusion. However, there seems little guarantee that, once mobilized, state litigants will desist. They have the use of stable legal resources in a way that private litigants do not and can therefore continually play for further rules when suits meet with success. If suits fail, state actors may have strong inducements to continue litigation if they are taking on a galvanizing political opponent. Under such circumstances, a landmark ruling appears likely either to produce more rather than less work for the appellate judiciary or to produce a rule whose consequences would run contrary to the preferences of an increasingly conservative appeals judiciary by cutting off the most significant legal avenue for challenging the activity of the federal administrative state. The resolution of this issue, then, is one that will demand either more than incremental judicial creativity or a continued search for means of settling cases in a way that avoids a direct ruling on legal questions that may appear to have no acceptable answer.

How Far Can State Policies Diverge?

For many practical purposes, state governments have become markedly more powerful than they were a generation ago. State executives are an influential force in the federal policy-making process. The federal turn toward private action to enforce rights and an expansive waiver model in social welfare provision have afforded states ample scope to define for themselves the form and extent of social protections available to residents. States' success in litigation against the federal government has further strengthened their bargaining position in policy development and rulemaking; litigation and administrative maneuvering, combined, offer a wide range of passive and active techniques to shape or resist federal policy. In many policy matters, the initiative rests with states for the simple reason that political divisions have made the federal government unproductive. The Trump administration's agenda of formal deregulation and attrition in federal administrative capacity promises a still-broader role for states in areas where federal involvement wanes, by reduction in either the scope and volume of regulations on the books or the inclination or practical ability to carry out what is written.

All these factors are conducive to significant state-to-state divergence in both policy behaviors and related social outcomes. And it seems likely that states will seek to make meaningful use of expanded power or discretion: the body of this book is, among other things, an extensive catalog of the ways in which conservative preferences for state control have gone well beyond cheap talk. Given that such a large proportion of state governments are in the firm control of one party or the other, the present situation seems to be one that could result in extreme fragmentation or in two cohesive, opposing approaches to regulation and social welfare provision that could yield, in practice, two Americas with two very different worlds of social policy. The following sets out what promise to be some pertinent factors for the scope of potential divergence in state policy.

A first consideration is whether there is symmetry in the legal authority available to states depending on their ideological leanings. In areas of policy such as immigration and elections administration, it appears that the legal conditions are amenable to very distinct policy regimes. It is conceivable that some states would make immigration status nearly irrelevant for most practical purposes and meaningfully shield immigrant populations from federal enforcement efforts while others might make immigration status visible in a host of circumstances and actively seek to enforce federal immigration law independently or in active coordination with federal authorities.[6] The same could be said of elections, where some states could make registration virtually automatic and provide ample opportunities and means to cast a ballot while others could impose tight documentary and time limitations on voting, engage in active maintenance of voter rolls, and seek to make criminal penalties for fraud highly visible throughout the process. The same could be said of delegated social welfare programs, where there are sharp state divergences in the coverage available and in the proportion of potentially eligible beneficiaries actually receiving benefits. Although it appears legally feasible for a state to move fully to one extreme or the other in these areas, no state has done so. In the final analysis, inertia and states' limited policy resources may be the most significant check on extremely divergent outcomes, particularly in matters where no new federal activity obliges states to alter the status quo.[7]

A second relevant factor is the degree to which, for a given area of policy, attitudes about levels of government are distinct from partisan preferences in general. Increased partisan polarization in the United States has been driven to a considerable extent by strengthened associations between party allegiances and particular positions on policy. In consequence, these partisan associations are usually strong enough to supersede beliefs about the appropriate level of government at which policy ought to be made. Where partisan considerations are markedly stronger than federalist ones—as they presently appear to be in most cases—functional devolution of authority to states under unified party control seems likely to promote divergent policies, particularly when viewed in light of high concentration of power in elected state executive offices.

A notable exception to this general subordination of federalist thinking to partisan thinking can be found in what has been taken to be an exceptionally divisive issue: environmental protection and natural resource management, admittedly not an area where this book has painted a very rosy picture. There is often a public preference for greater environmental involvement at lower levels of government irrespective of ideological leanings (e.g., Mills and Gore 2016), and conservatives are measurably more supportive of environmental action at the state level than at the federal (Jacobs 2017). On matters such as renewable energy and water management, conservative states have shown a meaningful readiness to take significant action even if the form of this action differs from liberal states' responses to similar issues (Hess, Mai, and Brown 2016; Hess et al. 2017). This is, very possibly, an area where the opportunity for cooperation across state and partisan lines may persist. It is notable, for instance, that managing surface water scarcity prompted the rise of interstate compacts in the twentieth century; the compact approach to water management has been a qualified success and also promoted innovative use of the compact form in a way that has facilitated cooperation in a great many other areas of policy over the past century.

Finally, the degree of state policy innovation and policy divergence in a given area will depend on the extent to which new policy requires new state administrative capacity. There exists a clear asymmetry in how readily competing ideological visions for state government could be realized. Politically and practically, in recent years it has proved much easier to reduce state government capacity than it is to expand it. Further, the present fiscal climate is one that is challenging for all states, more or less irrespective of political outlook. Only some states have, like Kansas, taken up the reduction in the scope of state government as a positive, vigorously pursued program. But all states have faced the problem of dealing with outstanding pension obligations and deferred infrastructure maintenance, and all have, to meaningful degrees, embraced efficiency-oriented, collaborative models of government service provision.[8] Whatever its political inclination, then, no state is likely to find it easy to build extensive capacity to fill in roles vacated by federal agencies or undertake new kinds of activity. Fiscally, it may be especially difficult for states to build capacity to pursue new, progressive policy objectives for several reasons. In some cases, such as immigration, pursuing such objectives may require forgoing federal funds. If the federal tax reforms create revenue shortfalls, some of this effect will assuredly be passed down to the states. Further, the federal cap on deductions for state and local taxes makes the raising of more revenue at lower levels of government a more expensive proposition for individual taxpayers—and thus, very possibly, a more difficult political proposition, as well.

What Will Liberals Seek to Learn from Conservatism?

This book has described a conjunction of processes working in two different sorts of time: the regular ebb and flow of partisan fortunes in elections and the slower and less predictable evolution of legal and policy institutions. The deepening of partisan divisions in America is both a palpable fact of everyday life and a development that has been studied very thoroughly by political scientists and sociologists. The drift in legal doctrines and administrative powers has been a subtler phenomenon but one whose development has been traced out by scholars in law and public administration. Conservative behavior since 2010 has shown that this drift, coupled with partisan divisions, has created conditions that afford a remarkably wide scope of action for sufficiently determined state officeholders. With the benefit of ideas and findings from all four of these disciplines and from the interdisciplinary community of interest in law and society, this book has reconstructed how that structure of opportunity developed. This book's own findings suggest that the opportunity for states is likely to persist. The sections immediately above have shown that the ultimate scope and consequences of states' freedom of action will, however, depend partly on processes that are not strictly predictable: the continued development of judicial ideas and the ability or willingness of state governments to pursue existing policy ideas toward one extreme or another.

But, although this development is not predictable, it will not fall to simple chance: a last uncertainty about what this will mean for the structure of American federalism is what liberal and progressive actors will seek to learn from conservative success in state government. Without going so far as to say that legal and administrative techniques have no inherent ideological valence, it is clear that these can be coupled with political objectives in a number of ways. The success of the state-level officeholders discussed in this book is, to a great degree, the culmination of a long-term process by which conservatives have sought to learn from and emulate the successes of liberals and progressives over much of the twentieth century, coupling those ideas to new, conservative objectives. It is worth recalling, at the end of a scholarly book on the subject, how important the academy was in that process and how it may figure in what happens next.

Teles's (2008) remarkable history of the conservative legal movement lays out how the legal and political landscape would have looked to conservatives in the 1970s. The preceding decades had seen the rapid expansion of an administrative state that was highly reliant on field-specific expertise and policy ideas originating in academic disciplines. Shifts in judicial doctrine had sought to promote dramatic progressive social change. Those shifts had involved an extraordinary widening in both the kinds of legal questions the judiciary was willing to consider and the sorts of remedies it was prepared to use. The architects of the conservative legal movement proceeded from a recognition that this was a landscape in which liberals held the high ground. Conservatives lagged behind in legal ideas and, just as significantly, in their influence on the social structures by which legal ideas were produced, legitimated, and circulated. Under such conditions, no hasty effort to secure a particular office or win a certain court case could seriously hope to produce a larger change.

Those core actors therefore pursued a slower strategy. Through a focus on the academy, they sought to produce conservative legal ideas, make it legitimate to discuss those ideas seriously, position conservative thinkers in influential positions, and create pathways for ideas—and graduates steeped in those ideas—to move from the legal academy to key sites in government and the appellate judiciary. *Conservative*, in this case, was deliberately given a broad definition meant to curb intellectual factionalism. Although all those worldviews combined remain a minority position in the legal academy, this larger effort to reshape legal ideas has undoubtedly transformed the law. Operating in approximate parallel to the legal movement Teles describes was the long-term development of an infrastructure for producing, legitimating, and circulating policy ideas, including nonscholarly intellectual magazines, think tanks, and policy networks—a process chronicled by Medvetz (2012b). Although the development of this policy infrastructure has not involved as concerted an effort to secure particular outcomes within the academy, economics is an academic field widely recognized as an important source of such ideas (Fourcade, Ollion, and Algan 2015). It can be argued that this is also true to some degree of political theory and institutes and centers within schools of policy and government where economic and political ideas intermingle.

The practical success of this conservative movement was meaningfully associated with a readiness to learn from liberal and progressive opponents. In this respect, the conservative legal movement is a very much an intellectual movement, not an anti-intellectual movement. In addition to acknowledging the importance of influence within the legal academy, it worked out how to emulate the strategic litigation structures that yielded such remarkable changes in law. Setting state-initiated litigation entirely aside, there is a case to be made that conservative public interest litigators are more successful than progressives in cooperating to play for major outcomes (Hollis-Brusky and Wilson 2017). This work has also noted more specific borrowings in the legal domain: the Goldwater Institute's recognition of the strategic uses of state positive rights guarantees or Secretary Kobach's acknowledgment of the role of state government in the Progressives' success. And, although the state conservative actors this book has examined clearly favor a general goal of limited government, that preference is much more than an anti-intellectual opposition to the state—they have shown a remarkable curiosity about the possibilities opened by active engagement with the legal and administrative capacities of state government. States have long been styled as America's "laboratories of democracy," and figures like Governor Brownback have been keen to experiment with a wide range of available apparatus.

With regard to state government, contemporary liberals, broadly defined, are arguably in a situation rather similar to that facing legal conservatives around the time that Teles's account begins (see Hertel-Fernandez and Skocpol 2016). It is not simply the case that Republicans hold a larger number of important state offices. Conservatives have a well-developed vision of state government. Conservative think tanks and policy networks are more widely dispersed and better established in state capitols. And conservative state policies have become, in crucial cases, reliant on expert use of administrative techniques pioneered by the Progressives. It is apparent that this is an approach for which modern liberals lack judicially compelling objections or in many cases a strong opposing political narrative. The extent of this asymmetry is suggested, in part, by the fact that an argument for state government over federal government or a claim for states' rights is likely to be received as a conservative argument almost by definition—this despite the central role that state governments have played in liberal and progressive political change, both past and present.

The practical role of state government has widened and is likely to continue widening—among other things, liberals' opposition to the Trump administration is proceeding along legal and administrative lines likely to consolidate the successes won by state-based conservatives, whether this structural outcome is desired by liberals or not. What this shift will mean for the direction of American government ultimately depends on the degree to which liberals produce a competing, robust vision of state government and an intellectual, legal, and policy infrastructure to make that vision real.

Just as was true for the conservative legal movement, it appears likely that, if it occurs, the development of such a competing vision will occur in the academy. It is the social sciences that are equipped with the tools to understand the current moment as an intelligibly structured outgrowth of the past rather than a continuous succession of news cycles. In contrast to America's nonacademic intellectual communities, which are highly concentrated in a few coastal cities and have shown a relatively limited interest in the operation of state governments, the academic social sciences are dispersed across the country. This affords them a distinctive vantage point from which to look deeply into the working of state governments—and, perhaps, to reimagine them, just as scholars did as the academic social sciences took shape at the opening of the twentieth century. This book, by design, is not one that provides firm bases for offering a normative vision of state government. But it has laid out a descriptive precondition for those who wish to develop a new vision. It will be necessary for disciplines that have long paid disproportionate attention to the federal government to pay considerably more attention to state governments and to the inner workings of intergovernmental relations. That task will also require a deeper and more considered engagement with conservatism.

Notes

Chapter One

1. Although it is hardly formal evidence, I can attest from personal experience that this view enjoys a great deal of currency. In years of discussing this research at conferences, colloquia, and so on, I cannot recall any extended formal or informal discussion of my topic in which ALEC was *not* mentioned.

2. As a passing remark, it may be said that there is nothing very mysterious about the means by which those organizations shape policy—practices like campaign donations, advertising, lobbying, and canvassing. What is unusual about the political behavior of the Kochs is precisely that they spend according to political principle, whether they stand to benefit from the realization of those principles directly or not.

3. Though the study of Kansas comes last in this book's exposition, it was the starting point for my research. As originally conceived, this was to be a study based on interviews and observation—a conception that reflected a belief that the study would involve significant initial labor to gain access. An important early lesson was that this access was not needed and that state government behavior was surprisingly easy to study; many of the activities examined in this work produce large volumes of public information that is generally ignored. Where already-public information was not adequate to develop the argument, routine open records requests answered the need; such requests are relatively underutilized in the social sciences. The simple failure to request information can contribute to a perception—often erroneous—that governments are secretive or hard to study (Greenberg 2015).

Chapter Two

1. This count employs criteria that differ slightly from those used by Nolette (2014). Nolette counts a case as partisan if 80 percent of state attorneys general

come from a single party; here, this requirement is relaxed to 67 percent in cases where at least six states briefed on one side of a case. In substance, this change only slightly expands the number of cases included in the count but allows Mississippi, West Virginia, and Wyoming to be counted. The attorneys general in these states became Republican during the time period discussed here; whatever their party affiliation, these officers were undoubtedly conservative, by any conventional understanding of the word.

2. It can be added that party and interbranch conflict at the federal level has made Congress more likely to divide enforcement powers or use adversarial law as an enforcement device (Farhang and Yaver 2015).

3. An important exception, discussed in greater detail in chapter 4, has been major new law about civil rights, civil liberties, and criminal justice. In the postwar period, this law has been to a great degree judge made (Grossman and Swedlow 2015, 14) and comes with few attendant administrative powers.

4. The attorney general is a partisan, elected constitutional officer in forty-three US states but appointed by the governor in Alaska, Hawaii, New Hampshire, New Jersey, and Wyoming, appointed by the state supreme court in Tennessee, and elected by the legislature in Maine.

5. The Federalist Society does not publish its list of members. However, inclusion on its list of experts is suggestive not only of membership but also of some degree of active involvement in the organization and its goals. Nearly all the attorneys general who are highly active in litigation against the federal government are listed as experts by the Federalist Society.

6. This is in many respects analogous to Epp's (1998) discussion of reforms in criminal procedure during the interwar period. The Supreme Court did not seek to develop a criminal procedure agenda—rather, a mobilization designed to create a high volume of cases effectively compelled the Court to do so, in part to deal with variation in lower courts.

7. The EPA cases have begun to establish cost as a persuasive consideration in judicial review of agency rules. Earlier, this chapter noted that appellate judicial review of agency rulemaking is awkward because rulemaking is not a quasi-judicial process. Judicial employment of the cost-benefit standards in general use in the federal bureaucracy is one conceivable means of aligning the relevant forms of reasoning—one urged by proponents of law and economics modes of reasoning (see Posner 2007), though it would do so by making federal courts in some regards a quasi-administrative body. As chapter 4 will suggest, the handling of statistical and social scientific evidence poses a substantial and inadequately resolved problem for the federal judiciary.

8. Existing understandings of federal immigration law oblige employers to collect relevant documents and forms from employees but not to confirm the validity of those materials; the fact of collecting such materials provides employers with an affirmative defense (see Calavita 2016).

9. Patterns of adoption of these measures indicate the existence of a strong split on immigration enforcement among Republicans. As chapter 1 noted, this stance on immigration divides Republicans to a much greater degree than many other policies discussed in this book. Business actors, led by the Chamber of Commerce, generally oppose laws that require stringent verification of eligibility for employment; the failure of Kobach's proposals in Kansas likely owes to vocal opposition from the Chamber of Commerce and related organizations (see Alvord, Menjívar, and Gómez Cervantes 2018). Owing to resistance from business actors, direct democratic mechanisms such as ballot measures have figured in the passage of such immigration laws (Reich and Barth 2012). The enactment of these laws is strongly associated with a pair of conditions: state-level economic distress and pronounced increases in the Hispanic immigrant population (Ybarra, Sanchez, and Sanchez 2015).

10. During this same period, many states have also considered, and in some cases adopted, new state laws oriented toward religious freedom, such as the Religious Freedom Restoration Acts passed after major Supreme Court rulings on same-sex marriage or the Healthcare Sharing Ministries Acts passed after Supreme Court rulings on the ACA. These measures reflect a similar dynamic of legal interaction between states and the federal courts but are perhaps slightly different in substance: they do not create new rights claims but rather seek to formalize the scope of the right to the free exercise of religion already implicitly or overtly recognized in court rulings.

11. This pattern of funding in Michigan is also suggestive of the increasingly central role of legal activity in furthering the political goals of the state executive. Governor Snyder, elected in 2010, has sought something near a 50 percent increase in the funds available to the attorney general even as he has maintained that the state is in the midst of a fiscal crisis of almost apocalyptic severity.

12. State office control by movement actors is central to resolving the standing problem. The Roberts Court has, on the whole, tended toward a stricter standing doctrine. In *Hollingsworth v. Perry*, it also recognized that the relaxation of state standing requirements poses potential problems; there, the court held that California could not depute authority to litigate its ban on same-sex marriage to private proponents of the ban (Davis 2016). This can be understood as, in effect, a ruling that obliges states to assume the responsibility of litigating.

Chapter Three

1. In recent years, critics of the size and continued growth of the federal deficit have noted that, in proportional terms, the national debt rivals that of countries such as Greece that have experienced severe crises. One obvious difference between the United States and Greece is, of course, that the United States is a

global political and economic power—and undoubtedly benefits in various ways from the central role of the dollar in global financial markets. It can be added that the legal and administrative strength of America's tax-collection system is another difference; as Piketty (2014) notes, problems arising from government indebtedness are compounded in a country like Greece by the limited ability to enumerate taxable economic activity and holdings adequately and actually collect. The United States has the advantage of a strong capacity both to enumerate and to collect (see Morgan and Prasad 2009) as well as a rather different civic attitude about taxation: though many Americans express grievances about taxation, these grievances are also an indication that one's status as a taxpayer is a central symbolic dimension of civic identity for many Americans, hardly the case for a polity like Greece.

2. And it should be remembered that this *is* an assumption. The fact that state-level officials in the United States have often been prepared to let fiscal considerations take precedence over ideological or sovereignty considerations does not mean that it must always be so or that it is the only normal or rational way for a region-level polity to behave. Movements for regional separation or autonomization in other democratic polities provide a strong illustration that officials and electorates are often prepared to trade national-level money for devolved powers.

3. Not all interstate compacts require congressional consent, and the question of when consent is required has been sporadically litigated. The Supreme Court's landmark 1893 decision in *Virginia v. Tennessee* established what remains the core principle: consent is required when the provisions of a compact would have a relative effect on the sovereignty of nonmember states.

4. One can readily see how this proposal might also have broached a different set of legal questions concerning which governments recognize important documents from other jurisdictions and for what purposes. For instance, the federal REAL ID Act provides that drivers' licenses cannot be considered proof of identity for certain purposes, depending on a state's initial documentary requirements for issuing a license. Similarly, *Obergefell v. Hodges* dealt with the questions not only of whether states must license same-sex marriages but also of whether states not licensing same-sex marriages were obliged to recognize marriages duly licensed in states that did permit them. The Court's reasoning in that case developed along lines that did not require a sustained engagement with the matter of reciprocal recognition, but it is a question that might very plausibly be urged on the Court as states' policies on immigration diverge.

5. Gramm-Rudman-Hollings has not had a notable effect on federal budget deficits, but it certainly contributed to procedural transformation in the congressional budgeting process, the most notable example of the emergence of unconventional lawmaking (Sinclair 2011).

6. All counts were produced by employing a variety of full text and keyword

search terms on Lexis-Nexis State Capital. The websites for the respective convention efforts were also consulted to confirm the soundness of these search results. States submitting a convention petition since 2010 are Alabama, Alaska, Florida, Georgia, Louisiana, Michigan, Mississippi, Nebraska, New Hampshire, North Dakota, Ohio, South Dakota, Tennessee, and Utah. States where petitions cleared at least one legislative chamber are Arizona, Arkansas, Colorado, Indiana, Iowa, Kentucky, Missouri, New Mexico, Oklahoma, South Carolina, Texas, Virginia, Wisconsin, and Wyoming.

7. The high rate of favorable action in committee is particularly notable: just as in Congress, the great majority of proposed measures in state legislatures die in committee, generally without receiving any consideration.

8. This discussion relies on a collection of minutes, transcripts, written testimony, and recordings of all public hearings on convention petitions in 2014 and 2015. (Such proposals have excited less interest since 2016.) This body of material is imperfect: the resources available to state legislatures vary widely, as does the scope of state laws on open records and open meetings. In many cases, state legislatures do not produce or publish detailed records of committee hearings; in other cases, it is possible to view complete video recordings of committee hearings or read transcripts and exhibits associated with hearings. Though incomplete, this material is sufficient to suggest an explanation for the widely divergent outcomes for the three organizations in committee hearings.

9. It may be added that efforts by congressional caucuses to enforce various forms of budgetary discipline or restrictions have historically foundered because of basic collective action problems reminiscent of those relevant here (see Vasi, Strang, and van de Rijt 2014; and Wallner 2015).

10. The enactment of the Twenty-Seventh Amendment, which provides that a congressional pay increase cannot take effect until after the following election, could conceivably have provided an occasion to resolve some of these procedural questions, but it did not elicit any legal opposition. In addition to enjoying the imprimatur of the Founders, it is an uncontroversial policy with extremely limited impact on the behavior of government.

11. The NOMINATE score for the average sponsor seeking to rescind a constitutional convention petition was 1.31 (data from Shor 2014).

Chapter Four

1. Kansas serves as a useful example of how dramatically one person, one vote has changed state legislative apportionment. The districting map for Kansas drawn after the 2010 Census has produced one of the largest partisan efficiency gaps in the United States—comparable in magnitude to the gap in Wisconsin, which is the subject of a Supreme Court case on partisan gerrymandering.

Under the 2010 map, Republicans won 85 of 125 seats in the Kansas House in the 2016 general election. In the 1950s, 105 of 125 Kansas House districts were given to individual counties, with only 20 allocated on the basis of population. A vote in many Western counties was hundreds of times more powerful in state legislative elections than a vote in Kansas City (Ansolabehere and Snyder 2008, 29–30). This allocation method was by no means the most unrepresentative of its time. If the 2016 election had allocated seats using the apportionment scheme in place in Kansas in the mid-twentieth century, Republicans would have won 118 of 125 seats in the Kansas House.

2. In many ways, felon disenfranchisement laws have an awkward place in the argument presented here. Nearly all states disenfranchise convicted felons during their incarceration and often for a considerable time afterward. These laws are not new: in many states, felon disenfranchisement predates the Civil War. In the South, such laws were often enacted as Reconstruction collapsed (Behrens, Uggen, and Manza 2002); offenses such as vagrancy—a wholly discretionary and flatly racial charge—were included among disqualifying crimes. In the last fifteen years, felon disenfranchisement laws have displayed a paradoxical quality. Legally, the general trend has been one of liberalization. However, owing to extraordinarily high incarceration rates in the United States, these laws affect an increasing number of potential voters even though the laws are not more stringent than they were in the past and are often less stringent. Their effect on opportunities to participate also depends on the mechanism and administrative efficiency by which voting rights are restored—many states are notably dilatory in processing restorations of rights. Though this issue is, in the strict legal sense, distinct from the voting rights matters considered here, many scholars view mass incarceration, felon disenfranchisement, and voter restriction as arising from a single system of politicized racial domination (see, e.g., Blessett 2015; and Pettit and Sykes 2015).

3. Many scholars and commentators have taken the lack of evidence to suggest that political actors use the risk of fraud as a mere pretext for enacting laws whose effects are likely to be discriminatory (for a summary, see Ellis [2014]). It is, of course, extremely difficult to ascertain what political actors really believe, particularly under these circumstances. However, it bears mention that public belief in the prevalence of voter fraud is certainly real. Survey research reveals strong, persistent partisan differences in beliefs about the prevalence of voter fraud (Ansolabehere and Persily 2008; Wilson and Brewer 2013). Recent work has also shown that enactment of voter identification laws significantly increases Republican voters' confidence in state elections (Bowley and Donovan 2016). The judiciary's blanket acknowledgment of an interest in safeguarding perceived electoral credibility renders the grounds for those perceptions legally irrelevant, however practically consequential they may be.

4. The view in this case is consistent with a judicial distinction between le-

gitimate partisan interests and unlawful racial animus that is employed in assessments of the drawing of electoral districts. The distinction is a very fine one when applied to districts in states, such as North Carolina, where race is a powerful predictor of partisan support and most supporters of a major party are members of a racial minority. There, Republicans drawing a district that disfavors Democrats will also, almost by definition, involve a body of mostly white elected officials drawing a district that may disfavor an African American community.

5. Katz notes the curious fact that the same Court that has weakened protections to a recognized fundamental right to vote had recognized a new fundamental right for same-sex couples to marry. The different outcomes of these two groups of cases, she argues, reflect an emerging line of judicial reasoning that "separates conduct that targets members of a minority group for disfavored treatment based on animus from conduct that targets them for more particularized, instrumental reasons," such as electoral advantage (Katz 2015: 213). On this view, challenges to restrictive voting laws may have failed, in part, because they have not advanced strong claims about individual dignity of the kind that proved persuasive in the same-sex marriage cases.

6. Although dispersion may facilitate legal defenses, it is wholly possible that it is a consequence of political dynamics rather than anticipated judicial challenges, particularly when viewed in light of more general patterns of fragmentation in legislative activity discussed elsewhere in this book. Changes to election law are controversial, and, after the wave of HAVA-related state legislation, enactment rates for election-related bills have been low. The overall enactment rate for election-related bills in state legislatures from 2003 through 2015 was around 11 percent, according to National Conference of State Legislatures data. The rate is significantly lower for bills dealing with issues such as election crimes or registration procedures. Dispersion may increase the chances that some portion of an election law agenda is enacted while also reducing the political scrutiny directed toward any given bill.

7. This geography, of course, overlaps in important ways with that of the 1960s. As the dissenters in *Shelby County* noted, the states subject to preclearance have also remained far more likely to lose cases under Section 2 of the VRA, which provides remedies against electoral practices that have discriminatory effects. The core disagreement in *Shelby County* has widely been construed as one about state vs. individual rights. Yet it can also be readily understood as a disagreement about time and history. The majority effectively took the view that the VRA had been devised to combat a historically specific mode of racial discrimination and pointed to evidence that the sharpest contours of that pattern of extreme racial inequality in electoral participation had been worn down in the ensuing fifty years. The majority, further, gave very serious weight to the finding in *South Carolina v. Katzenbach* that preclearance was justified as an exceptional and temporary intervention. The temporal metaphors in the Court and

dissenting opinions in *Shelby County* are thus quite different: the Court viewed preclearance as a curative "strong medicine" administered against the "infection" of racial discrimination in voting; the dissent saw an "umbrella" providing continuous protection in an ongoing "rainstorm."

8. However, it is notable that this decision involved two concurring opinions from Justices Thomas and Alito. In these concurrences, both justices stress that they do not acknowledge one person, one vote to be a constitutionally valid principle and adduce other reasons for holding that Texas could not be compelled to apportion on the basis of eligible voter population.

9. Many states have modified their voter identification laws to remove any directly imposed administrative costs on voters as some courts may treat these as a poll tax. See the dissent in *Veasey v. Perry*.

10. Although the proof-of-citizenship provision alone certainly did not determine the outcome of the election, it likely had a large effect on the margin of victory: 21,473 new registrations were suspended on the eve of an election decided by 32,096 votes. Based on party affiliation and voting patterns, it is likely that some 75 percent of suspended registrants would have voted against Brownback (data are drawn from Gruver 2014; and Kansas Secretary of State 2014). Expert testimony in *Fish v. Kobach* described persistently high rates of registration suspensions while this provision remained in effect.

11. Older or physically disabled voters are more likely to vote absentee, so such restrictions can make it particularly difficult for these populations to register; restrictive provisions are based in the view that these populations can also be more susceptible to coercion or deception. In some cases, relevant information for absentee voting is intentionally dispersed. In Indiana, a 2012 law mandated that absentee voter applications must provide the individual's voter identification number, but a 2013 law provides that registrars may not include this number in correspondence with registered voters, making it difficult for individuals to obtain a datum necessary for absentee voting.

12. North Dakota is excluded from this count: it requires identification, but it is the only state that does not employ voter registration.

13. States can also seek to foreground this possible confusion, suggested in the contrasting language on state voter registration forms in use in Kansas and Missouri in 2016. The first piece of text on the Kansas Voter Registration Application reads: "*Warning: If you submit a false voter registration application, you may be convicted and sentenced to up to 17 months in prison.*" Missouri places its warning in much smaller print at the bottom of its voter registration application, in rather more passive language that makes no specific reference to the registration form itself: "Warning: Conviction for making a false statement may result in imprisonment of up to five years and/or a fine of up to $10,000."

14. These felony penalties for handling the absentee ballot of a nonrelative are intended to prevent vote buying, which is illegal throughout the United

States. However, these prohibitions on handling of absentee ballots do not deal with intent and could in principle be used to prosecute individuals for providing innocuous assistance.

15. Though it can also be noted that early voting provides a fine example of the difficulties of predicting how administrative practices will interact with voting behavior. In the 2016 general election, many states experienced record rates of early voting; given the evidence of past elections, this suggested that overall turnout would be exceptionally high. Early voting rates in Kansas, e.g., led the Office of the Kansas Secretary of State to predict overall turnout at well over 70 percent, a remarkably high figure, especially in a state whose top-of-ticket races were not competitive. However, turnout in 2016 was generally comparable to or lower than turnout in 2012, suggesting that high-propensity voters simply voted early in response to messaging that stressed the importance of early voting and the hazard of long lines on Election Day.

16. In 2015, the Texas State Legislature mandated participation in Crosscheck, evidently making it the first state to join by legislative rather than administrative means. Legislatures in other states have voted against participation. The most notable refusal has been Wisconsin, where the Government Accountability Board (GAB), a unique administrative entity, mounted very stiff opposition to Crosscheck and related voter roll maintenance practices (Cheng et al. 2013; Haas 2015). The GAB's stance on voter list maintenance was the stated reason behind the Wisconsin Senate's efforts to abolish the GAB in 2015 (Richmond 2015).

17. Fifteen of the twenty-one state pairs in which the number of migrants exceeded the number of Crosscheck matches included Idaho, Nebraska, or South Dakota, whose overall match rates were far lower than those of other participating states. These are also the least populous and most homogeneous states in Crosscheck—as the following analysis will suggest, match rates in them were probably low because fewer of the matches were spurious.

18. The preceding discussion sets forth a view of population structure that suggests a greater likelihood of spurious matches among members of minority groups, and the analysis presented here is consistent with that view. However, it should of course be borne in mind that these regressions are reliant on an ecological mode of reasoning. A direct comparison of voter rolls would provide a stronger test of the hypothesized cause of excess matches offered here.

19. Many scholars have also evinced a preference for a more thoroughly administrative approach to the regulation of elections in the United States (for a summary, see Zipkin [2012]). This view has been less pronounced after *Shelby County*, not only because that decision adversely affects the legal plausibility of the federal administration argument, but also because it challenges more basic political assumptions underpinning this view (King and Smith 2016).

484 NOTES
Chapter Five

1. This book's claims for the importance of studying state governments rest partly on a view that any particular state or grouping of states possesses important legal and administrative power. But that power is more than a legal abstraction: states have distinctive histories, political cultures, and institutions, and these must be understood in order to fill out the picture. This chapter suggests that Kansas is a case that is particularly illuminating. Two others would also merit particular attention. Arizona has an unusually expansive set of direct democratic devices that have played a role in the state's immigration, elections, and union policy. The account offered in this book takes the dispositions of the electorate mainly as a background enabling condition for the activity of executive officeholders, rather than something to be explained. But, of course, voters do matter, and Arizona might provide an unusually clear view of the connection between citizen participation, ideas of citizenship, and state government. In Michigan, racial divisions, the fiscal consequences of deindustrialization, and the extraordinarily strong executive powers wielded by Governor Rick Snyder have created exceedingly sharp conflicts between the state government and municipalities. On some regulatory matters, such conflict is common across states with Republican-controlled governments (Warner and Shapiro 2013; Fisk 2016; Einstein and Glick 2017). However, a study of Michigan would be especially revealing for understanding the second-order consequences of conflicts within the fiscal and administrative structure of federalism (Anderson 2014; Peck 2014; Kirkpatrick 2016), including how these figured in one of the great policy calamities and environmental injustices of recent American history: the Flint water crisis.

2. This is, itself, a likely cause of the state's movement away from varieties of political radicalism; Populism was a distinctly rural phenomenon. So, to a substantial degree, was the state's labor radicalism, which centered on mining and oil drilling. William Allen White's famous condemnation of Populism was, among other things, a city dweller's view of rural politics.

3. Although these key figures are well to the right of the state's overall political sentiment, it is evident that they must have fashioned some coalition, even if transient, to win election. The coalition is similar to the one that narrowly elected Scott Walker in Wisconsin: a combination of rural voters with diminished faith in the ability of government to serve their interests and suburban voters who are willing to support state government contraction and provide relevant public goods locally (see Cramer 2016).

4. Much the same can be said of the state's other major recent foray into electronic government: the use of electronic filing in the state court system, the main purpose of which is to deal with the effects of high caseload with reduced staff.

5. Social scientists have taken a strong interest in the promise and failings of online political participation in general and electronic government practices in particular. (This sets wholly aside the effects of social media platforms on news consumption and engagement and considers only direct interaction with government.) Online forms of political activity have prompted some increase in engagement (Polletta and Chen 2013; but see also Oser, Hooghe, and Marien 2013), but they are generally the domain of those with the same high socioeconomic status characteristic of American political participation offline (Best and Krueger 2005; Scholzman, Verba, and Brady 2010). Further, partisan practices and dynamics have migrated online. For instance, astroturfing, in which private actors create a semblance of public support for desired policy changes, has been a major tool for those seeking to reduce state regulation (Lyon and Maxwell 2004; Fallin, Grana, and Glantz 2014). Online astroturfing is common (Klotz 2007; Conover et al. 2012; Mix and Waldo 2015). Electronic government efforts provide online frameworks for citizens to participate in policy-making activity. These are ordinarily meant to promote openness and transparency (Bingham 2010; Bryson et al. 2013, 25–26) and are strongly analogous to offline contexts of participation (Boehle and Riehm 2013; Duvivier 2013). The digitization of the federal agency notice-and-comment rulemaking process did not substantially alter the structure of the rulemaking framework, which has existed since the 1940s (Benjamin 2006): citizen contributions are generally of little use to agency regulators (Coglianese 2006; Farina et al. 2012; Epstein, Newhart, and Vernon 2014). At the same time, electronic rulemaking has allowed the extension of tactics used in lobbying legislatures by electronic means, with generally undesirable results (Zavestoski, Shulman, and Schlosberg 2006; Shulman 2009; Shkabatur 2012). Large volumes of form letter comments are of little use to rulemakers (Mendelson 2010; Merriman 2017).

6. The Tennessee office has, as a legislative rather than an executive entity, different commitments but has approached such proposals similarly: it forwarded all suggestions to the legislature but noted that many of them were "policy decisions" (Barnes and Himes 2015; Garrett and Himes 2016). By taking a very narrow view of its own mandate, the Tennessee office claimed that it could take no position on these proposals.

Chapter Six

1. Likewise, Trump's campaign rhetoric and public persona have undoubtedly strengthened social scientific interest in populism, including classification of varieties and definitions of populist politics. The Brexit referendum, Trump's election in the United States, and the spike in support for right-populist parties such as France's National Front and the Alternative for Germany serve as important

prods to intensify a thoughtful program of research already under way before these events (see, e.g., Bonikowski and DiMaggio 2016; and Bonikowski and Gidron 2016). Populism will not be discussed here, for the simple reason that the Trump administration's major policy actions have not inclined seriously in that direction.

2. His vacated Senate seat was initially filled by Alabama attorney general Luther Strange—and it may be recalled here that, during Strange's tenure, Alabama was the state that most often signed amicus briefs in state-initiated suits against the Obama administration and that Strange was chairman of the Republican Attorneys General Association. He was President Trump's initial choice in the special election.

3. A notable exception was Gorsuch's regularly finding in favor of Indian tribes during his tenure on the Tenth Circuit (Dossett 2018)—a pattern arguably consistent with his relatively favorable view of states' claims.

4. And, here, one may note similarities between the quick formation of the Climate Alliance in response to the withdrawal from the Paris Climate Accords and an earlier liberal campaign modeled on the state balanced-budget campaigns discussed in chapter 3. WolfPAC—a group led by liberal activists—arose to coordinate spontaneous state opposition to the Supreme Court's campaign finance ruling in *Citizens United v. FEC*. It sought to use state petitions to secure a limited constitutional convention to pass an amendment regulating campaign finance. It had some initial success in gaining introduction of its proposal in state legislatures, and at least five states formally adopted its petition.

5. Thus, there were high legal as well as political stakes in *Gill v. Whitford*, a case that challenged partisan (rather than racial) gerrymandering: there, the petitioners asked the Court to adopt a purely empirically derived figure (an 8 percent partisan efficiency gap in the first election under a new districting scheme) as a legal test. The Court was unanimous that such evidence was not sufficient to establish standing.

6. Although the legal matters are not settled in either case, the drift of judicial reasoning is such that courts could conceivably uphold the legality of both California's law forbidding local cooperation with civil detainer requests and Texas' law compelling such cooperation.

7. To the matter of symmetry can be added the issue of comity. The possibility that states could use litigation to seek remedies against other states is a potential check on divergence (Gerken and Holtzblatt 2014), though it is evidently a weak and slow one. Interstate environmental externalities are common (Monogan, Konisky, and Woods 2017) even though they are likely legally actionable. And the example of interstate water compacts shows that state governments typically prefer to allocate minimal resources and authority to compact administrations even when relatively modest increases in appropriations and power might make it much easier to resolve disagreements cooperatively (see Heikkila, Schlager,

and Davis 2011; and Merriman 2017). Given that judicial remedies for interstate water disputes can be extraordinarily costly, slow, and unpredictable, it appears that states often prefer a ton of cure to an ounce of prevention.

8. One can find considered arguments that the phenomenon of neoliberalism is, in essence, a strictly necessary result of the political economy of post-industrial capitalism, leading to the conclusion that the demise of the welfare state is more or less inevitable (e.g., Streeck 2016) as well as some less considered arguments that it is a purely ideological phenomenon. But most work on the phenomenon maintains some distinction between neoliberalism as a scholarly idea, a political program, and a necessary result of the political economy of postindustrial capitalism (see Mudge 2008). State-to-state variation in the turn toward efficiency, partnership, and a client orientation in service provision seems an especially good demonstration that the truth is somewhere in the middle. No American state has been able to afford to preserve a public bureaucracy structured on classic Wilsonian lines, but only a handful of states can be said to have sought to make markets the guiding principle of government structure.

Works Cited

Abbott, Andrew. 1999. *Department and Discipline: Chicago Sociology at One Hundred*. Chicago: University of Chicago Press.

Adut, Ari. 2012. "A Theory of the Public Sphere." *Sociological Theory* 30 (4): 238–62.

Ahler, Douglas J. 2014. "Self-Fulfilling Misperceptions of Public Polarization." *Journal of Politics* 76 (3): 607–20.

Ahlquist, John S., Kenneth R. Mayer, and Simon Jackman. 2014. "Alien Abduction and Voter Impersonation in the 2012 U.S. General Election: Evidence from a Survey List Experiment." *Election Law Journal* 13 (4): 460–75.

Aistrup, Joseph A. 1996. *The Southern Strategy Revisited: Republican Top-Down Advancement in the South*. Lexington: University Press of Kentucky.

Albiston, Catherine. 2010. *Institutional Inequality and the Mobilization of the Family and Medical Leave Act*. New York: Cambridge University Press.

Albiston, Catherine R., and Laura Beth Nielsen. 2014. "Funding the Cause: How Public Interest Law Organizations Fund Their Activities and Why It Matters for Social Change." *Law and Social Inquiry* 39 (1): 62–95.

Aldrich, John H. 2011. *Why Parties? A Second Look*. Chicago: University of Chicago Press.

Alvord, Daniel. 2018. "Small Businesses and the Kansas Tax Cuts: An Odd Case of Business Mobilization." Paper presented at the twentieth Chicago Ethnography Conference, Chicago, March 2018.

Alvord, Daniel R., Cecilia Menjívar, and Andrea Gómez Cervantes. 2018. "The Legal Violence in the 2017 Executive Orders: The Expansion of Immigrant Criminalization in Kansas." *Social Currents*. https://doi.org/10.1177/2329496518762001.

Ambar, Saladin M. 2012. *How Governors Built the Modern American Presidency*. Philadelphia: University of Pennsylvania Press.

Amenta, Edwin. 1998. *Bold Relief: Institutional Politics and the Origins of Modern American Social Policy*. Princeton, NJ: Princeton University Press.

Amenta, Edwin, Neal Caren, Tina Fetner, and Michael P. Young. 2002. "Challenges and States: Toward a Political Sociology of Social Movements." *Sociological Views on Political Participation in the 21st Century* 10:47–83.

Anderson, Margo J. 2015. *The American Census: A Social History.* 2nd ed. New Haven, CT: Yale University Press.

Anderson, Michelle Wilde. 2014. "The New Minimal Cities." *Yale Law Journal* 123:1118–1227.

Ansell, Christopher K. 2011. *Pragmatist Democracy: Evolutionary Learning as Public Philosophy.* New York: Oxford University Press.

Ansolabehere, Stephen, and Nathaniel Persily. 2008. "Vote Fraud in the Eye of the Beholder: The Role of Public Opinion in the Challenge to Voter Identification Requirements." *Harvard Law Review* 121 (7): 1737–74.

Ansolabehere, Stephen, and James M. Snyder. 2008. *The End of Inequality: One Person, One Vote and the Transformation of American Politics.* New York: Norton.

Ashbee, Edward. 2011. "Bewitched—the Tea Party Movement: Ideas, Interests, and Institutions." *Political Quarterly* 82 (2): 157–64.

Aylsworth, Leon E. 1931. "The Passing of Alien Suffrage." *American Political Science Review* 25 (1): 114–16.

Babbitt, Bruce. 1982. "Federalism and the Environment: An Intergovernmental Perspective on the Sagebrush Rebellion." *Environmental Law* 12 (4): 847–62.

Bader, Robert Smith. 1986. *Prohibition in Kansas: A History.* Lawrence: University Press of Kansas.

———. 1988. *Hayseeds, Moralizers, and Methodists: The Twentieth-Century Image of Kansas.* Lawrence: University Press of Kansas.

Bailey, Michael A., Jonathan Mummolo, and Hans Noel. 2012. "Tea Party Influence: A Story of Activists and Elites." *American Politics Research* 40 (5): 769–804.

Baker, Zeke. 2017. "Climate State: Science-State Struggles and the Formation of Climate Science in the US from the 1930s to 1960s." *Social Studies of Science.* https://doi.org/10.1177/0306312717725205.

Balz, Dan. 2010. "The Republican Takeover in the States." *Washington Post,* November 14, 2010.

Banaszak, Lee Ann. 2005. "Inside and Outside the State: Movement Insider Status, Tactics, and Public Policy Achievements." In *Routing the Opposition: Social Movements, Public Policy, and Democracy,* ed. David S. Meyer, Valerie Jenness, and Helen Ingram, 149–76. Minneapolis: University of Minnesota Press.

Banks, Antoine J. 2014. *Anger and Racial Politics: The Emotional Foundation of Racial Attitudes in America.* New York: Cambridge University Press.

Barber, Michael J. 2016. "Ideological Donors, Contribution Limits, and the Polarization of American Legislatures." *Journal of Politics* 78 (1): 296–310.

Barnes, Joseph, and Douglas Himes. 2015. *Office of the Repealer—2014 Annual Report*. Nashville: General Assembly of Tennessee Office of Legal Services. http://www.capitol.tn.gov/joint/staff/legal/2014%20Office%20of%20the%20Repealer.pdf.

Barrilleaux, Charles, and Carlisle Rainey. 2014. "The Politics of Need: Examining Governors' Decisions to Oppose the 'Obamacare' Medicaid Expansion." *State Politics and Policy Quarterly* 14 (4): 437–60.

Barron, David J., and Todd D. Rakoff. 2013. "In Defense of Big Waiver." *Columbia Law Review* 113 (2): 265–345.

Barry, Francis S. 2009. *The Scandal of Reform: The Grand Failures of New York's Political Crusaders and the Death of Nonpartisanship*. New Brunswick, NJ: Rutgers University Press.

Bartels, Larry M. 2006. "What's the Matter with *What's the Matter with Kansas?*" *Quarterly Journal of Political Science* 1:201–26.

Baum, Lawrence. 2014. "Hiring Supreme Court Law Clerks: Probing the Ideological Linkage between Judges and Justices." *Marquette Law Review* 98 (1): 333–60.

Baumgartner, Frank R., and Bryan D. Jones. 2015. *The Politics of Information: Problem Definition and the Course of Public Policy in America*. Chicago: University of Chicago Press.

Beckwith, Kate. 2015. "Narratives of Defeat: Explaining the Effects of Loss in Social Movements." *Journal of Politics* 77 (1): 2–13.

Bednar, Jenna. 2011. "The Political Science of Federalism." *Annual Review of Political Science* 7:269–88.

Behrens, Angela, Christopher Uggen, and Jeff Manza. 2002. "Ballot Manipulation and the 'Menace of Negro Domination': Racial Threat and Felon Disenfranchisement in the United States, 1850–2002." *American Journal of Sociology* 109 (3): 559–605.

Beienberg, Sean. 2014. "Contesting the U.S. Constitution through State Amendments: The 2011 and 2012 Elections." *Political Science Quarterly* 129 (1): 55–85.

Benetsky, Megan J., Charlynn A. Burd, and Melanie A. Rapino. 2015. "Young Adult Migration: 2007–2009 to 2010–2012." American Community Survey Reports, ACS-31. Washington, DC: US Census Bureau.

Benjamin, Gerald, and Zachary Keck. 2011. "Executive Orders and Gubernatorial Authority to Reorganize State Government." *Albany Law Review* 74 (4): 1611–34.

Benjamin, Stuart Minor. 2006. "Evaluating E-Rulemaking: Public Participation and Political Institutions." *Duke Law Journal* 55 (5): 893–941.

Bensel, Richard F. 1990. *Yankee Leviathan: The Origins of Central State Authority in America, 1859–1877*. New York: Cambridge University Press.

Benson, Jocelyn Friedrichs. 2009. "Voter Fraud or Voter Defrauded? Highlighting an Inconsistent Consideration of Election Fraud." *Harvard Civil Rights–Civil Liberties Law Review* 44:1–42.

Bentele, Keith G., and Erin E. O'Brien. 2013. "Jim Crow 2.0? Why States Consider and Adopt Restrictive Voter Access Policies." *Perspectives on Politics* 11 (4): 1088–1126.

Bernstein, Richard B. 1992. "The Sleeper Wakes: The History and Legacy of the Twenty-Seventh Amendment." *Fordham Law Review* 61:497–558.

Best, Samuel J., and Brian S. Krueger. 2005. "Analyzing the Representativeness of Internet Political Participation." *Political Behaviour* 27 (2): 183–216.

Biggers, Daniel R., and Michael J. Hanmer. 2015. "Who Makes Voting Convenient? Explaining the Adoption of Early and No-Excuse Absentee Voting in the American States." *State Politics and Policy Quarterly* 15 (2): 192–210.

Binder, Sarah. 2015. "The Dysfunctional Congress." *Annual Review of Political Science* 18:85–101.

Bingham, Lisa Blomgren. 2010. "The Next Generation of Administrative Law: Building the Legal Infrastructure for Collaborative Governance." *Wisconsin Law Review* 2010:297–356.

Black, Earl, and Merle Black. 2002. *The Rise of Southern Republicans*. Cambridge, MA: Harvard University Press.

Black, Ryan C., Ryan J. Owens, Justin Wedeking, and Patrick C. Wohlfarth. 2016. *US Supreme Court Opinions and Their Audiences*. New York: Cambridge University Press.

Blessett, Brandi. 2015. "Disenfranchisement: Historical Underpinnings and Contemporary Manifestations." *Public Administration Quarterly* 39 (1): 3–50.

Block, Fred L., and Margaret Somers. 2014. *The Power of Market Fundamentalism: Karl Polanyi's Critique*. Cambridge, MA: Harvard University Press.

Bloemraad, Irene. 2006. "Citizenship Lessons of the Past: The Contours of Immigrant Naturalization in the Early 20th Century." *Social Science Quarterly* 87 (5): 927–53.

Blum, John Morton. 1993. *Liberty, Justice, Order: Essays on Past Politics*. New York: Norton.

Boehle, Knud, and Ulrich Riehm. 2013. "E-Petition Systems and Political Participation: About Institutional Challenges and Democratic Opportunities." *First Monday* 18, no. 7. https://doi.org/10.5210/fm.v18i7.4220.

Bolick, Clint. 2011. "Save Our Secret Ballot." *Defining Ideas: A Hoover Institution Journal*, July 15. https://www.hoover.org/research/save-our-secret-ballot.

———. 2012. "State Constitutions as a Bulwark for Freedom." *Oklahoma City University Law Review* 37 (1): 1–16.

Bolleyer, Nicole. 2009. *Intergovernmental Cooperation: Rational Choices in Federal Systems and Beyond*. New York: Oxford University Press.

Bonica, Adam. 2014. "Mapping the Ideological Marketplace." *American Journal of Political Science* 58 (2): 367–86.

Bonikowski, Bart, and Paul DiMaggio. 2016. "Varieties of American Popular Nationalism." *American Sociological Review* 81 (5): 949–80.

Bonikowski, Bart, and Noam Gidron. 2016. "Multiple Traditions in Populism Research: Toward a Theoretical Synthesis." *APSA Comparative Politics Newsletter* 26 (12): 7–14.

Boushey, Graeme T., and Robert J. McGrath. 2016. "Experts, Amateurs, and Bureaucratic Influence in the American States." *Journal of Public Administration Research and Theory.* https://doi.org/10.1093/jopart/muw038.

Bowley, Shaun, and Todd Donovan. 2016. "A Partisan Model of Electoral Reform: Voter Identification Laws and Confidence in State Elections." *State Politics and Policy Quarterly.* https://doi.org/10.1177/1532440015624102.

Bowman, Ann O'M. 2004. "Horizontal Federalism: Exploring Interstate Relations." *Journal of Public Administration Research and Theory* 14 (4): 535–46.

Bowman, Ann O'M., and Neal D. Woods. 2007. "Strength in Numbers: Why States Join Interstate Compacts." *State Politics and Policy Quarterly* 7 (4): 347–68.

Brennan, Thomas E. 2014. *The Article V Amendatory Constitutional Convention: Keeping the Republic in the Twenty-First Century.* Lanham, MD: Lexington.

Brodkin, Evelyn Z., and Malay Majmundar. 2010. "Administrative Exclusion: Organizations and the Hidden Costs of Welfare Claiming." *Journal of Public Administration Research and Theory* 20 (4): 827–48.

Brownback, Sam. 2011. *Executive Order 11-01.* Topeka: Office of the Governor of Kansas. https://kslib.info/DocumentCenter/View/3182.

Bryson, John M., Kathryn S. Quick, Carissa Shively Slotterback, and Barbara C. Crosby. 2013. "Designing Public Participation Processes." *Public Administration Review* 73 (1): 23–34.

Bullock, Charles S. 2010. *Redistricting: The Most Political Activity in America.* Lanham, MD: Rowman & Littlefield.

Bullock, Charles S., Ronald Keith Gaddie, and Justin J. Wert. 2016. *The Rise and Fall of the Voting Rights Act.* Norman: University of Oklahoma Press.

Bulman-Pozen, Jessica. 2014. "Partisan Federalism." *Harvard Law Review* 127 (4): 1077–1146.

———. 2016. "Executive Federalism Comes to America." *Virginia Law Review* 102 (4): 953–1030.

Bulman-Pozen, Jessica, and Heather K. Gerken. 2009. "Uncooperative Federalism." *Yale Law Journal* 118:1256–1310.

Bulman-Pozen, Jessica, and Gillian E. Metzger. 2016. "The President and the States: Patterns of Contestation and Collaboration under Obama." *Publius: The Journal of Federalism* 46 (3): 308–36.

Burbank, Stephen B., and Sean Farhang. 2017. *Rights and Retrenchment: The Counterrevolution against Federal Litigation.* New York: Cambridge University Press.

Burbank, Stephen B., Sean Farhang, and Herbert Kritzer. 2013. "Private Enforcement." *Lewis and Clark Law Review* 17 (3): 637–722.

Burch, Traci. 2011. "Turnout and Party Registration among Criminal Offenders in the 2008 General Election." *Law and Society Review* 45 (3): 699–730.

Burden, Barry C., David T. Canon, Kenneth R. Mayer, and Donald P. Moynihan. 2011. "Early Voting and Election Day Registration in the Trenches: Local Officials' Perceptions of Election Reform." *Election Law Journal* 10 (2):
89–102.

———. 2014. "Election Laws, Mobilization, and Turnout: The Unanticipated
Consequences of Election Reform." *American Journal of Political Science*
58 (1): 95–109.

Burden, Barry C., David T. Canon, Kenneth R. Mayer, Donald P. Moynihan,
and Jacob R. Neiheisel. 2016. "What Happens at the Polling Place: Using Administrative Data to Look Inside Elections." *Public Administration Review.*
https://doi.org/10.1111/puar.12592.

Burke, Brendan F. 2014. "Understanding Intergovernmental Relations, Twenty-
Five Years Hence." *State and Local Government Review* 46 (1): 63–76.

Burstein, Paul. 1991. "Legal Mobilization as a Social Movement Tactic: The
Struggle for Equal Employment Opportunity." *American Journal of Sociology* 96 (5): 1201–25.

———. 2014. *American Public Opinion, Advocacy, and Policy in Congress: What
the Public Wants and What It Gets.* New York: Cambridge University Press.

Butters, Gerald B. 2007. *Banned in Kansas: Motion Picture Censorship, 1915–
1966.* Columbia: University of Missouri Press.

Calavita, Kitty. 2016. *Invitation to Law and Society: An Introduction to the
Study of Real Law.* 2nd ed. Chicago: University of Chicago Press.

Callen, Zachary. 2016. *Railroads and American Political Development: Infrastructure, Federalism, and State Building.* Lawrence: University Press of
Kansas.

———. 2017. "Repurposing the Administrative State." *The Forum: A Journal of
Applied Research in Contemporary Politics* 15 (2): 379–94.

Cammisa, Anne Marie. 1995. *Governments as Interest Groups: Intergovernmental Lobbying and the Federal System.* Westport, CT: Greenwood.

Carpenter, Tim. 2007. "Kansas GOP Forming 'Loyalty Committee.'" *Topeka
Capital-Journal*, July 31, 2007.

Cheng, Dorothy, Brett Halverson, John Magnino, Daniel Marlin, Matthew
Mayeshiba, and Mai Choua Thao. 2013. *Voter List Maintenance in Wisconsin: A Cost-Benefit Analysis.* Madison: Wisconsin Government Accountability Board.

Cho, Wendy K. Tam, James G. Gimpel, and Iris S. Hui. 2013. "Voter Migration
and the Geographic Sorting of the American Electorate." *Annals of the Association of American Geographers* 103 (4): 856–70.

Cho, Wendy K. Tam, James G. Gimpel, and Daron R. Shaw. 2012. "The Tea Party Movement and the Geography of Collective Action." *Quarterly Journal of Political Science* 7:105–33.

Christensen, Ray, and Thomas J. Schultz. 2014. "Identifying Election Fraud Using Orphan and Low Propensity Voters." *American Politics Research* 42 (2): 311–37.

Chu, Johan S. G., and Gerald F. Davis. 2016. "Who Killed the Inner Circle? The Decline of the American Corporate Interlock Network." *American Journal of Sociology* 122 (3): 714–54.

Cigler, Allan J., Mark Joslyn, and Burdett A. Loomis. 2003. "The Kansas Christian Right and the Evolution of Republican Politics." In *The Christian Right in American Politics*, ed. John C. Green, Mark J. Rozell, and Clyde Wilcox, 145–66. Washington, DC: Georgetown University Press.

Citrin, Jack, Donald P. Green, and Morris Levy. 2014. "The Effects of Voter ID Notification on Voter Turnout: Results from a Large-Scale Field Experiment." *Election Law Journal* 13 (2): 228–42.

Clemens, Elisabeth S. 1997. *The People's Lobby: Organizational Innovation and the Rise of Interest Group Politics in the United States, 1890–1925.* Chicago: University of Chicago Press.

Coggins, George Cameron, and Doris K. Nagel. 1990. "Nothing Beside Remains: The Legal Legacy of James G. Watt's Tenure as Secretary of the Interior on Federal Land Law and Policy." *Boston College Environmental Affairs Law Review* 17:473–550.

Coglianese, Cary. 2006. "Citizen Participation in Rulemaking: Past, Present, and Future." *Duke Law Journal* 55 (5): 943–68.

Cohen, Marty, David Karol, Hans Noel, and John Zaller. 2009. *The Party Decides: Presidential Nominations Before and After Reform.* Chicago: University of Chicago Press.

Colby, Thomas. 2016. "In Defense of the Equal Sovereignty Principle." *Duke Law Journal* 65 (6): 1087–1171.

Collins, Jane. 2012. "Theorizing Wisconsin's 2011 Protests: Community-Based Unionism Confronts Accumulation by Dispossession." *American Ethnologist* 39 (1): 6–20.

Commons, John R. 1907. *Race and Immigrants in America.* New York: Macmillan.

Conlan, Timothy. 1998. *From New Federalism to Devolution: Twenty-Five Years of Intergovernmental Reform.* Washington, DC: Brookings Institution Press.

Connell, Raewyn, and Nour Dados. 2014. "Where in the World Does Neoliberalism Come From? The Market Agenda in Southern Perspective." *Theory and Society* 43:117–38.

Conover, Michael D., Bruno Goncalves, Alessandro Flammini, and Filippo Menczer. 2012. "Partisan Asymmetries in Online Political Activity." *EPJ Data Science* 1 (6): 1–19.

Cowan, Sarah. 2015. "Periodic Discordance between Vote Equality and Representational Equality in the United States." *Sociological Science* 2:442–53.

Cramer, Katherine J. 2016. *The Politics of Resentment: Rural Consciousness in Wisconsin and the Rise of Scott Walker.* Chicago: University of Chicago Press.

Cremin, Lawrence. 1961. *The Transformation of the School: Progressivism in American Education.* New York: Knopf.

Cronin, Thomas E. 1989. *Direct Democracy: The Politics of Initiative, Referendum, and Recall.* Cambridge, MA: Harvard University Press.

Cross, Frank B. 2007. *Decision Making in the U.S. Court of Appeals.* Stanford, CA: Stanford University Press.

Cunningham, Dayna L. 1991. "Who Are to Be the Electors? A Reflection on the History of Voter Registration in the United States." *Yale Law and Policy Review* 9 (2): 370–404.

Dahl, Robert. 2003. *How Democratic Is the American Constitution?* New Haven, CT: Yale University Press.

Daniels, Gilda R. 2010. "Outsourcing Democracy: Redefining Public-Private Partnerships in Election Administration." *Denver University Law Review* 88:1–34.

Dannin, Ellen. 2012. "Privatizing Government Services in the Era of ALEC and the Great Recession." *University of Toledo Law Review* 43:503–32.

Davidson, Chandler, Tanya Dunlap, Gale Kenny, and Benjamin Wise. 2008. "Vote Caging as a Republican Ballot Security Technique." *William Mitchell Law Review* 34 (2): 533–62.

Davis, Seth. 2015. "Equal Sovereignty as a Right against a Remedy." *Louisiana Law Review* 76 (1): 83–119.

———. 2016. "Standing Doctrine's State Action Problem." *Notre Dame Law Review* 91:585–648.

DeMoss, Harold R. 2015. "HB 2326—Compact for a Balanced Budget: Written Testimony for the Arizona State Legislature." Phoenix: Arizona House of Representatives Committee on Federalism and States' Rights, February 11.

DeMuth, Christopher. 2016. "Can the Administrative State Be Tamed?" *Journal of Legal Analysis* 8 (1): 121–90.

Desmarais, Bruce A., Jeffrey J. Harden, and Frederick J. Boehmke. 2015. "Persistent Policy Pathways: Inferring Diffusion Networks in the American States." *American Political Science Review* 109 (2): 392–406.

DiGrazia, Joseph. 2017. "Using Internet Search Data to Produce State-Level Measures: The Case of Tea Party Mobilization." *Sociological Methods and Research* 46 (4): 898–925.

Dinan, John. 2014. "Implementing Health Reform: Intergovernmental Bargaining and the Affordable Care Act." *Publius: The Journal of Federalism* 44 (3): 399–425.

DiSalvo, Daniel. 2015. *Government against Itself: Public Union Power and Its Consequences*. New York: Oxford University Press.

Dobbs, Nate. 2015. "The Pitfalls of the Kansas SAFE Act Voter Identification Provision and the Resulting Negative Impact on Provisional Voters." *UMKC Law Review* 83 (2): 427–48.

Docking Institute of Public Affairs. 2015. *Kansas Speaks 2015 Statewide Opinion Survey*. Hays, KS: Fort Hays State University, Docking Institute of Public Affairs.

Dossett, John. 2018. "Justice Gorsuch and Federal Indian Law." *Human Rights* 43, no. 1. https://www.americanbar.org/groups/crsj/publications/crsj-human-rights-magazine/vol--43/vol--43--no--1/justice-gorsuch-and-federal-indian-law.html.

Douglas, Joshua A. 2015. "(Mis)Trusting States to Run Elections." *Washington University Law Review* 92 (3): 553–602.

Drake, Ian J. 2014. "Federal Roadblocks: The Constitution and the National Popular Vote Interstate Compact." *Publius: The Journal of Federalism* 44 (4): 681–701.

Dranias, Nick. 2014. "Introducing 'Article V 2.0': The Compact for a Balanced Budget." Heartland Institute Policy Studies 134. Chicago: Heartland Institute.

Drury, James W. 1970. *The Government of Kansas*. Rev. ed. Lawrence: University Press of Kansas.

———. 1993. *The Government of Kansas*. 4th ed. Lawrence: University of Kansas KU Capitol Center.

Dubin, Michael J. 2007. *Party Affiliations in the State Legislatures: A Year by Year Summary, 1796–2006*. London: McFarland.

Duvivier, K. K. 2013. "E-Legislating." *Oregon Law Review* 92:9–76.

Edelman, Lauren. 2016. *Working Law: Courts, Corporations, and Symbolic Civil Rights*. Chicago: University of Chicago Press.

Edwards, Harry T., and Michael A. Livermore. 2009. "Pitfalls of Empirical Studies That Attempt to Understand the Factors Affecting Appellate Decisionmaking." *Duke Law Journal* 58 (8): 1895–1990.

Einstein, Katherine Levine, and David M. Glick. 2017. "Cities in American Federalism: Evidence on State-Local Government Conflict from a Survey of Mayors." *Publius: The Journal of Federalism* 47 (4): 599–621.

Eisenach, Eldon J. 1994. *The Lost Promise of Progressivism*. Lawrence: University Press of Kansas.

Ellis, Abita R. 2014. "The Meme of Voter Fraud." *Catholic University Law Review* 63 (4): 879–916.

Elmendorf, Christopher S. 2015. "Advisory Rulemaking and the Future of the Voting Rights Act." *Election Law Journal* 14 (3): 260–77.

Elmendorf, Christopher S., and Douglas M. Spencer. 2015. "Administering Section 2 of the Voting Rights Act after *Shelby County*." *Columbia Law Review* 115 (8): 2143–2217.

Environmental Protection Agency. 2012. "National Emission Standards for Hazardous Air Pollutants from Coal- and Oil-Fired Generating Units and Standards of Performance for Fossil-Fuel-Fired Electric Utility, Industrial-Commercial-Institutional, and Small Industrial-Commercial-Institutional Steam Generating Units." *Federal Register* 77 (32): 9304–9513.

———. 2014. "Carbon Pollution Emission Guidelines for Existing Stationary Sources: Electric Utility Generating Units." *Federal Register* 79 (117): 34830–958.

———. 2015. "Clean Water Rule: Definition of 'Waters of the United States.'" *Federal Register* 80 (124): 37054–127.

Epp, Charles R. 1998. *The Rights Revolution: Lawyers, Activists, and Supreme Courts in Comparative Perspective*. Chicago: University of Chicago Press.

———. 2008. "Implementing the Rights Revolution: Repeat Players and the Interpretation of Diffuse Legal Messages." *Law and Contemporary Problems* 71 (2): 41–52.

———. 2010. *Making Rights Real: Activists, Bureaucrats, and the Creation of the Legalistic State*. Chicago: University of Chicago Press.

Epstein, Dmitry, Mary Newhart, and Rebecca Vernon. 2014. "Not by Technology Alone: The 'Analog' Aspects of Online Public Engagement in Policymaking." *Government Information Quarterly* 31:337–44.

Epstein, Lee, William Landes, and Richard Posner. 2013. *The Behavior of Federal Judges: A Theoretical and Empirical Study of Rational Choice*. Cambridge, MA: Harvard University Press.

Epstein, Lee, and Eric A. Posner. 2017. "The Decline of Supreme Court Deference to the President." Public Law and Legal Theory Working Paper no. 618. Chicago: University of Chicago Law School.

Epstein, Lee, Jeffrey A. Segal, Harold J. Spaeth, and Thomas G. Walker. 2015. *The Supreme Court Compendium: Data, Decisions, and Developments*. 6th ed. Thousand Oaks, CA: CQ Press.

Fallin, Amanda, Rachel Grana, and Stanton A. Glantz. 2014. "'To Quarterback behind the Scenes, Third-Party Efforts': The Tobacco Industry and the Tea Party." *Tobacco Control* 23 (4): 322–31.

Farhang, Sean. 2010. *The Litigation State: Public Regulation and Private Lawsuits in the United States*. Princeton, NJ: Princeton University Press.

Farhang, Sean, and Miranda Yaver. 2015. "Divided Government and the Fragmentation of American Law." *American Journal of Political Science*. https://doi.org/10.1111/ajps.12188.

Farina, Cynthia R., Mary Newhart, Josiah Heidt, and Cornell eRulemaking Initiative. 2012. "Rulemaking vs. Democracy: Judging and Nudging Public Participation That Counts." *Michigan Journal of Environmental and Administrative Law* 2 (1): 123–71.

Federal Elections Commission. 2013. "Official 2012 Presidential Election Results." https://transition.fec.gov/pubrec/fe2012/2012presgeresults.pdf.

———. 2017. "Official 2016 Presidential Election Results." https://transition.fec.gov/pubrec/fe2016/2016presgeresults.pdf.

Feinman, Ronald L. 1981. *The Twilight of Progressivism: The Western Republican Senators and the New Deal.* Baltimore: Johns Hopkins University Press.

Fenton, William B. 1965. *The Office of the Kansas Revisor of Statutes.* Lawrence, KS: Governmental Research Center.

Filene, Peter G. 1970. "An Obituary for the 'Progressive Movement.'" *American Quarterly* 22 (1): 20–34.

Finley, Keith M. 2008. *Delaying the Dream: Southern Senators and the Fight against Civil Rights, 1938–1965.* Baton Rouge: Louisiana State University Press.

Fisher, Dana. 2006. *Activism, Inc.: How the Outsourcing of Grassroots Campaigns Is Strangling Progressive Politics in America.* Stanford, CA: Stanford University Press.

Fisk, Jonathan M. 2016. "Fractured Relationships: Exploring Municipal Defiance in Colorado, Texas, and Ohio." *State and Local Government Review* 48 (2): 75–86.

FitzGerald, David Scott, and David Cook-Martin. 2014. *Culling the Masses: The Democratic Origins of Racist Immigration Policy in the Americas.* Cambridge, MA: Harvard University Press.

Fleming, Rick A. 2011. "100 Years of Securities Law: Examining a Foundation Laid in the Kansas Blue Sky." *Washburn Law Journal* 50:583–610.

Flentje, H. Edward, and Joseph A. Aistrup. 2010. *Kansas Politics and Government: The Clash of Political Cultures.* Lincoln: University of Nebraska Press.

Foner, Eric. 2014. *Reconstruction: America's Unfinished Revolution, 1863–1877.* Updated ed. New York: Perennial.

Fourcade, Marion, Etienne Ollion, and Yann Algan. 2015. "The Superiority of Economists." *Journal of Economic Perspectives* 29 (1): 89–113.

Fox, Cybelle, and Thomas A. Guglielmo. 2012. "Defining America's Racial Boundaries: Blacks, Mexicans, and European Immigrants, 1890–1945." *American Journal of Sociology* 118 (2): 327–79.

Fraga, Bernard L., and Julie Lee Merseth. 2016. "Examining the Causal Impact of the Voting Rights Act Language Minority Provisions." *Journal of Race, Ethnicity, and Politics* 1 (1): 31–59.

Frank, Thomas. 2004. *What's the Matter with Kansas? How Conservatives Won the Heart of America.* New York: Metropolitan.

Franklin, John Hope. 1980. *From Slavery to Freedom: A History of Negro Americans.* New York: Knopf.

Frederickson, H. George. 1994. *Public Policy and the Two States of Kansas.* Lawrence: University Press of Kansas.

Freeman, Jody, and Adrian Vermeule. 2007. "*Massachusetts v EPA*: From Politics to Expertise." *Supreme Court Review* 2007 (1): 51–110.

Frohnen, Bruce P., and George W. Carey. 2016. *Constitutional Morality and the Rise of Quasi-Law.* Cambridge, MA: Harvard University Press.

Galanter, Marc. 1974. "Why the 'Haves' Come Out Ahead: Speculations on the Limits of Legal Change." *Law and Society Review* 9 (1): 95–160.

Gardbaum, Stephen. 1997. "New Deal Constitutionalism and the Unshackling of the States." *University of Chicago Law Review* 64 (2): 483–566.

Garrett, Karen, and Douglas Himes. 2016. *Office of the Repealer—2015 Annual Report.* Nashville: General Assembly of Tennessee Office of Legal Services. http://www.capitol.tn.gov/joint/staff/legal/2015%20Office%20of%20the%20Repealer.pdf.

Garrett, Kristin N., and Joshua M. Jansa. 2015. "Interest Group Influence in Policy Diffusion Networks." *State Politics and Policy Quarterly* 15 (3): 387–417.

Gerken, Heather. 2013a. "Exit, Voice, and Disloyalty." *Duke Law Journal* 62:1349–86.

———. 2013b. "The Federalis(m) Society." *Harvard Journal of Law and Public Policy* 36:941–47.

———. 2014. "The Loyal Opposition." *Yale Law Journal* 123:101–37.

Gerken, Heather, and Ari Holtzblatt. 2014. "The Political Safeguards of Horizontal Federalism." *Michigan Law Review* 113 (1): 57–120.

Gluck, Abbe R., Anne Joseph O'Connell, and Rosa Po. 2015. "Unorthodox Lawmaking, Unorthodox Rulemaking." *Columbia Law Review* 115:1789–1865.

Goelzhauser, Greg, and Nicole Vouvalis. 2012. "State Coordinating Institutions and Agenda Setting on the U.S. Supreme Court." *American Politics Research* 41 (5): 819–38.

Goodnow, Frank K. 2002. *Politics and Administration.* Reprint, New Brunswick, NJ: Transaction. First published in 1900 by Macmillan.

Gormley, William T. 2006. "Money and Mandates: The Politics of Intergovernmental Conflict." *Publius: The Journal of Federalism* 36 (4): 523–40.

Gosling, James J. 2015. *Budgetary Politics in American Governments.* New York: Routledge.

Graham, James M. 1972. "Law's Labor Lost: Judicial Politics in the Progressive Era." *Wisconsin Law Review* 1972:447–76.

Grantham, Dewey W. 1983. *Southern Progressivism: The Reconciliation of Progress and Tradition.* Knoxville: University of Tennessee Press.

Greenberg, Pierce. 2015. "Strengthening Sociological Research through Public Records Requests." *Social Currents.* https://doi.org/10.1177/2329496515629646.

Griggs, Burke W. 2017. "The Political Cultures of Irrigation and the Proxy Battles of Interstate Water Litigation." *Natural Resources Journal* 57:1–73.

Grossman, Matt, and David A. Hopkins. 2015. "Ideological Republicans and Group Interest Democrats: The Asymmetry of American Party Politics." *Perspectives on Politics* 13 (1): 119–39.

Grossman, Matt, and Brendon Swedlow. 2015. "Judicial Contributions to US National Policy Change since 1945." *Journal of Law and Courts* 3 (1): 1–35.

Gruver, Deb. 2014. "More Than 21,000 Kansas' Voter Registrations in Suspense Because of Proof of Citizenship." *Wichita Eagle*, October 31, 2014.

Haas, Michael. 2015. "Testimony of Michael Haas, Elections Division Administrator, Wisconsin Government Accountability Board." Madison: Wisconsin Assembly Committee on Campaigns and Elections, May 19.

Hacker, Jacob S., and Paul Pierson. 2015. "Confronting Asymmetric Polarization." In *Solutions to Political Polarization in America*, ed. Nathaniel Persily, 59–72. New York: Cambridge University Press.

Haeder, Simon F., and David L. Weimer. 2013. "You Can't Make Me Do It: State Implementation of Insurance Exchanges under the Affordable Care Act." *Public Administration Review* 73, suppl. 1:S34–S47.

Haines, Michael R. 2006. "Population, by Sex and Race: 1790–1990." In *Historical Statistics of the United States* (millennial ed.), ed. Susan B. Carter, 48–51. New York: Cambridge University Press.

Hajnal, Zoltan, Nazita Lajevardi, and Lindsay Nielson. 2017. "Voter Identification Laws and the Suppression of Minority Votes." *Journal of Politics* 79 (2): 363–79.

Hale, Kathleen, and Ramona McNeal. 2010. "Election Administration Reform and State Choice: Voter Identification Requirements and HAVA." *Policy Studies Journal* 38 (2): 281–302.

Hall, Jean P., Noelle K. Kurth, Shawna L. C. Chapman, and Theresa I. Shireman. 2015. "Medicaid Managed Care: Issues for Beneficiaries with Disabilities." *Disability and Health Journal* 8 (1): 130–35.

Hall, Matthew E. K. 2011. *The Nature of Supreme Court Power.* New York: Cambridge University Press.

Hamburger, Philip. 2014. *Is Administrative Law Unlawful?* Chicago: University of Chicago Press.

Hansen, John Mark. 1991. *Gaining Access: Congress and the Farm Lobby, 1919–1981.* Chicago: University of Chicago Press.

Harder, Marvin A., and Raymond G. Davis. 1979. *The Legislature as an Organization: A Study of the Kansas Legislature.* Lawrence: University Press of Kansas.

Harrison, Robert. 1997. *State and Society in Twentieth-Century America.* New York: Longman.

Haveman, Heather A. 2015. *Magazines and the Making of Modern America.* Princeton, NJ: Princeton University Press.

Hawley, George. 2016. *Right-Wing Critics of American Conservatism.* Lawrence: University Press of Kansas.

Hayduk, Ron. 2015. "Political Rights in the Age of Migration: Lessons from the United States." *Journal of International Migration and Integration* 16 (1): 99–118.

Hays, Samuel P. 1964. "The Politics of Reform in Municipal Government in the Progressive Era." *Pacific Northwest Quarterly* 55 (4): 157–69.

Heckelman, Jac C. 1995. "The Effect of the Secret Ballot on Voter Turnout Rates." *Public Choice* 82:107–24.

Heikkila, Tanya, Edella Schlager, and Mark W. Davis. 2011. "The Role of Cross-Scale Institutional Linkages in Common Pool Resource Management: Assessing Interstate Compacts." *Policy Studies Journal* 39 (1): 121–45.

Herd, Pamela. 2015. "How Administrative Burdens Are Preventing Access to Critical Income Supports for Older Adults: The Case of the Supplemental Nutrition Assistance Program." *Public Policy and Aging Report* 25 (2): 52–55.

Herron, Michael C., and Daniel A. Smith. 2012. "Souls to the Polls: Early Voting in Florida in the Shadow of House Bill 1355." *Election Law Journal* 11 (3): 331–47.

Hertel-Fernandez, Alexander. 2014. "Who Passes Business's 'Model Bills'? Policy Capacity and Corporate Influence in U.S. State Politics." *Perspectives on Politics* 12 (3): 582–602.

———. 2016. "American Employers as Political Machines." *Journal of Politics.* https://doi.org/10.1086/687885.

Hertel-Fernandez, Alexander, and Konstantin Kashin. 2015. "Capturing Business Power across the States with Text Reuse." https://projects.iq.harvard.edu/files/govposters/files/hertelfernandez_kashin.pdf.

Hertel-Fernandez, Alexander, and Theda Skocpol. 2016. "How the Right Trounced Liberals in the States." *Democracy* 39:45–59.

Hertel-Fernandez, Alexander, Theda Skocpol, and Daniel Lynch. 2016. "Business Associations, Conservative Networks, and the Ongoing Republican War over Medicaid Expansion." *Journal of Health Politics, Policy and Law.* https://doi.org/10.1215/03616878-3476141.

Hess, David J., Quan D. Mai, and Kate Pride Brown. 2016. "Red States, Green Laws: Ideology and Renewable Energy Legislation in the United States." *Energy Research and Social Science* 11:19–28.

Hess, David J., Christopher A. Wold, Scott C. Worland, and George M. Hornberger. 2017. "Measuring Urban Water Conservation Policies: Toward a Comprehensive Index." *Journal of the American Water Resources Association* 53 (2): 442–55.

Hicks, William D. 2015. "Partisan Competition and the Efficiency of Lawmaking in American State Legislatures, 1991–2009." *American Politics Research*
43 (5): 743–70.

Hicks, William D., Seth C. McKee, Mitchell D. Sellers, and Daniel A. Smith.
2015. "A Principle or a Strategy? Voter Identification Laws and Partisan
Competition in the American States." *Political Research Quarterly* 68 (1):
18–33.

Hicks, William D., Seth C. McKee, and Daniel A. Smith. 2016. "The Determi-
nants of State Legislator Support for Restrictive Voter ID Laws." *State Politics and Policy Quarterly*. https://doi.org/10.1177/1532440016630752.

Hill, Seth J., and Chris Tausanovitch. 2015. "A Disconnect in Representation?
Comparison of Trends in Congressional and Public Polarization." *Journal of
Politics* 77 (4): 1058–75.

Hobby, Bill, Mark P. Jones, Jim Granato, and Renee Cross. 2015. "The Texas
Voter ID Law and the 2014 Election: A Study of Texas's 23rd Congressional
District." http://bakerinstitute.org/media/files/files/e0029eb8/Politics-Voter
ID-Jones-080615.pdf.

Hofstadter, Richard. 1949. "From Calhoun to the Dixiecrats." *Social Research*
16 (2): 135–50.

———. 1955. *The Age of Reform: From Bryan to FDR*. New York: Knopf.

———. 1963. *Anti-intellectualism in American Life*. New York: Knopf.

———. 1969. *The Idea of a Party System: The Rise of Legitimate Opposition in
the United States, 1780–1840*. Berkeley and Los Angeles: University of California Press.

Hollis-Brusky, Amanda. 2011. "Support Structures and Constitutional Change:
Teles, Southworth, and the Conservative Legal Movement." *Law and Social
Inquiry* 36 (2): 516–36.

———. 2013. "'It's the Network': The Federalist Society as a Supplier of Intellectual Capital for the Supreme Court." *Studies in Law, Politics, and Society*
61:137–78.

Hollis-Brusky, Amanda, and Joshua C. Wilson. 2017. "Playing for the Rules:
How and Why New Christian Right Public Interest Law Firms Invest in Sec-
ular Litigation." *Law and Policy* 39 (2): 121–41.

Hood, M. V., and Charles S. Bullock. 2012. "Much Ado about Nothing? An Empirical Assessment of the Georgia Voter Identification Statute." *State Politics
and Policy Quarterly* 12 (4): 394–414.

Hood, M. V., Quentin Kidd, and Irwin L. Morris. 2001. "The Key Issue: Constit-
uency Effects and Southern Senators' Roll-Call Voting on Civil Rights." *Legislative Studies Quarterly* 26 (4): 599–621.

Hooghe, Liesbet, and Gary Marks. 2003. "Unraveling the Central State, but
How? Types of Multi-level Governance." *American Political Science Review*
97 (2): 233–43.

Howard, Christopher. 2002. "Workers' Compensation, Federalism, and the Heavy Hand of History." *Studies in American Political Development* 16 (1): 28–47.

Huebner, Daniel R. 2014. *Becoming Mead: The Social Process of Academic Knowledge.* Chicago: University of Chicago Press.

Huffman, James. 2016. "The New Sagebrush Rebels." *Defining Ideas: A Hoover Institution Journal*, January 21. https://www.hoover.org/research/new-sage brush-rebels.

Hume, Robert J. 2006. "The Use of Rhetorical Sources by the U.S. Supreme Court." *Law and Society Review* 40 (4): 817–44.

Institute on Taxation and Economic Policy. 2012. "Latest Kansas Tax Bill Carries $680 Million Price Tag and Raises Taxes on Those Least Able to Pay." May 17. https://itep.org/latest-kansas-tax-bill-carries-680-million-price-tag -and-raises-taxes-on-those-least-able-to-pay.

Jacobs, Nicholas. 2017. "An Experimental Test of How Americans Think about Federalism." *Publius: The Journal of Federalism* 47 (4): 572–98.

Jansa, Joshua M., Eric R. Hansen, and Virginia H. Gray. 2018. "Copy and Paste Lawmaking: Legislative Professionalism and Policy Reinvention in the States." *Legislative Studies Quarterly.* https://doi.org/10.1177/1532673X18776628.

Jensen, Jennifer M. 2016. *The Governors' Lobbyists: Federal-State Relations Offices and Governors Associations in Washington.* Ann Arbor: University of Michigan Press.

Jochim, Ashley, and Lesley Lavery. 2015. "The Evolving Politics of the Common Core: Policy Implementation and Conflict Expansion." *Publius: The Journal of Federalism* 45 (3): 380–404.

Johnson, Kevin R. 2015. "Immigration in the Supreme Court, 2009–13: A New Era of Immigration Law Unexceptionalism." *Oklahoma Law Review* 68:57–118.

———. 2016. "Doubling Down on Racial Discrimination: The Racially Disparate Impacts of Crime-Based Removals." *Case Western Reserve Law Review* 66 (4): 993–1037.

Johnson, Kimberley S. 2007. *Governing the American State: Congress and the New Federalism, 1877–1929.* Princeton, NJ: Princeton University Press.

Jones, David K., Katharine W. V. Bradley, and Jonathan Oberlander. 2014. "Pascal's Wager: Health Insurance Exchanges, Obamacare, and the Republican Dilemma." *Journal of Health Politics, Policy and Law* 39 (1): 97–137.

Jones, Jennifer, and Hana E. Brown. 2017. "American Federalism and Racial Formation in Contemporary Immigration Policy: A Processual Analysis of Alabama's HB56." *Ethnic and Racial Studies.* https://doi.org/10.1080/01419870.2017.1403033.

Kalmijn, Matthijs. 1993. "Trends in Black/White Intermarriage." *Social Forces* 72 (1): 119–46.

Kansas Department of Revenue. 2013. "Estimated Effect of Tax Reductions and Increases Enacted since 1995." http://www.ksrevenue.org/pdf/EstEffect.pdf.

———. 2015. "2014 Annual Report." http://ksrevenue.org/pdf/ar14a.pdf.

Kansas Legislative Division of Post Audit. 2018. "Medicaid: Evaluating Kan-Care's Effect on the State's Medicaid Program." http://www.kslpa.org/media/files/reports/r-18-006.pdf.

Kansas Legislative Research Department. 2013. "Executive Reorganization Orders." http://www.kslegresearch.org/KLRD-web/Publications/StateLocalGovt/ERO_memo_2013_update.pdf.

Kansas Secretary of State. 2014. "2014 General Election Official Turnout." Topeka: Office of the Secretary of State. http://www.kssos.org/elections/elections_statistics.html.

———. 2017. "Kobach Secures Ninth Voter Fraud Conviction." Topeka: Office of the Secretary of State. http://www.kssos.org/other/news_releases/PR_2017/NR_2017_5_3.pdf.

Kansas State Library. n.d. "Kansas Governors' Executive Orders." https://kslib.info/Archive.aspx?AMID=41.

Kansas Statistical Abstract. 2014. 49th ed. Lawrence, KS: Institute for Policy and Social Research.

Karch, Andrew, Sean C. Nicholson-Crotty, Neal D. Woods, and Ann O'M. Bowman. 2016. "Policy Diffusion and the Pro-innovation Bias." *Political Research Quarterly* 69 (1): 83–95.

Kasdan, Diana. 2012. *State Restrictions on Voter Registration Drives*. New York: Brennan Center for Justice.

Katz, Ellen D. 2015. "What the Marriage Equality Cases Tell Us about Voter ID." *University of Chicago Legal Forum* 2015:211–42.

Katznelson, Ira, Kim Geiger, and Daniel Kryder. 1993. "Limiting Liberalism: The Southern Veto in Congress, 1933–1950." *Political Science Quarterly* 108 (2): 283–306.

Keiter, Robert B., and John C. Ruple. 2014. "A Legal Analysis of the Transfer of Public Lands Movement." White Paper no. 2014-2. Salt Lake City: University of Utah, Wallace Stegner Center for Land, Resources and the Environment.

Kersch, Ken I. 2011. "Ecumenicalism through Constitutionalism: The Discursive Development of Constitutional Conservatism in *National Review*, 1955–1980." *Studies in American Political Development* 25 (1): 86–116.

Kerwin, Cornelius M., and Scott R. Furlong. 2011. *Rulemaking: How Government Agencies Write Law and Make Policy*. 4th ed. Washington, DC: CQ Press.

Keyssar, Alexander. 2000. *The Right to Vote: The Contested History of Democracy in the United States*. New York: Basic.

Kim, Ae-sook, and Edward Jennings. 2012. "The Evolution of an Innovation:

Variations in Medicaid Managed Care Program Extensiveness." *Journal of Health Politics, Policy and Law* 37 (5): 815–49.

Kincaid, John D. 2016. "The Rational Basis of Irrational Politics: Examining the Great Texas Political Shift to the Right." *Politics and Society.* https://doi.org/10.1177/0032329216674003.

King, Desmond S., and Rogers M. Smith. 2016. "The Last Stand? *Shelby County v. Holder,* White Political Power, and America's Racial Policy Alliances." *Du Bois Review* 13 (1): 25–44.

Kirkpatrick, L. Owen. 2016. "The New Urban Fiscal Crisis: Finance, Democracy, and Municipal Debt." *Politics and Society* 44 (1): 45–80.

Klotz, Robert J. 2007. "Internet Campaigning for Grassroots and Astroturf Support." *Social Science Computer Review* 25 (1): 3–12.

Kobach, Kris W. 1994. "Rethinking Article V: Term Limits and the Seventeenth and Nineteenth Amendments." *Yale Law Journal* 103 (7): 1971–2007.

———. 2005. "The Quintessential Force Multiplier: The Inherent Authority of Local Police to Make Immigration Arrests." *Albany Law Review* 69:179–236.

———. 2007. "Attrition through Enforcement: A Rational Approach to Illegal Immigration." *Tulsa Journal of Comparative and International Law* 15:155–64.

———. 2008. "Reinforcing the Rule of Law: What States Can and Should Do to Reduce Illegal Immigration." *Georgetown Immigration Law Journal* 22:459–84.

Kolb, Felix. 2007. *Protest and Opportunities: The Political Outcomes of Social Movements.* New York: Campus.

Konings, Martijn. 2015. *The Emotional Logic of Capitalism: What Progressives Have Missed.* Stanford, CA: Stanford University Press.

Konisky, David M., and Neal D. Woods. 2016. "Environmental Policy, Federalism, and the Obama Presidency." *Publius: The Journal of Federalism.* https://doi.org/10.1093/pjw004.

Kousser, J. Morgan. 1974. *The Shaping of Southern Politics: Suffrage Restriction and the Establishment of the One-Party South, 1880–1910.* New Haven, CT: Yale University Press.

Kousser, Thad, and Mathew D. McCubbins. 2005. "Social Choice, Crypto-Initiatives, and Policymaking by Direct Democracy." *Southern California Law Review* 78:949–84.

Kramer, Larry D. 2000. "Putting the Politics Back into the Political Safeguards of Federalism." *Columbia Law Review* 100 (1): 215–93.

Krehbiel, Jay N. 2016. "The Politics of Judicial Procedures: The Role of Public Oral Hearings in the German Constitutional Court." *American Journal of Political Science.* https://doi.org/10.1111/ajps.12229.

Krinsky, John. 2013. "The New Tammany Hall? Welfare, Public Sector Unions,

Corruption, and Neoliberal Policy Regimes." *Social Research* 80 (4): 1087–1118.

Kurzman, Charles. 1991. "Convincing Sociologists: Values and Interests in the Sociology of Knowledge." In *Ethnography Unbound: Power and Resistance in the Modern Metropolis*, ed. Michael Burawoy, 250–68. Berkeley and Los Angeles: University of California Press.

Kwak, Sunjoo. 2016. "Cyclical Asymmetry in State Fiscal Policy: Is It Biased toward Big or Small Government?" *American Review of Public Administration*. https://doi.org/10.1177/0275074016638482.

La Forte, Robert Sherman. 1974. *Leaders of Reform: Progressive Republicans in Kansas, 1900–1916*. Lawrence: University Press of Kansas.

Lang, Corey, and Shanna Pearson-Merkowitz. 2015. "Partisan Sorting in the United States, 1972–2012: New Evidence from a Dynamic Analysis." *Political Geography* 48:119–29.

Langholz, Samuel P. 2008. "Fashioning a Constitutional Voter-Identification Requirement." *Iowa Law Review* 93:731–800.

La Roja, Raymond. 2009. "Redistricting: Reading between the Lines." *Annual Review of Political Science* 12:203–23.

Larson, Rhett B. 2015. "Interstitial Federalism." *UCLA Law Review* 62:908–68.

Laumann, Edward O., and David Knoke. 1987. *The Organizational State: Social Choice in National Policy Domains*. Madison: University of Wisconsin Press.

Laversuch, I. M. 2011. "'May Change Name and Pretend to Be Free': A Corpus Linguistic Investigation of Surnames Adopted by Fugitive Slaves as Advertised in Colonial American Newspapers between 1729 and 1818." *Names* 59 (4): 191–203.

Lawson, Gary. 1994. "The Rise and Rise of the Administrative State." *Harvard Law Review* 107 (6): 1231–54.

Lee, Mordecai. 2008. *Bureaus of Efficiency: Reforming Local Government in the Progressive Era*. Milwaukee: Marquette University Press.

Lefler, Dion. 2011. "Opponents: ID Plan Suppresses Voters." *Wichita Eagle*, January 20, 2011.

Lemos, Margaret H. 2012. "Aggregate Litigation Goes Public: Representative Suits by State Attorneys General." *Harvard Law Review* 126 (2): 486–549.

Lemos, Margaret H., and Kevin M. Quinn. 2015. "Litigating State Interests: Attorneys General as Amici." *New York University Law Review* 90:1229–68.

Leonard, Elizabeth Weeks. 2012. "The Rhetoric Hits the Road: State Resistance to Affordable Care Act Implementation." *University of Richmond Law Review* 46:781–822.

Leshy, John D. 1980. "Unraveling the Sagebrush Rebellion: Law, Politics, and Federal Lands." *University of California at Davis Law Review* 14:317–55.

Levendusky, Matthew. 2009. *The Partisan Sort: How Liberals Became Demo-

crats and Conservatives Became Republicans. Chicago: University of Chicago Press.

Levine, Helisse, and Eric Scorsone. 2011. "Institutional Change in the Public Employment Relationship: Implications for State and Local Governments." *State and Local Government Review* 43 (3): 208–14.

Levinson, Daryl J., and Richard H. Pildes. 2006. "Separation of Parties, Not Powers." *Harvard Law Review* 119 (8): 2311–86.

Lienesch, Michael. 2016. "Creating Constitutional Conservatism." *Polity* 48 (3): 387–413.

Link, William A. 1992. *The Paradox of Southern Progressivism, 1880–1930.* Chapel Hill: University of North Carolina Press.

Loomis, Burdett A. 1994. *Time, Politics, and Policies: A Legislative Year.* Lawrence: University Press of Kansas.

Lowry, Bryan. 2015. "Kobach's Voter Prosecutions Draw Scrutiny to Proof-of-Citizenship Requirement." *Wichita Eagle,* October 18, 2015.

Lyon, Thomas P., and John W. Maxwell. 2004. "Astroturf: Interest Group Lobbying and Corporate Strategy." *Journal of Economics and Management Strategy* 13 (4): 561–97.

Macías-Rojas, Patrisia. 2016. *From Deportation to Prison: The Politics of Immigration Enforcement in Post–Civil Rights America.* New York: New York University Press.

Mahoney, Paul G. 2003. "The Origins of the Blue-Sky Laws: A Test of Competing Hypotheses." *Journal of Law and Economics* 46 (1): 229–51.

Markowitz, Peter L. 2015. "Undocumented No More: The Power of State Citizenship." *Stanford Law Review* 67:869–915.

Martin, Isaac W. 2008. *The Permanent Tax Revolt: How the Property Tax Transformed American Politics.* Stanford, CA: Stanford University Press.

———. 2013. *Rich People's Movements: Grassroots Campaigns to Untax the One Percent.* New York: Oxford University Press.

Martin, John Levi. 2009. *Social Structures.* Princeton, NJ: Princeton University Press.

———. 2011. *The Explanation of Social Action.* New York: Oxford University Press.

Mashaw, Jerry L. 2012. *Creating the Administrative Constitution: The Lost One Hundred Years of American Administrative Law.* New Haven, CT: Yale University Press.

Mashaw, Jerry L., and Dylan S. Calsyn. 1996. "Block Grants, Entitlements, and Federalism: A Conceptual Map of Contested Terrain." *Yale Law and Policy Review* 14 (2): 297–324.

Masket, Seth E. 2009. *No Middle Ground: How Informal Party Organizations Control Nominations and Polarize Legislatures.* Ann Arbor: University of Michigan Press.

———. 2016. *The Inevitable Party: Why Attempts to Kill the Party System Fail and How They Weaken Democracy.* New York: Oxford University Press.

Maxwell, Angie, and T. Wayne Parent. 2012. "The Obama Trigger: Presidential Approval and Tea Party Membership." *Social Science Quarterly* 93 (5): 1384–1401.

McCann, Charles R. 2012. *Order and Control in American Socio-economic Thought: Social Scientists and Progressive Era Reform.* New York: Routledge.

McCannon, Kevin. 2016. "Challenges of Health Care Devolution: Problems of Legitimacy, Consumer Knowledge, and Work Transfer in Kansas Medicaid." PhD diss., University of Kansas, Department of Sociology.

McCormick, Peter J. 1995. "The 1992 Secession Movement in Southwest Kansas." *Great Plains Research* 15:247–58.

McCormick, Richard L. 1986. *The Party Period and Public Policy: American Politics from the Age of Jackson to the Progressive Era.* New York: Oxford University Press.

McCright, Aaron M., Riley E. Dunlap, and Chenyang Xiao. 2014. "Increasing Influence of Party Identification on Perceived Scientific Agreement and Support for Government Action on Climate Change in the United States, 2006–12." *Weather, Climate, and Society* 6 (2): 194–201.

McCright, Aaron M., Chenyang Xiao, and Riley E. Dunlap. 2014. "Political Polarization on Support for Government Spending on Environmental Protection in the USA, 1974–2012." *Social Science Research* 48:251–60.

McGerr, Michael. 2003. *A Fierce Discontent: The Rise and Fall of the Progressive Movement in the United States, 1870–1920.* New York: Free Press.

McKee, Seth C. 2015. "Politics Is Local: State Legislator Voting on Restrictive Voter Identification Legislation." *Research and Politics.* https://doi.org/10.1177/2053168015589804.

McKee, Seth C., Ian Ostrander, and M. V. Hood III. 2017. "Out of Step and Out of Touch: The Matter with Kansas in the 2014 Midterm Election." *The Forum: A Journal of Applied Research in Contemporary Politics* 15 (2): 291–312.

McNitt, Andrew D. 2014. "The Tea Party Movement and the 2012 House Elections." *PS: Political Science and Politics* 47 (4): 799–805.

McVeigh, Rory, Kraig Bayerlein, Burrel Vann Jr., and Priyamvada Trivedi. 2014. "Educational Segregation, Tea Party Organizations, and Battles over Distributive Justice." *American Sociological Review* 79 (4): 630–52.

Medvetz, Thomas. 2012a. "'Scholar as Sitting Duck': The Cronon Affair and the Buffer Zone in American Public Debate." *Public Culture* 24 (1): 47–53.

———. 2012b. *Think Tanks in America.* Chicago: University of Chicago Press.

Mendelson, Nina A. 2010. "Rulemaking, Democracy, and Torrents of Email." *George Washington Law Review* 79:1343–80.

Mendez, Matthew S., and Christian R. Grose. 2018. "Doubling Down: Inequality in Responsiveness and the Policy Preferences of Elected Officials." *Legislative Studies Quarterly.* https://doi.org/10.1111/lsq.12204.

Menjívar, Cecilia, Andrea Gómez Cervantes, and Daniel Alvord. 2018. "The Expansion of 'Crimmigration,' Mass Detention, and Deportation." *Sociology Compass* 12, no. 4. https://doi.org/10.1111/soc4.12573.

Merriman, Ben. 2017. "Testing the Great Lakes Compact: Administrative Politics and the Challenge of Environmental Adaptation." *Politics and Society* 45 (3): 441–66.

——. 2018. "Modern State-Federal Conflict: The Central Role of Administration and Administrative Law." In *Handbook of American Public Administration*, ed. H. George Frederickson and Edmund Stazyk, 67–80. Northampton, MA: Elgar.

Mettler, Suzanne. 2011. *The Submerged State: How Invisible Government Policies Undermine American Democracy.* Chicago: University of Chicago Press.

Metzger, Gillian E. 2008. "Administrative Law as the New Federalism." *Duke Law Journal* 57 (2): 2023–2109.

——. 2015. "Agencies, Polarization, and the States." *Columbia Law Review* 115:1739–87.

——. 2017. "1930s Redux: The Administrative State under Siege." *Harvard Law Review* 131 (1): 1–95.

Meyer, David S., and Debra C. Minkoff. 2004. "Conceptualizing Political Opportunity." *Social Forces* 82 (4): 1457–92.

Meyer, Keith G. 1972. "Arrest under the New Kansas Criminal Code." *University of Kansas Law Review* 20:685–744.

Michigan State Budget Office. 2018. *Executive Budget, Fiscal Years 2019 and 2020.* http://www.michigan.gov/documents/budget/FY19_Exec_Budget_613184_7.pdf.

Milkman, Ruth. 2013. "Back to the Future? US Labour in the New Gilded Age." *British Journal of Industrial Relations* 51 (4): 645–65.

Miller, Banks. 2010. "Describing the State Solicitors General." *Judicature* 93 (6): 238–46.

Mills, C. Wright. 1956. *The Power Elite.* New York: Oxford University Press.

Mills, Sarah, and Christopher Gore. 2016. "Public and Local Government Leader Opinions on Environmental Federalism: Comparing Issues and National Contexts." *State and Local Government Review* 48 (3): 165–74.

Miner, Craig. 2002. *Kansas: A History of the Sunflower State, 1854–2000.* Lawrence: University Press of Kansas.

Mix, Tamara L., and Kristin G. Waldo. 2015. "Know(ing) Your Power: Risk Society, Astroturf Campaigns, and the Battle over the Red Rock Coal-Fired Plant." *Sociological Quarterly* 56 (1): 125–51.

Mizruchi, Mark. 2013. *The Fracturing of the American Corporate Elite.* Cambridge, MA: Harvard University Press.

Mizruchi, Mark, and Mikell Hyman. 2014. "Elite Fragmentation and the Decline of the United States." *Political Power and Social Theory* 26:147–94.

Molitor, Abigail B. 2014. "Understanding Equal Sovereignty." *University of Chicago Law Review* 81:1839–82.

Moncrieff, Gary F., and Peverill Squire. 2017. *Why States Matter: An Introduction to State Government*. Lanham, MD: Rowman & Littlefield.

Monogan, James E., David M. Konisky, and Neal D. Woods. 2017. "Gone with
  the Wind: Federalism and the Strategic Location of Air Polluters." *American
  Journal of Political Science* 61 (2): 257–70.

Moran, Rachel F. 2010. "What Counts as Knowledge? A Reflection on Race, Social Science, and the Law." *Law and Society Review* 44 (3–4): 515–52.

Morgan, Kimberly J., and Monica Prasad. 2009. "The Origins of Tax Systems:
  A French-American Comparison." *American Journal of Sociology* 114 (5):
  1350–94.

Moynihan, Donald, and Pamela Herd. 2010. "Red Tape and Democracy: How
  Rules Affect Citizenship Rights." *American Review of Public Administration* 40 (6): 654–70.

Moynihan, Donald, Pamela Herd, and Hope Harvey. 2015. "Administrative Burden: Learning, Psychological, and Compliance Costs in Citizen-State Interactions." *Journal of Public Administration Research and Theory* 25 (1):
  43–69.

Moynihan, Donald, Pamela Herd, and Elizabeth Rigby. 2013. "Policymaking
  by Other Means: Do States Use Administrative Barriers to Limit Access
  to Medicaid?" *Administration and Society*. https://doi.org/10.1177/0095399
  713503540.

Moynihan, Donald, and Stephane Lavertu. 2012. "Cognitive Biases in Governing: Technology Preferences in Election Administration." *Public Administration Review* 72 (1): 68–77.

Mudge, Stephanie L. 2008. "What Is Neo-Liberalism?" *Socio-Economic Review*
  6 (4): 703–31.

Muller, Derek T. 2007. "The Compact Clause and the National Popular Vote Interstate Compact." *Election Law Journal* 6 (4): 372–93.

Nackenoff, Carol. 2014. "The Private Roots of American Political Development:
  The Immigrants' Protective League's 'Friendly and Sympathetic Touch,'
  1908–1924." *Studies in American Political Development* 28 (2): 129–60.

Nall, Clayton. 2015. "The Political Consequences of Spatial Policies: How Interstate Highways Facilitated Geographic Polarization." *Journal of Politics* 77
  (2): 394–406.

National Commission on Federal Election Reform. 2002. *To Assure Pride and
  Confidence in the Electoral Process: Report of the National Commission on
  Federal Election Reform*. Washington, DC: Brookings Institution Press.

NeJaime, Douglas. 2012. "The Legal Mobilization Dilemma." *Emory Law Journal* 61:663–736.

Newport, Frank. 2013. "Alabama, North Dakota, Wyoming Most Conservative States." http://www.gallup.com/poll/160196/alabama-north-dakota-wyoming -conservative-states.aspx#1.

Nicholson-Crotty, Sean. 2012. "Leaving Money on the Table: Learning from Recent Refusals of Federal Grants in the American States." *Publius: The Journal of Federalism* 42 (3): 449–66.

———. 2015. *Governors, Grants, and Elections: Fiscal Federalism in the American States.* Baltimore: Johns Hopkins University Press.

Nicholson-Crotty, Sean S., Neal D. Woods, Ann O'M. Bowman, and Andrew Karch. 2014. "Policy Innovativeness and Interstate Compacts." *Policy Studies Journal* 42 (2): 305–24.

Nickerson, David W. 2015. "Do Voter Registration Drives Increase Participation? For Whom and When?" *Journal of Politics* 77 (1): 88–101.

Noble, Jason. 2012. "Secretary of State's Voter Eligibility Investigation on Hold After Judge Issues Injunction." *Des Moines Register*, September 14.

Nolette, Paul. 2014. "State Litigation during the Obama Administration: Diverging Agendas in an Era of Polarized Politics." *Publius: The Journal of Federalism* 44 (3): 451–74.

———. 2015. *Federalism on Trial: State Attorneys General and National Policymaking in Contemporary America.* Lawrence: University Press of Kansas.

Nou, Jennifer. 2013. "Sub-regulating Elections." *Supreme Court Review* 2013 (1): 135–82.

Nugent, John Douglas. 2009. *Safeguarding Federalism: How States Protect Their Interests in National Policymaking.* Norman: University of Oklahoma Press.

Nugent, Walter. 2013. *The Tolerant Populists: Kansas Populism and Nativism.* 2nd ed. Chicago: University of Chicago Press.

Nussbaumer, Kirsten. 2013. "The Election Law Connection and U.S. Federalism." *Publius: The Journal of Federalism* 43 (3): 392–427.

Oates, Wallace E. 1972. *Fiscal Federalism.* New York: Harcourt Brace Jovanovich.

O'Neill, Karen M. 2002. "Why the TVA Remains Unique: Interest Groups and the Defeat of New Deal River Planning." *Rural Sociology* 67 (2): 163–82.

Opheim, Cynthia, Landon Curry, and Patricia M. Shields. 1994. "Sunset as Oversight: Establishing Realistic Objectives." *American Review of Public Administration* 24 (3): 253–68.

Orbach, Barak Y., Kathleen S. Callahan, and Lisa M. Lindemenn. 2010. "Arming States' Rights: Federalism, Private Lawmakers, and the Battering Ram Strategy." *Arizona Law Review* 52:1161–1206.

Orren, Karen. 2012. "Doing Time: A Theory of the Constitution." *Studies in American Political Development* 26 (1): 71–81.

———. 2014. "Constitutional, Criminal, Civil." *Review of Politics* 76:635–59.

Orren, Karen, and Stephen Skowronek. 2004. *The Search for American Political Development*. New York: Cambridge University Press.

Oser, Jennifer, Marc Hooghe, and Sofie Marien. 2013. "Is Online Participation Distinct from Offline Participation? A Latent Class Analysis of Participation Types and Their Stratification." *Political Research Quarterly* 66 (1): 91–101.

Owen, Randall, Tamar Heller, and Anne Bowers. 2016. "Health Services Appraisal and the Transition to Medicaid Managed Care from Fee for Service." *Disability and Health Journal* 9 (2): 239–47.

Owens, Ryan J., and Patrick C. Wohlfarth. 2014. "State Solicitors General, Appellate Expertise, and State Success before the U.S. Supreme Court." *Law and Society Review* 48 (3): 657–85.

Pacewicz, Josh. 2015. "Playing the Neoliberal Game: Why Community Leaders Left Party Politics to Partisan Activists." *American Journal of Sociology* 121 (3): 826–81.

———. 2016. *Partisans and Partners: The Politics of the Post-Keynesian Society*. Chicago: University of Chicago Press.

Pagliari, Stefano, and Kevin Young. 2015. "The Interest Ecology of Financial Regulation: Interest Group Plurality in the Design of Financial Regulatory Policies." *Socio-Economic Review*. https://doi.org/10.1093/ser/mwv024.

Palmer, Donald, Justin Riemer, and Matthew Davis. 2014. *Annual Report on Voter Registration List Maintenance Activities*. Richmond: Virginia State Board of Elections.

Parker, Christopher S., and Matt A. Barreto. 2013. *Change They Can't Believe In: The Tea Party and Reactionary Politics in America*. Princeton, NJ: Princeton University Press.

Patty, John. 2016. "Signaling through Obstruction." *American Journal of Political Science* 60 (1): 175–89.

Paulsen, Michael Stokes. 2011. "How to Count to Thirty-Four: The Constitutional Case for a Constitutional Convention." *Harvard Journal of Law and Public Policy* 34:837–72.

Peck, Jamie. 2014. "Pushing Austerity: State Failure, Municipal Bankruptcy, and the Crises of Fiscal Federalism in the USA." *Cambridge Journal of Regions, Economy and Society* 7 (1): 17–44.

Perez, Myrna. 2008. *Voter Purges*. New York: Brennan Center for Justice.

———. 2017. *Election Integrity: A Pro-voter Agenda*. New York: Brennan Center for Justice.

Perrin, Andrew J., J. Micah Roos, and Gordon W. Gauchat. 2014. "From Coalition to Constraint: Modes of Thought in Contemporary American Conservatism." *Sociological Forum* 29 (2): 285–300.

Petit, Jeanne D. 2010. *The Men and Women We Want: Gender, Race, and the*

Progressive Era Literacy Test Debate. Rochester, NY: University of Rochester Press.

Pettit, Becky, and Bryan L. Sykes. 2015. "Civil Rights Legislation and Legalized Exclusion: Mass Incarceration and the Masking of Inequality." *Sociological Forum* 30, suppl. 1: 589–611.

Phillips, James C. 2016. "Why Are There So Few Conservatives and Libertarians in Legal Academia? An Empirical Exploration of Three Hypotheses." *Harvard Journal of Law and Public Policy* 39:1–56.

Piketty, Thomas. 2014. *Capital in the Twenty-First Century.* Cambridge, MA: Harvard University Press.

Pildes, Richard H. 2013. "Institutional Formalism and Realism in Constitutional and Public Law." *Supreme Court Review* 2013 (1): 1–54.

Pitts, Michael J. 2014. "Empirically Measuring the Impact of Photo ID over Time and Its Impact on Women." *Indiana Law Review* 48:605–30.

Polletta, Francesca, and Pang Ching Bobby Chen. 2013. "Gender and Public Talk: Accounting for Women's Variable Participation in the Public Sphere." *Sociological Theory* 31 (4): 291–317.

Popp-Berman, Elizabeth, and Laura M. Milanes-Reyes. 2013. "The Politicization of Knowledge Claims: The 'Laffer Curve' in the U.S. Congress." *Qualitative Sociology* 36 (1): 53–79.

Popper, Frank J. 1984. "The Timely End of the Sagebrush Rebellion." *Public Interest* 76:61–73.

Posner, Richard. 2007. *Economic Analysis of Law.* 7th ed. Austin, TX: Aspen.
———. 2008. *How Judges Think.* Cambridge, MA: Harvard University Press.

Prasad, Monica. 2006. *The Politics of Free Markets: The Rise of Neoliberal Economic Policies in Britain, France, Germany, and the United States.* Chicago: University of Chicago Press.

Prasad, Monica, Steve G. Hoffman, and Kieran Bezila. 2016. "Walking the Line: The White Working Class and the Economic Consequences of Morality." *Politics and Society* 44 (2): 281–304.

Presidential Commission on Election Administration. 2014. "The American Voting Experience: Report and Recommendations of the Presidential Commission on Election Administration." https://www.eac.gov/assets/1/6/Amer-Voting-Exper-final-draft-01-09-14-508.pdf.

Preston, Julia. 2012. "Republican Immigration Platform Backs 'Self-Deportation.'" *New York Times*, August 23.

Priest, Chelsea. 2015. "Dual Registration Voting Systems: Safer and Fairer?" *Stanford Law Review Online* 67:101–10.

Provine, Doris Marie, Monica W. Varsanyi, Paul G. Lewis, and Scott H. Decker. 2016. *Policing Immigrants: Local Law Enforcement on the Front Lines.* Chicago: University of Chicago Press.

Provost, Colin. 2010. "When Is AG Short for Aspiring Governor? Ambition and

Policy Making Dynamics in the Office of State Attorney General." *Publius: The Journal of Federalism* 40 (4): 597–616.

Pruitt, E. Scott. 2015. "Written Testimony on 'Impacts of the Proposed Waters of the United States Rule on State and Local Government.'" Joint Hearing of House Committee on Transportation and Infrastructure and Senate Committee on Environment and Public Works, February 4. https://transportation.house.gov/uploadedfiles/2015-02-04-pruitt.pdf.

Qian, Zhenchao, and Daniel T. Lichter. 2007. "Social Boundaries and Marital Assimilation: Interpreting Trends in Racial and Ethnic Intermarriage." *American Sociological Review* 72 (1): 68–94.

Read, James H. 2016. "Constitutionalizing the Dispute: Federalism in Hyperpartisan Times." *Publius: The Journal of Federalism* 46 (3): 337–65.

Reeves, Andrew, and Jon C. Rogowski. 2018. "The Public Cost of Unilateral Action." *American Journal of Political Science.* https://doi.org/10.1111/ajps.12340.

Reich, Gary, and Jay Barth. 2012. "Immigration Restriction in the States: Contesting the Boundaries of Federalism?" *Publius: The Journal of Federalism* 42 (3): 422–48.

Richmond, Todd. 2015. "Senate GOP Votes to Overhaul Campaign Finance, Revamp Elections Board in Late-Night Session." *Minneapolis Star-Tribune*, November 7.

Riddell, Chris. 2004. "Union Certification Success under Voting versus Card-Check Procedures: Evidence from British Columbia, 1978–1998." *ILR Review* 57 (4): 493–517.

Robnett, Belinda, and Cynthia Feliciano. 2011. "Patterns of Racial-Ethnic Exclusion by Internet Daters." *Social Forces* 89 (3): 807–28.

Rohr, John A. 1986. *To Run a Constitution: The Legitimacy of the Administrative State.* Lawrence: University Press of Kansas.

Rose, Shanna. 2010. "Institutions and Fiscal Sustainability." *National Tax Journal* 63 (4): 807–38.

Rose, Shanna, and Cynthia J. Bowling. 2015. "The State of American Federalism, 2014–15: Pathways to Policy in an Era of Party Polarization." *Publius: The Journal of Federalism* 45 (3): 351–79.

Rose, Shanna, and Daniel L. Smith. 2015. "Federal Budget Reform: Lessons from State and Local Governments." In *Pathways to Fiscal Reform in the United States*, ed. John W. Diamond and George R. Zodrow, 135–62. Cambridge, MA: MIT Press.

Rosenberg, Gerald N. 2008. *The Hollow Hope: Can Courts Bring about Social Change?* 2nd ed. Chicago: University of Chicago Press.

Ross, Deuel. 2014. "Pouring Old Poison into New Bottles: How Discretion and the Discriminatory Administration of Voter ID Laws Recreate Literacy Tests." *Columbia Human Rights Law Review* 45:362–440.

Santoro, Wayne A., and Gail M. McGuire. 1997. "Social Movement Insiders:

The Impact of Institutional Activists on Affirmative Action and Comparable Worth Policies." *Social Problems* 44 (4): 503–19.

Sarine, L. Elizabeth. 2012. "The Supreme Court's Problematic Deference to Special Masters in Interstate Water Disputes." *Ecology Law Quarterly* 39 (2): 535–70.

Sawyers, Traci M., and David S. Meyer. 1999. "Missed Opportunities: Social Movement Abeyance and Public Policy." *Social Problems* 46 (2): 187–206.

Scherer, Nancy, and Banks Miller. 2009. "The Federalist Society's Influence on the Federal Judiciary." *Political Research Quarterly* 62 (2): 366–78.

Schifeling, Todd. 2013. "Defense against Recession: U.S. Business Mobilization, 1950–1970." *American Journal of Sociology* 119 (1): 1–34.

Schifeling, Todd, and Mark Mizruchi. 2014. "The Decline of the American Corporate Network, 1960–2010." In *The Power of Corporate Networks: A Comparative and Historical Perspective*, ed. Thomas David and Gerarda Westerhuis, 31–47. New York: Routledge.

Schiller, Wendy, and Charles Haines Stewart. 2015. *Electing the Senate: Indirect Democracy Before the Seventeenth Amendment*. Princeton, NJ: Princeton University Press.

Schlager, Edella, and Tanya Heikkila. 2009. "Resolving Water Conflicts: A Comparative Analysis of Interstate River Compacts." *Policy Studies Journal* 37 (3): 367–92.

Schmitt, Jeffrey M. 2016. "In Defense of *Shelby County*'s Principle of Equal State Sovereignty." *Oklahoma Law Review* 68 (2): 209–62.

Scholzman, Kay Lehman, Sidney Verba, and Henry E. Brady. 2010. "Weapon of the Strong? Participatory Inequality and the Internet." *Perspectives on Politics* 8 (2): 487–509.

Schruben, Francis W. 1969. *Kansas in Turmoil, 1930–1936*. Columbia: University of Missouri Press.

Schumaker-Matos, Edward. 2011. "Birthright Battles That Miss the Mark." *Washington Post*, January 8, A11.

Sears, David O., and Jack Citrin. 1985. *Tax Revolt: Something for Nothing in California*. Cambridge, MA: Harvard University Press.

Seifter, Miriam. 2014. "States as Interest Groups in the Administrative Process." *Virginia Law Review* 100 (5): 953–1025.

Shah, Seema, and Patricia Zettler. 2010. "From a Constitutional Right to a Policy of Exceptions: Abigail Alliance and the Future of Access to Experimental Therapy." *Yale Journal of Health Policy, Law, and Ethics* 10:135–96.

Sharkey, Catherine M. 2009. "Federalism Accountability: 'Agency-Forcing' Measures." *Duke Law Journal* 58 (8): 2125–92.

Shelley, Bryan. 2008. "Rebels and Their Causes: State Resistance to No Child Left Behind." *Publius: The Journal of Federalism* 38 (3): 444–68.

Shkabatur, Jennifer. 2012. "Transparency With(out) Accountability: Open Government in the United States." *Yale Law and Policy Review* 31:79–140.

Shor, Boris. 2014. "July 2014 Update: Aggregate Data for Ideological Mapping of American Legislature." *Harvard Dataverse*. https://doi.org/10.7910/DVN/26799.

Shor, Boris, and Nolan McCarthy. 2011. "The Ideological Mapping of American Legislatures." *American Political Science Review* 105 (3): 530–51.

Shortridge, James R. 1995. *Peopling the Plains: Who Settled Where in Kansas.* Lawrence: University Press of Kansas.

Shulman, Stuart W. 2009. "The Case against Mass E-Mails: Perverse Incentives and Low-Quality Public Participation in U.S. Federal Rulemaking." *Policy and Internet* 1 (1): 23–53.

Silverstein, Gordon. 2009. *Law's Allure: How Law Shapes, Constrains, Saves, and Kills Politics.* New York: Cambridge University Press.

Sinclair, Barbara. 2011. *Unorthodox Lawmaking: New Legislative Processes in the U.S. Congress.* 4th ed. Washington, DC: CQ Press.

Skocpol, Theda. 1997. *Boomerang: Health Care Reform and the Turn against Government.* New York: Norton.

Skocpol, Theda, and Alexander Hertel-Fernandez. 2016. "The Koch Network and Republican Party Extremism." *Perspectives on Politics* 14 (3): 681–99.

Skocpol, Theda, and Vanessa Williamson. 2012. *The Tea Party and the Remaking of Republican Conservatism.* New York: Oxford University Press.

Skowronek, Stephen. 1982. *Building a New American State: The Expansion of National Administration, 1877–1920.* Ithaca, NY: Cornell University Press.

———. 2006. "The Reassociation of Ideas and Purposes: Racism, Liberalism, and the American Political Tradition." *American Political Science Review* 100 (3): 385–401.

Smith, Alexander Thomas T. 2010. "Faith, Science and the Political Imagination: Moderate Republicans and the Politics of Embryonic Stem Cell Research." *Sociological Review* 58 (4): 623–37.

———. 2013. "Democracy Begins at Home: Moderation and the Promise of Salvage Ethnography." *Sociological Review* 61, suppl. 2: 119–40.

Smith, Daniel A., and Caroline J. Tolbert. 2004. *Educated by Initiative: The Effects of Direct Democracy on Citizens and Political Organizations in the United States.* Ann Arbor: University of Michigan Press.

Southworth, Ann. 2008. *Lawyers of the Right: Professionalizing the Conservative Coalition.* Chicago: University of Chicago Press.

Stearns, Linda Brewster, and Paul Almeida. 2004. "The Formation of State Actor–Social Movement Coalitions and Favorable Policy Outcomes." *Social Problems* 51 (4): 478–504.

Steil, Justin Peter, and Ion Bogdan Vasi. 2014. "The New Immigration Contestation: Social Movements and Local Immigration Policy Making in the United States, 2000–2011." *American Journal of Sociology* 119 (4): 1104–55.

Stenehjem, Wayne. 2015. "Letter to the Honorable Gina McCarthy and the Honorable Jo Ellen Darcy." July 28. https://ag.ks.gov/docs/default-source/documents/ag-wotus-letter.pdf?sfvrsn=2.

Stewart, Charles, III. 2013. "Voter ID: Who Has Them? Who Shows Them?" *Oklahoma Law Review* 66:21–52.

Stock, Margaret D. 2016. "American Birthright Citizenship Rules and the Exclusion of 'Outsiders' from the Political Community." In *Citizenship in Question*, ed. Benjamin N. Lawrance and Jacqueline Stevens, 179–99. Durham, NC: Duke University Press.

Storey, Tim. 2010. "GOP Makes Historic State Legislative Gains in 2010." *Rasmussen Reports*, December 10. http://www.rasmussenreports.com/public_content/political_commentary/commentary_by_tim_storey/gop_makes_historic_state_legislative_gains_in_2010.

Stoughton, Kathleen M. 2013. "A New Approach to Voter ID Challenges: Section 2 of the Voting Rights Act." *George Washington Law Review* 81: 292–328.

Strach, Kim, Marc Burris, and Veronica Degraffenreid. 2014. "North Carolina State Board of Elections Presentation to Joint Legislative Elections Oversight Committee." April 2. https://www.ncleg.net/documentsites/committees/JLElectionsOC/2013-2014/Meeting%20Documents/April%202,%202014/SBOE_JointCommittee_April%202014.pdf.

Streeck, Wolfgang. 2016. *How Will Capitalism End? Essays on a Failing System*. London: Verso.

Stromquist, Shelton. 2006. *Reinventing "The People": The Progressive Movement, the Class Problem, and the Origins of Modern Liberalism*. Urbana: University of Illinois Press.

Sunstein, Cass R. 1987. "Constitutionalism After the New Deal." *Harvard Law Review* 101 (2): 421–510.

———. 2006. "Chevron Step Zero." *Virginia Law Review* 92 (2): 187–249.

Sunstein, Cass R., and Adrian Vermeule. 2016. "The New Coke: On the Plural Aims of Administrative Law." *Supreme Court Review* 2015 (1): 41–88.

Tamanaha, Brian Z. 2009. *Beyond the Formalist-Realist Divide: The Role of Politics in Judging*. Princeton, NJ: Princeton University Press.

Tani, Karen M. 2016. *States of Dependency: Welfare, Rights, and American Governance, 1935–1972*. New York: Cambridge University Press.

Tausanovitch, Chris, and Christopher Warshaw. 2013. "Measuring Constituent Policy Preferences in Congress, State Legislatures, and Cities." *Journal of Politics* 75 (2): 330–42.

Taylor, Verta. 1989. "Social Movement Continuity: The Women's Movement in Abeyance." *American Sociological Review* 54 (5): 761–75.

Teles, Steven M. 2008. *The Rise of the Conservative Legal Movement*. Princeton, NJ: Princeton University Press.

Thierault, Sean M. 2013. *The Gingrich Senators: The Roots of Partisan Warfare in Congress*. New York: Oxford University Press.

Thompson, Frank J., and Michael K. Gusmano. 2014. "The Administrative Presidency and Fractious Federalism: The Case of Obamacare." *Publius: The Journal of Federalism* 44 (3): 426–50.

Tichenor, Daniel J., and Alexandra Filindra. 2012. "Raising *Arizona v. United States*: Historical Patterns of American Immigration Federalism." *Lewis and Clark Law Review* 16:1215–47.

Titus, A. Constandina. 1981. "The Nevada 'Sagebrush Rebellion' Act: A Question of Constitutionality." *Arizona Law Review* 23:263–82.

Tokaji, Daniel P. 2008. "Voter Registration and Election Reform." *William and Mary Bill of Rights Journal* 17 (2): 453–506.

Tolbert, Pamela S., and Lynne G. Zucker. 1983. "Institutional Sources of Change in the Formal Structure of Organizations: The Diffusion of Civil Service Reform, 1880–1935." *Administrative Science Quarterly* 28 (1): 22–39.

Treadwell, Mead. 2017. "Advisory Memorandum Regarding the Congressional Resolution in the New Congress." Compact for a Balanced Budget Compact Commission. July 14. https://docs.wixstatic.com/ugd/e48202_c36f74ef02df4c729ec55d2e1c16174a.pdf.

Trump, Donald J. 2017a. "Border Security and Immigration Enforcement Improvements." *Federal Register* 82 (18): 8793–97.

——. 2017b. "Enforcing the Regulatory Reform Agenda." *Federal Register* 82 (39): 12285–87.

——. 2017c. "Enhancing Public Safety in the Interior of the United States." *Federal Register* 82 (18): 8799–8803.

——. 2017d. "Establishing Discipline and Accountability in the Environmental Review and Permitting Process for Infrastructure Projects." *Federal Register* 82 (163): 40463–69.

——. 2017e. "Establishment of Presidential Advisory Commission on Election Integrity." *Federal Register* 82 (93): 22389–90.

——. 2017f. "Expediting Environmental Reviews and Approvals for High Priority Infrastructure Projects." *Federal Register* 82 (18): 8657–58.

——. 2017g. "A Federal Strategy to Ensure Secure and Reliable Supplies of Critical Minerals." *Federal Register* 82 (246): 60835–37.

——. 2017h. "Implementing an America-First Offshore Energy Strategy." *Federal Register* 82 (84): 20815–18.

——. 2017i. "Minimizing the Economic Burden of the Patient Protection and Affordable Care Act Pending Repeal." *Federal Register* 82 (14): 8351–52.

——. 2017j. "Promoting Energy Independence and Economic Growth." *Federal Register* 82 (61): 16093–97.

———. 2017k. "Promoting Healthcare Choice and Competition Across the United States." *Federal Register* 82 (199): 48385–87.

———. 2017l. "Protecting the Nation from Foreign Terrorist Entry into the United States." *Federal Register* 82 (20): 8977–82.

———. 2017m. "Reducing Regulation and Controlling Regulatory Costs." *Federal Register* 82 (22): 9339–41.

———. 2017n. "Restoring the Rule of Law, Federalism, and Economic Growth by Reviewing the 'Waters of the United States' Rule." *Federal Register* 82 (41): 12497–98.

———. 2017o. "Review of Designations under the Antiquities Act." *Federal Register* 82 (82): 20429–31.

Uggen, Christopher, and Jeff Manza. 2002. "Democratic Contraction? Political Consequences of Felon Disenfranchisement in the United States." *American Sociological Review* 67 (6): 777–803.

US Census Bureau. 2012a. "Geographical Mobility: 2011 to 2012: Table 1, General Mobility, by Race and Hispanic Origin, Region, Sex, Age, Relationship to Householder, Educational Attainment, Marital Status, Nativity, Tenure, and Poverty Status: 2011 to 2012." https://www2.census.gov/programs-surveys/demo/tables/geographic-mobility/2012/cps-2012/tab01-01.xls.

———. 2012b. "Population: Estimates and Projections by Age, Sex, Race/Ethnicity, Table 10—Resident Population by Race, Hispanic Origin, and Age: 2000 and 2009." In *Statistical Abstract of the United States 2012.* https://www2.census.gov/library/publications/2011/compendia/statab/131ed/2012-statab.pdf.

———. 2013. "Voting and Registration in the Election of November 2012, Table 4b: Reported Voting and Registration by Sex, Race, and Hispanic Origin, for States: November 2012." https://www2.census.gov/programs-surveys/cps/tables/p20/568/table04b.xls.

———. 2014. "Frequently Occurring Surnames from the Census 2000, File A: Top 1000 Surnames." http://www2.census.gov/topics/genealogy/2000surnames/Top1000.xls.

———. 2015. "State-to-State Migration Flows, Detailed Tables: 2013." https://www2.census.gov/programs-surveys/demo/tables/geographic-mobility/2013/state-to-state-migration/state_to_state_migrations_table_2013.xls.

Vasi, Ion Bogdan, David Strang, and Arnout van de Rijt. 2014. "Tea and Sympathy: The Tea Party Movement and Republican Precommitment to Radical Conservatism in the 2011 Debt-Limit Crisis." *Mobilization* 19 (1): 1–22.

Vermeule, Adrian. 2009. *Law and the Limits of Reason.* New York: Oxford University Press.

Vile, John R. 2010. *Encyclopedia of Constitutional Amendments, Proposed Amendments, and Amending Issues, 1789–2010.* Santa Barbara, CA: ABC-Clio

Villazor, Rose Cuison. 2010. "'Sanctuary Cities' and Local Citizenship." *Fordham Urban Law Journal* 37:573–98.

Wagner-Pacifici, Robin, and Iddo Tavory. 2017. "Politics as a Vacation." *American Journal of Cultural Sociology* 5 (3): 307–21.

Waldo, Dwight. 1948. *The Administrative State: A Study of the Political Theory of American Public Administration*. New York: Ronald.

Walker, Edward T., and Christopher M. Rea. 2014. "The Political Mobilization of Firms and Industries." *Annual Review of Sociology* 40:281–304.

Wallner, James I. 2015. "The Problem of Credible Commitment in Congressional Budgeting." *Journal of Policy History* 27 (2): 382–403.

Walsh, Camille. 2018. *Racial Taxation: Schools, Segregation, and Taxpayer Citizenship, 1869–1973*. Chapel Hill: University of North Carolina Press.

Ward, Jason Morgan. 2011. *Defending White Democracy: The Making of a Segregationist Movement and the Remaking of Racial Politics, 1936–1965*. Chapel Hill: University of North Carolina Press.

Warner, Barbara, and Jennifer Shapiro. 2013. "Fractured, Fragmented Federalism: A Study in Fracking Regulatory Policy." *Publius: The Journal of Federalism* 43 (3): 474–96.

Wechsler, Herbert. 1954. "The Political Safeguards of Federalism: The Role of the States in the Composition and Selection of the National Government." *Columbia Law Review* 54:543–60.

Weinstein, James. 1968. *The Corporate Ideal in the Liberal State: 1900–1918*. Boston: Beacon.

Weiser, Wendy, and Erik Opsal. 2014. *The State of Voting in 2014*. New York: Brennan Center for Justice.

Weissert, Carol S., and David Blake Jones. 2015. "Devolution Paradox and the US South." *Regional and Federal Studies* 25 (3): 259–76.

Wenzel, Michael. 2007. "The Multiplicity of Taxpayer Identities and Their Implications for Tax Ethics." *Law and Policy* 29 (1): 31–50.

White, Ariel R., Noah L. Nathan, and Julie K. Faller. 2015. "What Do I Need to Vote? Bureaucratic Discretion and Discrimination by Local Election Officials." *American Political Science Review* 109 (1): 129–42.

Wilde, Melissa J., and Sabrina Danielsen. 2014. "Fewer and Better Children: Race, Class, Religion, and Birth Control Reform in America." *American Journal of Sociology* 119 (6): 1710–60.

Williamson, Heather J., Elizabeth A. Perkins, Bruce L. Levin, et al. 2017. "Implementation of Medicaid Managed Care Long-Term Services and Supports for Adults with Intellectual and/or Developmental Disabilities in Kansas." *Intellectual and Developmental Disabilities* 55 (2): 84–96.

Willis, Ellen. 2006. "Escape from Freedom: What's the Matter with Tom Frank (and the Lefties Who Love Him?)." *Situations* 1 (2): 5–20.

Wilson, David C., and Paul R. Brewer. 2013. "The Foundations of Public Opinion on Voter ID Laws: Political Predispositions, Racial Resentment, and Information Effects." *Public Opinion Quarterly* 77 (4): 962–84.

Wilson, Paul E. 1968. "New Bottles for Old Wine: Criminal Law Revision in
Kansas." *University of Kansas Law Review* 16:585–603.

Wong, Tung Sing. 2013. "Branded to Drive: Obstacle Preemption of North Carolina Driver's Licenses for DACA Grantees." *Hamline Law Review* 37:81–108.

Wood, Richard E. 2008. *Survival of Rural America: Small Victories and Bitter
Harvests*. Lawrence: University Press of Kansas.

Woods, Neal D., and Ann O'M. Bowman. 2011. "Blurring Borders: The Effect
of Federal Activism on Interstate Cooperation." *American Politics Research*
39 (5): 859–84.

Wright, Deil S. 1982. *Understanding Intergovernmental Relations*. 2nd ed. Mon-
terey, CA: Brooks/Cole.

Wuthnow, Robert. 2005. "Depopulation and Rural Churches in Kansas, 1950–
1980." *Great Plains Research* 15:117–34.

———. 2011. *Remaking the Heartland: Middle America since the 1950s*. Princeton, NJ: Princeton University Press.

Yancey, George. 2009. "Crossracial Differences in the Racial Preferences of Potential Dating Partners: A Test of the Alienation of African Americans and
Social Dominance Orientation." *Sociological Quarterly* 50 (1): 121–43.

Ybarra, Vickie D., Lisa M. Sanchez, and Gabriel R. Sanchez. 2015. "Anti-
immigrant Anxieties in State Policy: The Great Recessions and Punitive Immigration Policy in the American States, 2005–2012." *State Politics and Policy Quarterly*. https://doi.org/10.1177/1532440015605815.

Young, Ernest A. 2011. "'The Ordinary Diet of the Law': The Presumption
against Preemption in the Roberts Court." *Supreme Court Review* 2011 (1):
253–344.

Young, Frank W. 2013. "What's the Matter with Kansas? A Sociological Answer." *Sociological Forum* 28 (4): 864–72.

Young, Kevin, and Stefano Pagliari. 2015. "Capital United? Business Unity in
Regulatory Politics and the Special Place of Finance." *Regulation and Governance*. https://doi.org/10.1111/rego.12098.

Zackin, Emily. 2011. "What's Happened to American Federalism?" *Polity* 43
(3): 388–403.

———. 2013. *Looking for Rights in All the Wrong Places: Why State Constitutions Contain America's Positive Rights*. Princeton, NJ: Princeton University
Press.

Zavestoski, Stephen, Stuart Shulman, and David Schlosberg. 2006. "Democracy and the Environment on the Internet: Electronic Citizen Participation
in Regulatory Rule Making." *Science, Technology and Human Values* 31 (3):
1–26.

Zeidel, Robert F. 2004. *Immigrants, Progressives, and Exclusion Politics: The Dillingham Commission, 1900–1927.* DeKalb: Northern Illinois University Press.

Zettler, Patricia J., and Henry T. Greely. 2014. "The Strange Allure of State 'Right-to-Try' Laws." *JAMA Internal Medicine* 174 (12): 1885–86.

Zimmerman, Joseph F. 2012. *Horizontal Federalism: Interstate Relations.* Albany: State University of New York Press.

Zipkin, Saul. 2010. "Democratic Standing." *Journal of Law and Politics* 26:179–238.

——. 2012. "Administering Election Law." *Marquette Law Review* 95:641–708.

Cases Cited

Arizona v. Inter Tribal Council of Arizona, 570 U.S. — (2013).

Arizona v. United States, 567 U.S. — (2012).

Baker v. Carr, 369 U.S. 186 (1962).

Bush v. Gore, 531 U.S. 98 (2000).

Chamber of Commerce v. Whiting, 563 U.S. 582 (2011).

Chevron U.S.A., Inc. v. Natural Resources Defense Council, Inc., 467 U.S. 837 (1984).

Citizens United v. Federal Election Commission, 558 U.S. 310 (2010).

Colegrove v. Green, 328 U.S. 549 (1946).

Cooper v. Harris, 581 U.S. — (2017).

County of Santa Clara v. Trump, No. 17-cv-00574 (N.D. Cal. April 25, 2017).

Crawford v. Marion County Election Board, 553 U.S. 181 (2008).

Environmental Protection Agency v. EME Homer City, 572 U.S. — (2014).

Evenwel v. Abbott, 578 U.S. — (2016).

Fish v. Kobach, No. 16-3147 (10th Cir. October 19, 2016).

Gannon v. State, 298 Kan. 1107 (2014).

Gill v. Whitford, 585 U.S. — (2018).

Harper v. Virginia Board of Elections, 383 U.S. 663 (1966).

Hollingsworth v. Perry, 570 U.S. — (2013).

Husted v. A. Philip Randolph Institute, 584 U.S. — (2018).

Kobach v. United States Election Assistance Commission, No. 14-3062 (10th Cir. November 7, 2014).

League of Women Voters v. Newby, No. 16-5196 (D.C. Cir. September 26, 2016).

Loving v. Virginia, 388 U.S. 1 (1967).

Massachusetts v. Environmental Protection Agency, 549 U.S. 497 (2007).

Michigan v. Environmental Protection Agency, 576 U.S. — (2015).

National Federation of Independent Business v. Sebelius, 567 U.S. — (2012).

National Labor Relations Board v. Arizona, No. 11-CV-00913-PHX (D. Ariz. September 5, 2012).

Nevada v. U.S. Department of Labor, No. 16-cv-00731 (E.D. Tex. Nov. 22, 2016)

North Carolina Conference of Branches of NAACP v. McCrory, No. 14-1856 (4th Cir. October 1, 2014).

North Carolina State Conference of the NAACP v. North Carolina State Board of Elections, No. 16-CV-1274 (M.D. N.C. November 4, 2016).

Obergefell v. Hodges, 576 U.S. ——— (2015).

Rapanos v. United States, 547 U.S. 715 (2006).

Reynolds v. Sims, 377 U.S. 533 (1964).

Rideout v. Gardner, No. 15-2021 (1st Cir. September 28, 2016).

Sackett v. Environmental Protection Agency, 566 U.S. ——— (2012).

Shelby County v. Holder, 570 U.S. ——— (2013).

South Carolina v. Katzenbach, 383 U.S. 301 (1966).

Tarrant Regional Water District v. Herrmann, 569 U.S. ——— (2013).

Texas v. United States, No. 15-40239 (5th Cir. November 25, 2015).

Thornburg v. Gingles, 478 U.S. 30 (1986).

United States v. Texas, 579 U.S. ——— (2016).

United States v. Windsor, 570 U.S. ——— (2013).

Utility Air Regulatory Group v. Environmental Protection Agency, 573 U.S. ——— (2014).

Veasey v. Abbott, No. 14-41127 (5th Cir. August 5, 2015).

Veasey v. Perry, 574 U.S. ——— (2014).

Virginia v. Tennessee, 148 U.S. 503 (1893).

Washington v. Trump, No. 2:17-cv-00141 (W.D. Wash. Feb. 3, 2017).

Index

litigation (*continued*)
    of federal authority and, 41–46; Obama
    administration and, 3, 5, 30–32, 34,
    37–39, 41, 57, 65–66, 70, 145–46, 158–
    60, 164; slow court changes and, 31–
    32; state power and, 145, 176n5, 186n7;
    symmetry and, 186n7; Trump adminis-
    tration and, 146, 153, 156, 158–60, 163–
    67, 172; trying new arguments and, 31;
    voting rights and, 3, 93, 120, 164; Wa-
    ters of the United States Rule and, 30.
    See also specific cases
lobbying: conservative legal activism and,
    36, 48, 51; cross-government, 78; elec-
    tronic, 185n5; influencing Congress
    and, 11, 175n1; intergovernmental, 14,
    48, 60, 78, 139; interstate compacts and,
    60, 72–73, 78; Kansas Experiment and,
    130, 134–35, 139, 185n5
Louisiana, 113, 178n6
Loving v. Virginia, 116

Maine, 91, 176n4
Martin, Isaac W., 127, 143
Mashaw, Jerry L., 36
Massachusetts vs. EPA, 37–38, 41, 44, 93,
    164
McCannon, Kevin, 130
McCarthy, Gina, 30
Medicaid: eligibility for, 62; expansion of,
    19, 55, 62–63, 81, 121, 131–32, 154, 160;
    fee-for-service model and, 130; inter-
    state compacts and, 62, 81; KanCare
    and, 130; Kansas Experiment and, 121,
    130–32; limited uptake of, 101; Repub-
    licans and, 62; Trump administration
    and, 154, 160
Medicare, 154
Medvetz, Thomas, 172
Mendez, Matthew W., 95
Methodists, 128
Michigan, 33, 54, 100, 122, 129, 148,
    177n11, 178n6, 184n1
Michigan v. EPA, 41, 43, 45
Milanes-Reyes, Laura M., 130
mining, 153, 184n2
Minutemen, 76–77
Mississippi, 48, 50, 155, 175n1, 178n6
Missouri, 65, 126, 178n6, 183n13
Montana, 153

Moore v. Kobach, 115
Moynihan, Donald P., 92
Mudge, Stephanie L., 187n8
Multistate Non-Navigable Waters Com-
    pact, 66

NAACP v. McCrory, 114
Nathan, Noah L., 95
Nation, Carrie, 125
National Association for Gun Rights,
    76–77
National Commission on Federal Election
    Reform, 91
National Conference of State Legislatures
    Elections Legislation Database, 92
*National Federation of Independent Busi-
    nesses v. Sebelius*, 41, 58, 62, 66, 160
National Popular Vote Interstate Com-
    pact, 64
National Voter Registration Act (NVRA),
    90–91, 104, 107, 109, 119, 156
Native Americans, 86
naturalization papers, 101
Nebraska, 33, 178n6, 183n17
neoliberalism, 82, 152, 187n8
Nevada, 49, 89, 113
Nevada v. Department of Labor, 45
New Deal: conservative legal activism and,
    35–36, 52; Democrats and, 9, 29; federal
    power and, 1, 7–10, 12, 29; interstate
    compacts and, 59; Kansas Experiment
    and, 123–25; large national government
    and, 9–10; social welfare state and, 8,
    10, 59, 161–62; Supreme Court and, 12;
    US Constitution and, 12
New Federalism, 46
New Hampshire, 50, 106, 155, 176n4, 178n6
New Jersey, 160, 176n4
New York, 160
Nicholson-Crotty, Sean C., 61
Nineteenth Amendment, 86
Nixon administration, 16
NLRB v. Arizona, 52
Nolette, Paul, 34–35, 175n1
North Carolina, 17, 25, 45, 95–96, 100, 113–
    16, 180n4
*North Carolina State Conference of the
    NAACP v. North Carolina State Board
    of Elections*, 107
North Dakota, 178n6, 182n12